The Latino
student's guide to
college success

The Latino Student's Guide to College Success

THE LATINO STUDENT'S GUIDE TO COLLEGE SUCCESS

Second Edition, Revised and Updated

Leonard A. Valverde, Editor

 GREENWOOD

AN IMPRINT OF ABC-CLIO, LLC

Santa Barbara, California • Denver, Colorado • Oxford, England

Library of Congress Cataloging-in-Publication Data

The Latino student's guide to college success / Leonard A. Valverde, editor. —2nd ed., rev. and updated
    p. cm.
  Includes index.
  ISBN 978-0-313-39797-4 (hardback) — ISBN 978-0-313-39798-1 (ebook)
1. Hispanic Americans—Education (Higher)—Handbooks, manuals, etc.
2. Universities and colleges—United States—Directories.   I. Valverde, Leonard A.
  LC2670.6.H57 2012
  378.19'82968073—dc23   2012010827
ISBN: 978-0-313-39797-4
EISBN: 978-0-313-39798-1

16   15   14   13   12   1   2   3   4   5

This book is also available on the World Wide Web as an eBook.
Visit www.abc-clio.com for details.

Greenwood
An Imprint of ABC-CLIO, LLC

ABC-CLIO, LLC
130 Cremona Drive, P.O. Box 1911
Santa Barbara, California 93116-1911

This book is printed on acid-free paper ∞
Manufactured in the United States of America

To the many Latinos and Latinas of past generations who were capable but discouraged or not encouraged to go to college like Don Silva and to the many future Latino generations who will likely go, Little Olivia V., Sophia & baby sister Lila, Faith Isabel, and Delilah Madison

Contents

PART III
SHORT STORIES OF HOW I MADE IT IN COLLEGE

PART IV
COLLEGE AND UNIVERSITY DIRECTORIES

PART V
RESOURCE GUIDES

Introduction

The face of the United States is changing and it is looking more Latin in color, flavor, and taste. The latest census count confirms the change that started in the 1980s and is continuing until now. More importantly, the 2010 Census data are being used to predict the status of Latinos in the United States until the year 2050. And the Latino population trend looks even better than now. Briefly, here are the highlights taken from the U.S. Census Count, 2010. Latinos are the largest ethnic or racial group in the United States (50.5 million population or 16%) surpassing the African American population. Secondly, Latinos are the fasting growing subpopulation in the United States (more than 50% of the total population of the United States between 2000 and 2010 was due to Hispanic population increase) and now the youngest population (most of the Latinos are school age). This tremendous growth is due to two factors, immigration rate and high birth rates. Third, Latinos reside and work across the country. We are no longer a regional population. Instead, we are in the West (28%), Southwest, Midwest (7%), traditional southern states (15.9%), and the northeast (12.6%). Latinos are diverse in ancestry, that is, Mexican ancestry (63%), Puerto Rican (9.2%), Cuban (3.5%), and other (Middle and South Americans 24.3%). Because of the increased population numbers, young in age, and now a national population, attention is being focused on us. That is, businesses are advertising to have Latinos buy their goods and use their services. Politicians are seeking our votes. Schools are offering more ESL classes, and bilingual programs are expanding. At the college level, ethnic studies are being introduced, recruiters are going to high schools with large Hispanic student bodies, and more Latino staff and faculty are being hired.

Secondly, the nature of work is changing in the United States. The United States is now a service economy, using technology to conduct more business, and information sharing is a big commodity. Computers, Internet, and smart phones now provide society access to information and sharing it in high speed like never before. The future promises even more in this direction, for example, iPods and iPads are the latest innovations and Amazon Kindle has changed the way we buy and read books. Few drivers use printed road maps; instead we have GPS in cars to give us voice directions to get to places in town that were just built six months ago!

What does this have to do with you, you ask? There are two direct implications. First, you will be entering a new work environment, one that calls for creative and analytical thinking. The kind of academic preparation colleges provide for their graduates. In short, a high school diploma no longer is good enough to compete for jobs. Part of this first implication is that persons of the 21st century will change their careers more than once, unlike your parents who stayed in the same career and maybe even with the same employer. To change careers, you will probably need to retool or said another way, *go back to college* and retrain yourself. So getting a college education (degree) is becoming a necessity if one is going to be successful in life. College will permit you to have more opportunities and more options, giving you more probability to be successful and happier in life. This new status that colleges offer is above the old incentive. The old incentive was college graduates earn more money over their lifetime than a high school graduate. The Census Bureau study (Julian and Kominski, 2011) found that college graduates on an average earn $1 million more than a high school graduate! Even better, with a master's degree the earnings increase another half million dollars, and with a doctorate the earnings increased by another $1 million. So the more the college education, expect greater lifetime income, for example, $2.5 million. While this gap is large, in an era of high-tech industry and global economy, the salary gap promises to be even higher or wider than in the past!

The second implication is greater acceptability and much better odds in your favor. The more we grow in population number, the more society will come to learn about us. Our historical contributions will no longer be as forgotten or distorted as in the past. The more society knows about our history and our culture, the more they will come to recognize that we are more alike than different. In short, we will become more acceptable. Once we become more in the mainstream, we will be included instead of excluded as in the past. The inclusion has already begun. In government, we see more Latinos being elected, as mayor in large cities like Los Angeles and San Antonio, as governor in New Mexico, not to forget state legislatures and Congressional representatives. In education, particularly in higher education, Latinos and Latinas are being named presidents of community colleges and universities. As Latinos get into these leadership roles and positions, they open doors for others to go through. They open doors by way of educating staff and faculties about strengths and weaknesses of Latino populations, providing background information about situations and conditions faced by Latino students in high school, and so forth. In short, the United States will soon come to understand that the future of the country will be dependent on the education of Latinos and, in turn, their role in providing leadership in business, governance, medicine, justice system, and so forth. Some universities and colleges have already come to this realization and are changing their thinking about recruitment, admission, curriculum, and student services. In short, your chances of being accepted into a college are better than the previous generations. While the odds are better, you can and must improve your personal opportunity to not only get admitted, but also complete your college education with a degree.

This guide has been written to prepare you for success. Briefly, let me outline how this book guides you to being a college graduate. First, the book is divided into four major parts. Parts I and II are divided into eight chapters called steps. Part I has three steps starting with how to think positively about planning for college, how to think about where to start your college education, to making application, and understanding the multiple cost and funding available to students. Part II has five steps and provides you with information that will help you to be successful once you start taking classes. Universities and colleges have developed services to help their ever-growing student body. Chapter 4 helps you to know what is available and how to use it to your advantage. Chapter 5 shares valuable insight into being successful both academically and personally. Since colleges have incorporated high technology into their classrooms, faculty offices, and computer centers for students, Chapter 6 gives you tips and ideas to master computers and the Internet for success in your academic life. Chapter 7 addresses those of you who are starting your college education at the two-year or community-college level. You will want to read it so your transition from a two-year to a four-year college goes smoothly and cuts the cost down. Lastly, Chapter 8 both encourages you to think about preparing for an advanced degree while you are working toward your first college degree. As was stated earlier in this introduction, the BA or BS degree is replacing the high school diploma as entry point to work. In very short time, you will find that to be competitive for high paying professional jobs, you need a master's or a doctorate degree. So stay ahead of the curve.

Part III has six short stories by Latinas and Latinos, some writing about how they were successful in getting in and graduating from college. Others write about their experiences in getting an advanced degree. These are real people whose stories represent a cross section of Latinos. By reading these stories, you should be able to identify with one or more of them. You should be motivated and inspired. But remember there are hundreds upon hundreds of Latino stories.

Part IV is a directory of the top 50 four-year colleges and universities and the top 20 two-year colleges that graduate the most Latinos. Listed for your follow-up are website addresses so that you can look up any of the colleges that interest you to get more detailed information. When thinking about where you want to start your college education, you should consider those colleges and universities that have a strong track record in getting their Latino students to complete their education with a degree. In addition, since we are advocating to go beyond your first degree, we list the top 50 universities awarding master's degrees to Latinos and the top 50 universities awarding doctoral or terminal degrees to Latinos.

A few words about the contributing authors. You should know that all the chapter authors faced discouragement, or were not encouraged and faced difficulties in starting their higher education degree programs. But despite these barriers, they overcame hardships, weaknesses, and obstacles that you and others will face, such as lack of confidence, weak academic preparation, lack of money, and so forth. Not only did they face all the challenges, but after graduating from a university, they also became highly successful in their lives.

Thus, all of the contributing writers who are rich in experience and wise in counsel (read more about each of them in "About the Authors" section of this book) are of the strong belief that if you follow their steps, you will be successful in getting a college education and degree. In doing so you will earn more in your lifetime, contribute to your local community as a leader, and provide service to our nation. We end with the famous Vulcan saying as spoken by Mr. Spock from the TV series and motion picture *Star Trek*, "Live Long and Prosper!"

Leonard A. Valverde

References

U.S. Census Bureau, 2010 Count. *Hispanic Demographic Data*, www.census.gov/opulation/www/socdemo/hispanics.

Julian, Tiffany, and Kominski, Robert. "How Much Is a College Degree Worth?" U.S. Census Bureau, 2011.

Planning for College Success

"The only way to get his family out of the circle of poverty was to work his way up and send the kids to college!"*

Cesar Chavez
Community and Labor Leader
Born in Yuma, Arizona

---

*Source: "The Story of Cesar Chavez, the Beginning," United Farm Workers of America, http://www.ufw.org/.

Getting Ready for College: *Vamanos*

Leonard A. Valverde

This chapter provides valuable information about two main factors that lead to success in college. The first part of the chapter focuses on eliminating excuses about not going to college and building the *belief* that Latino and Latinas can be successful in college. The second part addresses what a Latina or Latino student needs to attend to in order to select a college that is the best fit for him or her, given their circumstances.

First Things First: Say Yes to College

Getting ready for college starts with you deciding in your mind that you want to go to college. The sooner you make this decision, the more time you will have to plan and prepare for college. However, if your decision comes late in life, no matter, it is never too late to go. Next, you can be successful in getting a college degree, whatever your situation might be. For example, if you were discouraged by teachers and others saying to you, "Don't think about going to college, you can't do it," like U.S. secretary of labor Linda Solis was told, you can still go to college. She did by going to Cal Poly Pomona (DOL/Secretary's webpage, 2012). Or, if you were not encouraged by school counselors; and/or no one spoke to you, even so you should think about going to college; you can still go to college. Or, after high school if you joined the military, or if you had to get a job to help support your parents, younger brothers, and sisters, or if you started a family of your own and had to earn money to take care of them, you can still start a college education. All of these situations can be overcome with a strong belief in self, a commitment to a goal, and working at fulfilling the necessary college requirements. In this chapter you will find ideas, information, checklists, and tips that will make you more self-confident about your abilities and successful in getting into a two-year or four-year college or a university. It will help you do what is necessary while in college so that you will earn a bachelor of arts or science degree and think early about going for an advanced degree, like a master's or a doctorate.

Part I: Believing in Self or *Si Se Puede*

Far too many students of any color (red for Indians, yellow for Asians, black for Africans) have doubts about doing well in college, but for brown people (Latinos) in particular, the doubts begin way before starting college. The authors of this book will help you to understand why it is important to have the right attitude—"I can do it." Many educators and I know there are ways to strengthen your self-imagination, discover what your strengths and weaknesses are and what you can do to increase your capacities as well as reduce your deficiencies. By doing so, you will be successful not only in college but also in work and life. Also, when thinking about yourself in these ways, you can and should assess where you are in life, for example, your age, your obligations to *familia*, your experiences so far, and so forth. Before writing about positive attitudes and thoughts, let us begin by eliminating negative beliefs or myths. By putting these falsehoods out of your mind, you can fill your mind with positive thoughts.

Forget the Excuses of Why You Can't Go to College

The following list presents some excuses you have been told and have come to believe why you can't go to college.

1. I am too old.
2. I don't have the money.
3. I am not smart enough.
4. I did not get a high school diploma.
5. I have family financial responsibilities, so don't have the time.
6. I did not take the right courses in high school to get into college.
7. I started in community college and dropped out.
8. I am too scared to try.
9. I can't move away from my parents.
10. I am a single parent.

11. I cannot get a high score on the SAT or ACT.

12. My parents are undocumented workers.

13. I am not a U.S. citizen.

None of these excuses are reasons to keep you from going to college! Every excuse we tell ourselves or have heard from someone else can be overcome. You can go to college, if you want to go! This book will help you to do two very important things: First, plan and prepare to start your college education. Second, it will guide you to successfully do all that is required to graduate with a college degree.

To prove that the preceding 13 excuses can be overcome, here are some quick but true answers. The answers are in the same order as the excuses.

1. There is no age limit to applying and going to college. During graduation, newspapers publish stories about atypical graduates. One common story is of persons who at the age of 60, 70, 80, or even 90 years get their BA or BS degree from a local college or university.

2. There are financial aids you can apply for and scholarships available to help pay for your college costs. In fact, Congress is increasing the loan limits and making it easier to apply for financial aid. (See Step 3 in the book for more details.)

3. Everyone has a brain. All you have to do is use it. There are college services that help you improve your learning skills, organize your time, and gain access to the latest technologies.

4. If you dropped out before finishing high school, you can study to get a general education diploma (GED).

5. You can go to school and work, continuing to take on your family's financial responsibility. There are services that help you to manage your time better.

6. If you did not take enough math, science, and English courses in high school, you can take courses in college to make up for this. All it will take is more time in college.

7. If you tried college and dropped out, you can reapply to a different college or the previous one again. Even if you left in bad academic standing, you can retake courses in order to get back into good academic standing. All that is required is more effort and time on your part.

8. You can overcome your fear of failure by talking with friends and family who believe in you. Fear is self-imposed. You can get rid of it by saying to yourself, "I have nothing to fear if I work at it."

9. Family is important and if there are reasons why you feel you can't leave home and your relatives, there are always ways to work things out with family and others. If you can't move away, apply to a *local* two-year college and drive to school or take a bus.

10. Being a single parent means that you will need to seek out and find help. Don't try and do everything by yourself. There are many sources: colleges and universities have services to help, employers have ways of helping their workers to improve themselves, and so forth.

11. You don't need to take either the SAT or ACT exam to enroll in a two-year community college. Community colleges have open enrollment, that is, all you need is a high school diploma or GED. In fact, most community colleges ask their students to take a general diagnostic exam to find what their weaknesses are. Then, you can plan a program of study that helps you overcome your deficiencies. See Step Six in this book for more details. From a community college, you can get a transfer to a four-year college or university.

12. By applying to a college for admission, you do not place your parents' status (undocumented) in jeopardy.

13. There are more than 3,300 colleges and universities in the United States. These fall into two basic categories, publicly supported by state legislatures and privates. The majority of private colleges and even some public colleges don't deny enrollment to students based on citizenship.

Attitudes or Behaviors to Make You Successful in College

Now let me share information about developing a way of overcoming the academic challenges created by K-12 teachers and college faculty perceptions, class assignments, college requirements, peer pressure, family expectations, and many more. University faculty and researchers (like Syracuse professor Vincent Tinto) have done studies to learn what contributes to students' graduating. Among the things they have identified are the following:

• *Persistence*: Stay with it, the difficulties will keep on coming, so you need to address them. Don't give up. Remember the old saying, "Quitters never win, winners never quit."

• *Self-discipline*: There are many things you can control. Even if you can't control everything, you can control some part of it. Ask yourself, what can I do by myself? Who controls the other parts and how do I influence them to act on my behalf?

• *Set goals and challenge yourself*: There are different types of goals, and at different times you can think about and set different goals for yourself. The best time to set goals is at the start, for example, set five- or six-year goals when you start your undergraduate degree program, yearly goals at the start of the academic year, and semester goals at the start of each semester. Be realistic about the goals you set; don't make them too easy (e.g., less courses to take) nor too hard (e.g., get all A's in courses).

- *Planning*: Plan for the short term (stepping stones) and the long term—ways to ensure reaching your major goals. For example, if you are taking a course in math and you have done badly in math in the past, find out where you can get some tutoring. Or, if you are taking one more course than you normally take, how can you schedule more time for study and still meet your work requirements? Do your planning in advance of starting a new semester of work.

- *Take action*: Follow your plans; on a monthly basis evaluate your progress. Did you do what you should have done? If not, what should you do to make up for it?

- *Manage time between work and school*: One of your best resources is your time. Also, you can control how you spend most of your time. If you are working part-time and going to college full time, then the majority of your time should be organized and divided to fulfill your academic responsibilities. Set up a daily and weekly calendar for yourself and stick to it. There will be times when you have to adjust your routine time schedule, for example, at the end of the semester, while getting ready for exams, you may have to reduce your work time. So inform your boss in advance about taking this time off. Most work places will accommodate this type of timely request.

- *Balance commitment to self and* familia: Every person's family situation is different, but family relationships are always important. You can't and neither should ignore family obligations or your desire to honor your role whatever it maybe (father, mother, son or daughter, older brother or sister, etc.). By balance we don't mean there must be an even balance (50/50) of time. For as we know, there are some times (such as birthdays or illness of a relative) when you will need to be a father more than a student, a daughter more than a student, and so forth. Again, some family responsibilities are predictable, so plan on responding to them, and let college faculty know in advance if, for example, you need to miss class.

- *Motivation*: You will need to find ways to sustain your energy level throughout your college years. Just like athletes train to keep their body in shape so they can compete in their sport, so too, must college students strengthen their will to compete in the classroom.

- *Refresh self*: Each person has his or her own way of relaxing. By doing so, he or she can remove stress that builds up over a semester. Stress comes at times of class exams or when you have to hand over class assignments. So, in between semesters, do things that refresh your energy, such as physical exercises, biking, reading for fun, attending social events, visit to family members, and so forth.

Start today to adopt these nine attitudes and behaviors. Think positively and act in the affirmative. By putting the excuses out of your thoughts and then replacing them with positives, you will start to be a new and better person and for sure a successful student.

Part II: What Kind of College Is Right for Me to Start My Higher Education?

There are many elements to consider when selecting a college to go to. Even when your options are limited, there are always alternatives to explore and decide on. For example, just when you think the only way to start your higher education experience is by enrolling in the local community college because you are location bound, there are four-year colleges (may be out of your state) that have started offering online courses, for example, the University of Phoenix. The wider your options, the more you have to consider. The more you have to think about, get help by talking with others. That is, don't make decisions by yourself; talk to others to find out what they think. Talk with friends, family, people in the college, and others. Ask questions, think out loud, and listen to others. Decisions are best made when you have information, so collect information. After you have the facts, let your discussion with others help you to organize the facts and think about the meaning or consequences of your choices. However, keep in mind, if after a month or more in the college of your choice makes you think your choice was wrong, you can always change things. No decision is irreversible.

This section is intended to help you, the prospective student, to think in an orderly way to choose the right college. The section is divided into two parts. First, to decide on a college, there are four questions you should ask yourself. The second part gives you ideas on where you can get information to help answer these four questions.

Question#1: What is your purpose for going to college?

Nowadays, very few people go to college for the purpose of gaining a broader knowledge of society and the world. The vast majority of people go to college in order to prepare themselves to enter the world of work and earn as much money as possible so they can have a good life. We typically ask ourselves the first question in this way: "What do I want to become?" The answer is usually a corporate lawyer, a medical doctor, a social worker, an educator, an engineer, a banker, and so forth. But what we are really saying is that college is a means to an end. College education paves the way to become a professional, who earns more salary than skilled workers. The college degree you earn when you graduate will qualify you to enter into the arena you have decided to work in. However, since society is advancing and being transformed with high-technology inventions, there are new professional jobs being created and long-standing professional areas are expanding with new types of occupations. So you should ask yourself: What profession am I interested in? For example, instead of answering narrowly like the preceding examples, of being a corporate lawyer, you should say I am interested in the legal profession. Instead of being a medical doctor, you should say you are interested in medicine, which will allow you to become a nurse, a technician, a surgeon, and so forth. This question of what you want to be is important because it tells you what kind of curriculum (courses to take early in college) or study program to emphasize and declare as your major, for example, if you are going into medicine, then take more science and math courses. You may think that all colleges have the required courses and faculty to provide you with the basics. Yes, but colleges are noted for certain emphases. For example, some emphasize the literal arts, whereas others the sciences. Some four-year colleges have developed reputations in certain fields. So when you are looking for colleges, keep these broad things in mind.

Question #2: What type of college are you thinking of going to (both starting and ending)? Basically you have the following types of colleges to consider.

- Two-year or community colleges: To earn a certificate, an associate of arts or science degree, or to transfer to a four-year college.
- Four-year college: For a BA or BS and possibly continuing on to earn a master's degree.
- University: For comprehensive research or Research I because you definitely want to get a terminal degree beyond a master's like a doctorate or professional degree, for example, jurisprudence (law).
- Public or private: Public colleges are supported by the state they are located in and they cost less than private colleges. Private colleges are supported mostly by student tuition and donors (usually alumni), so their cost is higher, but the benefit they provide in general is better, that is, they help their graduates get a job.
- Technical institutes: These are typically places where training is provided in specific trades, such as culinary arts. These are limited in what they prepare people to do and generally offer a certificate of successful completion, not a degree.

If the answer to the first question is like the examples provided (into a professional field, engineering or social work), you will probably want to think about a four-year college or university (either public or private). But for other reasons, you may have to start off at a local two-year college, commonly named a community college. Some reasons for choosing the community college are: you can't leave the area, don't have sufficient funds, lack a high enough SAT or ACT score, have low grade point average (GPA) in high school, or lack required English, math, and science courses, and so forth. More and more people are starting their higher education experience at community colleges. As a result, these are becoming very good learning institutions (emphasize teaching) and are establishing formal transfer agreements with four-year colleges. By this we mean that upon entering a community college, if you declare to the admission staff that you plan on transferring to a four-year college, and if they have a formal transfer agreement with a four-year college or university, all the courses you take should qualify for the transfer. You won't be wasting time and money taking courses that won't count toward transfer credit. This is important because it is now taking students much longer to finish a four-year degree program of study. The average is now five to six years.

If you are considering entering a four-year college or university at the very start, then you need to get information from them on the following basics:

- What are the requirements for admission into the institution? *Warning: In order for you to meet the many deadlines, you will have to act at lease a semester before or even a year ahead of time.* So plan ahead, but once you start you will be in the pipeline and you will know the college calendar. Typically most four-year colleges require the following in their applications:
  - SAT or ACT scores
  - GPA for high school
  - Official transcripts
  - Others:
    - if applying for financial aid, filled-out forms; or
    - if applying for scholarship, financial information, letters of references, a statement from you about your extracurricular activities.
- Program implications: What is the number of semester credit hours needed to complete the program of your choosing? How long (in years) does it take a student to typically finish?

Question #3: What personal factors will restrict or shape your decision about where to go to college?

College student bodies across the country are changing (Lewin, 2011). They are no longer homogenous (recent high school graduates, 18- to 22-year-olds, singles, full-timers, supported by parents, etc.). Instead, college student bodies have become diverse (whites and students of color, 24- to 30-year-olds, part-timers, working, married with family, etc.). Your decision about where and to which college to apply will be dependent on some personal factors. It will not be solely on what you aspire to become or your academic consideration. The personal factors may also influence your decision more than the academic consideration. Just to get you started, a few will be mentioned here.

- First, what is your status? Are you single or married? Are you a parent? If you are married or a parent, you may not be able to relocate your residence to another city or even another state.
- Family obligations—care for family or the need to work. You may be single, but find that you are the oldest of a large family and have to work to help support your brothers and sisters. Hence again, you may be able to move away, but not too far. That is, you may be able to find work near the college of your choice and send money home, but you may have to go back home frequently like once a month, or during holidays, and so forth.
- Location preference: depending on your point of view, you may want to go to a college setting that you are familiar with (e.g., if you grew up in a big city, you may not want to go to a college in a town). Then again you may want to try something different, that is, if your youth was on the East Coast, you may want to go to college on the West Coast.

Question #4: What is your financial status or what college education can you afford both short and long term? When thinking about your financial situation, you need to ask two types of question, one set is about your circumstances and the second set about the institution. Let's start with questions about you.

- What kind of financial resources are available to you; in particular, do you have a good size savings to help pay for your college education over the years?
- How much debt have you accumulated before starting college or how much debt can you assume while going to college?
- If you are dependent on your family for some assistance, how much will they be able to provide and over how much time? What other sources of support are available to you?

To answer the preceding questions you should ask yourself yet another set of questions, which are: How much are the tuition and fees of the college or university I am interested in applying to? And how many years will it take me to finish my degree?

The second set of questions is directed to the institution. Find out:

- What kind of financial assistance can the college offer?
- Do they have work study programs, scholarships, and tuition waivers? How many students can be supported per year?
- And if you are able to get some type of college support, how long are you eligible to receive the funds?

Since paying for a college education is becoming greater in amount with every passing year, financial considerations, specifically where can you get money to help cover the total cost, is a major consideration for many students. Chapter/Step 3 gives you detailed information about cost of education, where and how you can apply to get financial aid, as well as places for potential scholarships.

Now let us turn our attention on ways you can collect necessary information to help you answer the preceding four major questions and the sub-questions. There are three major ways of collecting information: (1) via the Internet, (2) from a local high school, and (3) from a campus visit. During your quest for information gathering, be sure to talk with your family members, be they parents, grandparents, *tios* and *tias*, wives or husbands, older *hermanos* or *hermanas*, and cousins to see if they have questions that you may not have thought of.

From the Internet

From the Internet, you can get a lot of information quickly at no cost. If you don't have a personal computer at home, you can go to a local public library. All colleges have a website that provides all sorts of information. Everything you want to know about the college can be found on their website. You will even be able to print out (or download) forms that colleges will require you to complete and return to them. The Internet allows you to view this information at any time of day or night. The website works 24/7. Since the website of the university is constantly being updated and added to, it is the best place to collect the following:

- General information about the college; the various programs of studies; faculty numbers and even information about their background; estimated cost per course, fees; types of support services for students, not just academic but medical; student body information, total enrollment; facilities, not just classrooms but recreational; campus activities of all types, and so forth.

- Dates for application and requirements for admission.
- Yearly and semester calendars: when classes start and end, exam week, add or drop classes, holidays, and so forth.
- Forms that can be downloaded for application and financial aids.

From Local High School

If you are still in high school or if you have graduated from a local high school and you still live near it, make an appointment with your former counselor. The purpose of the meeting for you is to collect general and specific information about applying to college from the counselor. Most high schools, but not all, have a day set aside for seniors and sometimes juniors to get some introductory information about going to college. At these large group sessions, you will be able to get only general information. What you should do is have a one-on-one meeting with a high school counselor, so you can ask questions that relate to your particular situation. If you are still in high school, you will probably want to have more than one visit with the counselor. If you are out of high school, you will probably have only a one-time visit with the counselor. If this is the case, write down questions before you visit with the counselor. If the counselor cannot answer a particular question, ask where you can get the information.

On-Campus Visit

Going to campus is important, but more than likely you will not be able to visit more than two campuses that you are interested in applying to, due to travel time and costs involved. The location of the college or university will determine the cost in taking an on-campus visit. Almost all four-year colleges conduct organized tours of the campuses. But you need to find out in advance when they conduct these scheduled tours and how you sign up for one. At the time you call to get signed up for a tour, ask what is typically seen on the tour, how long it takes, and what kind of information you get in order to make application. With such information in hand, you will be able to plan for visiting places on campus that may not be part of the visit, for example, visiting with financial aid staff. Make sure you ask specific questions and collect necessary forms at these meetings.

During the tour, either at the start or at the end, but before it is over, make sure you ask the question: Who teaches the freshman classes and how large are the class sizes? If the answer is regular full-time faculty and the classes are more than 100 students, you should inquire about small break-out discussion groups. If the reply is graduate students (working toward their doctorate) and class sizes are more than 100 students, then you should be concerned. Ask about university services, that is, tutors, developing your study skills like note taking, joining small study groups, and so forth.

Also, you will want to talk with students who have similar backgrounds as you. You will want to know what problems they faced on getting in, how they handled the difficulties, what things were unexpected, and so on. But most importantly, you will want to measure the feeling welcome temperature. As a Latino or Latina in high school, you probably were in the majority, that is, most of the student body was made up of Latinos. But in college, because so few go to college after high school, you may find yourself in the minority. Most colleges are large places. Community college campuses have more than 12,000 students and four-year colleges have 15,000 students or more. Universities typically have more than 20,000 students. With such large numbers, you need to feel like you belong there. This *bienvenido* factor is critical during the first year on campus. It is well known that most persons leave college before they finish their first year of college. How do you know you are welcome? Find out if there are:

• student groups or organizations that you want to join;
• ethnic studies and/or a Latino focus program;
• Latino faculty and staff: (go to Part IV, College and University Directory— College Profiles—in the book, regarding Latino student enrollments, costs and graduation rates, etc.);
• do they have annual events, such as *Cinco de Mayo* celebrations?

Deadlines, Forms, and Attachments

Once you begin to look into going to college, you will quickly come to know that there are deadlines to meet, forms that must be filled out completely, and additional information to get from other places and persons to attach to applications and requests. Once in college, you will come to know that deadlines, forms, and attachments will be with you every year and every semester. So don't resist or complain; it is only a waste of time and adds to your stress level. Welcome it by planning ahead or looking ahead. For example, the college always posts its calendar, containing holidays or no-class meeting dates and other important dates, on its website for class registration a year in advance. Look at it and make plans for yourself, for example, on your personal calendar, mark what classes you will enroll in next semester, what holidays you will take to travel back home to visit with family, and so forth. By doing so, you will be prepared, can get forms early, start to fill them out over time, and slowly put together whatever information you need to submit. You won't be rushed and overloaded all at once. (Remember that most deadlines come about the same time, either at the end of one semester or at the start of a new semester. In any event, these are the same times that you are studying for finals or getting registered in new courses.)

Special Note about Community Colleges

In the previous section about types of college, community colleges were included. Before ending this first chapter or first step, I want to end the way I began. There are a lot of myths or wrong impressions about Latinos and their ability to be successful in college. So too there is a general wrong view held about community colleges. Community colleges are fine institutions to get started. It is generally believed that these places are lesser in quality than four-year colleges. Not so! Most students get a better chance to start their higher education experience in community colleges than at four-year colleges. Why? They have open enrollment. All you need is a high school diploma or GED. Also, upon entering, most community colleges have their students take a diagnostic exam. This is different than the SAT or the ACT. A diagnostic exam tells you what your academic weaknesses or strengths are, that is, writing skills, reading comprehensive skills, and analytical thinking (math ability). These strengths and weaknesses are used to place you in the right level of academic courses. With the right placement, you will not be overwhelmed with the quantity of work required. But most importantly, community colleges provide a solid foundation for their students to go on and complete a four-year undergraduate degree somewhere else. How? Most of their courses are taught by persons holding an advance degree in their subject field or having practical work experience in the subject matter and years of experience as instructors. Secondly, class size is typically under 50. These two facts, instructor experience and class size, enhance your chances of learning more and doing better in other advance classes. So, if you have to start your higher education at a community college, feel good about this. It means you will more than likely be successful in getting not just a four-year undergraduate degree but an advanced degree as well.

Getting Started Is Usually the Hardest Part of the Journey

For many years, more and more students are graduating from high school but unable to read at 12th grade level, do math at 12th grade level, or express themselves either in writing or speaking at a reasonable level. Because large numbers of students are below grade level, SAT and ACT scores are lower, and more importantly, if they are admitted to college, before taking freshman English and other required entry level courses, they must take remedial courses. Remedial courses are classes that help students make up academic deficiencies. And typically, the student does *not* receive academic credit toward their degree for passing these courses. In short, you will be in college longer and paying more, since you will have to take more courses that are required for the degree. I bring this to your attention early because this news may be very discouraging to you. But think positively. First, if you have to take these remedial courses, it will help you overcome academic weaknesses, which means you will do better as you progress. Second, think of remediation as preventive health care. The more you do early to get your mind and body healthy, the stronger you will be when college problems and difficult academic courses are encountered, as they will be. Again, don't think negatively, think positively!

Empower Yourself with a College Education

Empowerment is the key to success, not just in college but throughout life. Having strong self-confidence in your ability to handle any situation is extremely important. Empowerment is a mental way of thinking. With the feeling of empowerment, you can overcome any obstacle or barrier you encounter; it is just a matter of putting in time, expending effort, and applying a strategy. Once you have the feeling of empowerment, then you can attend to satisfying all the challenges both informal and formal, starting with getting admitted into the college of your choice either at the start of your higher education experience or prior to making application by taking some preliminary steps, like taking remedial work over the Internet, entering into an open admission community college and then transferring to a four-year program. Or, your journey in higher education may be a start-and-stop affair, like starting in a two-year college, after earning an AA degree, staying out to work full time for a year or two, and then moving on to a four-year college. Or, another common path others have taken before you is after completing a four-year degree and working full time a few years in the professions of their major, enrolling in a university to earn an advanced degree (master's or doctorate) at a prestigious university, like Harvard and/or Yale in the East Coast or Stanford or UCLA on the West Coast. Just remember and believe that the sky is the limit provided you say to yourself—*Si Se Puede!*

Important Things to Remember about Your First Step

The journey to earning a college degree begins with *you*. Say yes to yourself—"I am going to college."

Put the negative idea that you can't go to college out of your mind and begin to think positively.

To decide on what kind of colleges are right for you (to start at and to end at), ask yourself four basic questions:

What do I want to do or be in life?

What is my personal situation?

Which type of college should I start with?

What is the cost of going to college?

Collect information to help you make decisions. You can get information in three ways:

Internet

At a local high school from a counselor

By visiting campuses and taking an organized tour

Talk to as many people to help you think through the information: parents, spouses, relatives, friends, college staffs, and so forth.

Start your planning and taking action at least a year in advance. You will discover that deadlines and forms to fill out and turn in usually are called for months in advance.

Don't get discouraged about all the rules, regulations, and procedures to meet, information requested, cost factors, forms to fill out, dates to meet, and so forth. Everyone has to do this. The more you look into going to college, the more you will know and be able to plan and prepare yourself.

When you face a challenge, a detour, or a roadblock, don't give up. Say to yourself: "I can overcome the issue." Many others in the past have been in your place and they got over it and succeeded! You can do it—*SI SE PUEDE!*

Translation

Spanish	*English*
Vamanos	Let's go
Familia	Family
Si se puede!	Yes, it can be done!
Tias or *Tios*	Aunts or uncles
Hermanos or *Hermanas*	Brothers or sisters
Bienvenido	Welcome

References

For college success student characteristics read writings by Vincent Tinto, professor of education at Syracuse University, NY.

Lewin, Tamar. "Complete College Report." *New York Times,* September 27, 2011.

Solis, Linda. Short biography can be found at www.dol.gov/sec/welcome.htm.

Success Starts with You: Getting in, Earning Your First Degree, and Considering Graduate School

Patricia L. Guerra

Now that you're in high school, do you ever think about going to college? If you make good grades and have parents with a college degree who provide academic guidance and financial support, this may already be your goal after graduation. But what if you don't? Going to college can appear to be an impossible dream, especially when your GPA is low, no one in your family has gone to college, money is tight, English is your second language, or you dropped out of school. But don't be disheartened because college is still attainable.

Anyone can succeed in college, provided he or she believes in himself or herself and puts time and effort into finishing all the requirements. Do you have the right attitude to be successful, or have you been told by too many for too long that college is not for you? If you do believe in yourself, then this chapter will give you more ideas of how to be successful. If you don't, don't worry. This chapter will help you say, "Yes I can, or *si se puede.*"

This chapter is divided into four sections. In the introductory section, Myths and Misperceptions, common beliefs that teachers, counselors, and administrators tell Latino students are presented and discussed to help you understand that these beliefs are inaccurate and college *is* for you regardless of your situation. The second section, Getting into College, outlines several paths to college and discusses strategies for getting in. Strategies That Will Help You Earn Your First Degree, the third section, provides ways for successfully managing the college experience and graduating, which are often not known to Latinos. Finally, students graduating with a bachelor's degree are encouraged to continue their education and consider earning a graduate degree in the fourth section, Considering Graduate School.

Myths and Misperceptions

1. "College is not for everyone."
2. "You're not college material."
3. "College is only for smart kids."
4. "You can't go to college if you were in special education."
5. "You don't have what it takes to make it at university so consider the community college."
6. "Ivy League schools like Harvard, Yale, and Princeton don't accept students like you."
7. "To do well in college you have to be a strong writer."
8. "You can't go to college if you only took remedial courses and didn't take literature, algebra, calculus, biology, and other college prep courses."
9. "Your GPA is too low to go to college."
10. "Colleges only accept well-rounded students who participate in extra-curricular activities such as bands, sports, and academic and social clubs. Working students are not usually viewed as good applicants for college."
11. "You already speak Spanish so you don't need to take two years of a foreign language to get into college."
12. "You can't go to college because you dropped out of high school."
13. "Students from poor families can't go to college because of the cost."
14. "With your family's lack of financial resources, perhaps you should work after high school and think about college later."
15. "The only way you can pay for college is through student loans."
16. "Only students whose parents have a college degree go to college."
17. "If you want to go to college your parents have to complete the college application forms."

Do any of these statements sound familiar? Have you ever heard a counselor, a teacher, or a principal at school make one or more of these remarks to you, a sibling, or a friend? These are the common myths that educators believe about many Latino students, particularly when students' grades are not good, their families are working class, their parents did not graduate from high school, and/or English is the second language. These myths are used to discourage Latino students from pursuing a college degree. If you have heard them at your school and any of them apply to you, they can be overcome! Do not give up your dream of going to college because these myths are not true.

Myths Related to Intelligence

Myths 1 through 7, which include "college is not for everyone," "college is only for smart kids," and "Ivy League schools like Harvard, Princeton, and Yale don't accept students like you," focus on students' perceived lack of intelligence. These examples and others in this category are told to Latino students by educators believing students are not smart enough to go to college or an Ivy League institution and be successful.

Because many educators (whites and of color) equate knowledge of English with intelligence, that is—the more you speak proper English, the smarter you are—they believe Latinos, as English language learners, lack the intelligence to go to college. They point to students' poor academic performance in high school as evidence that students do not have what it takes to get into college and graduate. However, educators fail to understand that school factors such as early exit from bilingual education programs, poorly trained English as second language (ESL) teachers, and staff with little knowledge of students and families' cultural backgrounds are the primary causes of this situation, *not* students' lack of intelligence.

Intelligence is not measured by proficiency in English but by the ability to learn, reason, and think abstractly. If you have these skills, then you can do college work. Of course, a certain level of English proficiency is required to succeed in college, but if you don't have strong reading and writing skills, these skills can be further developed in college. Many colleges, particularly community colleges offer preparation courses in reading and writing for English language learners and other students seeking to improve their language skills. In addition, individual assistance is available through college writing centers. So, do not let these myths prevent you from going to college.

Myth 4, "You can't go to college if you were in special education," is also related to students' intelligence. Unfortunately, many Latino students are *mistakenly* placed in special education classes because educators lack knowledge of second-language acquisition and culture. When they observe students converse in English but struggle to read and write it, they believe students are slow learners who require special instructions. Rather than understand that these behaviors are part of the second-language acquisition process and more bilingual education or ESL instruction is needed to acquire academic language, students are dismissed from these programs after only one to two years of instructions. Not receiving the five to seven years of second-language instructions they require, students struggle to read and write academic English throughout their school careers.

If you do struggle with reading and writing English, you need to take some prep courses to strengthen these skills. But again, these courses are offered in community colleges and at universities and should be taken prior to starting college course work. With time and hard work, you can learn the academic language needed to be successful in community college and can ultimately transfer to a four-year institution.

Another problem that contributes to Latino students *mistakenly* being placed in special education is the lack of cultural knowledge by many teachers. Culturally unaware teachers often perceive Latino students as passive, dependent, and needy because in class, students tend to wait to be recognized before speaking, prefer groups to independent working, seek teachers' directions and inputs often, and avoid direct conflicts. Believing students should be self-starters, outspoken, and work independently with little directions from teachers to be academically successful, educators view these differences as problems.

Do not believe these perceptions. Students with different learning and interaction styles do well in college. There is no one right way to learn and interact. In fact, to be successful, you are expected to use a variety of styles. For example, in the first two years of college when classes are large in size, students are expected to demonstrate individual initiative in completing the course work with little teacher direction. Sometimes containing as many as 300 students, students receive little individual attention in these huge classes, and multiple-choice exams are frequently used to measure students' learning. But once courses are taken in one's major (career choice), usually in years three and four, group work and project-based assessments are used. In these small classes of approximately 25–30, students are required to work collaboratively to produce projects that demonstrate their learning of course content.

If you do have a legally documented disability and special learning needs, by law, colleges must provide accommodation services for the specific disability. For example, classroom interpreters are provided for hearing impaired students, whereas additional time and a quiet testing place may be allocated for students with a learning disability. The goal is for students to be successful in college so the learning environment is tailored to fit the students' needs.

Myths Related to Academic Preparation

Myths 8 through 12, such as "you can't go to college if you only took remedial courses and didn't take literature, algebra, calculus, biology, and other college prep courses" and "your GPA is too low to go to college," address students' academic preparation. Latino students, especially those from working-class families, may not have as much academic preparation as their white classmates for several reasons. First, as previously discussed, schools generally do not provide the five to seven years of bilingual education that is needed to learn to read and write academic English. Second, teachers believe students lacking English proficiency are not very smart and often place students in remedial and vocational courses. Third, irrelevant lessons, textbooks, and boring instructions (i.e., drill and kill) in these courses neither challenge nor prepare students for college. Combine these factors with teachers who do not understand nor value students' or parents' cultures but instead believe students are unmotivated to learn, lazy, and not smart, and their parents don't value education and are uncaring and a perfect storm results. It is no wonder why there is a 15 percent dropout rate for Latino high school students who have attended U.S. schools, which is twice as high as the national average (Pew Hispanic Center, 2010).

Currently you may be in remedial classes at your high school or you may have already dropped out of school, but don't let this stop you from going to college. With some determination, hard work, and time, you can overcome these barriers. If you're in high school taking remedial courses, take advantage of the time left by putting in extra study time to improve your academic language skills and take and pass as many math, science, and social studies courses as possible. Seek additional help and tutoring from teachers and friends. Ask to take courses in the regular education track. The goal is to pass your courses and the state exit exam so you can graduate from high school. Although you may graduate with a low GPA don't worry because community colleges accept high school graduates even with low GPAs. All that is required is a high school diploma or GED. If you want to attend a four-year institution, you will first have to go to a community college and take courses to raise your GPA. After two years of course work and earning the required GPA you can then transfer to the college of your choice.

Once in college you may need to continue working on your writing skills or take literature, biology, algebra, and other preparation courses before beginning college courses. You can do this, especially at community college where courses are not only more affordable but are also offered in the evenings so you can work during the day.

If you're in the regular education track, study hard, request more challenging assignments, and ask to take college prep courses or advanced placement and honors courses. The goal is to take as many English, math, and science courses as you can in preparation for passing college entrance exams (SAT or ACT) and maintaining a good GPA.

But what if you dropped out of school, myth 12? Is attending college still possible? Yes, but first you must earn a GED and then you can apply for college. The GED exam can be taken online or at a local testing center. For more information, see "How to Get a GED: A Step-by-Step Process to Earn a GED" (Education-Portal.com, 2011).

"Colleges only accept well-rounded students who participate in extracurricular activities such as bands, sports, and academic and social clubs. Working students are not usually viewed as good applicants for college" (myth 10). If you want to attend college but have not participated in school activities such as sports, bands, and clubs because you are working part-time to help your family survive, then consider a community college. Participation in extracurricular activities is not required by community colleges. In addition, after successfully completing your basic requirements, you can transfer to a four-year institution without participation in these activities. But remember, even if you have a reasonable GPA and no extracurricular activities to report, you can still apply to a four-year university along with your application to community college. The university might accept you, knowing that you had to work while going to school, but be sure to indicate this on your college application. In addition, you can always decline admission to community college if accepted by the university.

If you prefer starting at a four-year institution, then participation in extracurricular activities is an important part of your college application. Participation in these activities shows you can handle multiple responsibilities, effectively manage your time, and provide service while still maintaining a good academic record. However, participation is not only limited to school-sponsored activities. Activities like Junior Reserve Officer Training Corps (ROTC) program, drill teams, church choir, hobbies, and community services at a homeless shelter, food bank, library, and church will all count as extracurricular activities. Working part-time along with employer recommendations will also count but may not replace participation in these activities.

"You already speak Spanish so you don't need to take two years of a foreign language to get into college" (myth 11). This is not true. In order to be accepted into college, high school students are generally required to take two years of a single foreign language regardless of whether they speak it or not, and some schools like Harvard and other top universities recommend three to four years. If you're not currently enrolled in a foreign language class now, make sure you do so as soon as possible or your application will most likely be rejected by a four-year institution. Even though you speak Spanish, you can still take it as your foreign language requirement, and if you don't read and write Spanish it's probably a good choice and will make you much more marketable after graduating from college. Just think of how much easier it will be for you to be successful in completing this foreign language requirement. Or, you can take French, Russian, Latin, or any other foreign language.

Community colleges will not prevent your admission if you do not have these two years but will require that you take them as part of your basic requirements. So start now and build on the skills you do have.

Myths Related to Paying for College

Myths 13 through 15 such as "students from poor families can't go to college because of the cost" or "the only way you can pay for college is through student loans" revolve around paying for college. Latino students often give up their dreams of college because of these myths. If your family does not have money to pay for college, you can still go. It may take more time and effort on your part, but it will be well worth the investment for you and your family. The return in employment income after college is large and good for over a lifetime. (See Chapter 3.)

One way to pay for college is to work and pay as you go, taking one to two courses a semester until a degree is earned. Many community colleges offer a full array of courses during the day and in the evening so students can attend classes and work. This route may take more time, but there will be no student loans to repay when you graduate from a local community college with your associates degree. Then you should transfer to a four-year institution where you can take classes and still work to pay for college. The costs will be higher and you will most likely have to obtain financial aid such as scholarships, grants, and student loans to help defray the costs. Colleges and universities have financial aid offices that provide assistance in identifying ways to pay for college. You should also search the Internet for websites such as Scholarships.com and the Hispanic College Fund. Scholarships.com lists various types of state and federal grant programs and scholarships offered by foundations, corporations, and community organizations (such as the Rotary Club), while the Hispanic College Fund features scholarships that are specifically for Hispanic students, such as the Sally Mae Fund First in My Family Scholarship Program or Google Hispanic College Fund Scholarship Program. Every year, private, governmental, and nonprofit organizations give money to high school and college students with a strong academic record or to those in need. So it is well worth the time to look and apply for these opportunities. Obtaining this type of financial aid means less reliance on student loans and less debt to repay once you graduate. But if you do have some student loans, don't worry because the investment you make in getting your college degree will be returned 10-fold. It will not only open the door to more and better job opportunities for you, but you will also earn much more money than you could with only a high school degree. With more income you can repay student loans over a number of years, give money to your parents, and provide a better life for your children once you have your own family.

If you have a high GPA in high school and you want to go directly to a university, another way to pay for college is through scholarships. If you are in the top 10 percent of your graduating class, you should approach your high school counselor and ask for information on scholarships and also conduct Internet searches for these financial resources. Students with a high GPA and whose family is poor are not only eligible for scholarships based on merit but also on need. So the chances are good that you will be awarded at least one scholarship.

Myths Related to Parental Support

Myths 16 and 17, "only students whose parents have a college degree go to college" and "if you want to go to college your parents have to complete the college application forms," focus on parental support. Having parents who attended college can make applying for and attending college easier. As parents have experienced the process, they have knowledge about it and can advise their children early on about the importance of taking the right classes, making good grades, being involved in extracurricular activities, taking college entrance exams, visiting colleges, and applying for scholarships. They also know how to complete college admission forms and financial-aid paperwork.

If your parents did not attend college, don't be disheartened. You can still complete this process with guidance from others. First, identify siblings, cousins, friends, classmates, your parents' coworkers, people at church, and other individuals who have attended college and ask for assistance and mentoring. People are usually very willing to help students who want to improve their lives. You only have to ask. Second, for example, in Texas, the Austin Chamber of Commerce hosts Financial Aid Saturdays in which free help is provided to students and families in completing complex college financial-aid forms. Additionally, Volunteer Corps for College attempts to connect faculty and staff from the University of Texas campuses across the state to first-generation college-going students and their families. Volunteers located in high schools or community centers provide guidance in college preparation including college admissions and completing financial-aid paperwork. Finally, there are a number of websites such as:

www.collegeboard.org

http://studentaid.ed.gov/students/attachments/siteresources/CollPrep.pdf

http://csopportunityscholars.org/

http://www.fafsaonline.com/

http://www.hsf.net/

on Internet that provide specific information and advice on preparing for college, applying for admission, searching for scholarships and financial aid, and making the move from high school to college. If you don't have a computer and Internet at your home, use one at school or the local library.

Do not let these myths stop you from pursuing your dream of creating a better life for you and your family. With determination, effort, time, and persistence you *can* go to college and be successful. If you're from a middle-class family, make good grades, and English is your first language, these myths may be unfamiliar to you. Instead, you may have heard "You're not like them," particularly if you're in advanced placement classes or in the college prep track at school. But don't be fooled. Although you may not have yet personally encountered these beliefs, you will at some point in college and in your career.

Getting into College

Know Yourself

When thinking about getting into college, it is important to know yourself and the path you are on because this information is helpful in guiding decision making related to college and identifying needed supports to be successful. To know yourself, first take stock of your assets. Identify your values, skills, abilities, talents, and interests by asking yourself several questions. When thinking about going to college, decide what is important to you? Is staying close to family important or moving away from home? Is saving money important or going to a prestigious university?

Next consider your skills, abilities, and talents by asking, "What can I do?" and "What am I good at?" Do you speak and write several languages, know computers, draw, enjoy talking to new people, play instruments, or are you good at math and science? Also ask, "What is of interest to you?" Do you like working with children, writing stories, doing research, debating and politics, or caring for animals? The answers to these questions are important because they will guide your decisions about college, that is, where to go and what to study. For example, if you want to stay close to home and save money, then attending a community college for the first two years and transferring to a university close to your home might be the best decision for you. However, if the local university does not have the major in which you're interested in or your city doesn't have a university, you will have to consider transferring to an out of city or out of state college or university.

The last question you should ask yourself is: "What do I want to be after college?" or "What will I do professionally?" You won't have to make this decision in the first two years of college because you don't have to declare a major until the start of the third year, but if you want to be a lawyer, doctor, or in business like a banker, your choice of a bachelor's degree is important. A degree in interdisciplinary studies or general studies will not serve you well since these degrees do little to prepare you for admission to a graduate program. Rather than focusing on one area of study in the last two years of the bachelor's degree, a variety of courses are taken in multiple disciplines such as literature, art, science, math, sociology, and anthropology. As a result, students graduate with a little knowledge about a lot of different subjects but lack deep knowledge of any one area. For example, graduating with a bachelor's degree in biology with approximately 60 hours of course work in science will prepare you much better for medical school than one three-hour introductory course in biology. It is for such reasons that it is important to think ahead and make strategic decisions when thinking about college.

The second step in taking stock of yourself is to identify your challenges because these too will influence your decisions about college. First, consider your academic challenges. Do you need to improve your writing skills? Is your GPA low? Have you only taken remedial courses and no college prep courses like algebra, biology, and literature? Do you have poor study habits? Also consider personal circumstances that may also present challenges. Will you have to work to pay for college? If so, how many work hours? Will you have to live at home to help with younger siblings? Will you have personal transportation to get to college or have to take a bus? The responses to these questions are important in deciding whether a community college or a four-year university is the right choice for you. If you are facing academic challenges it may be best to start at a community college to improve your academic skills and GPA and then transfer to a four-year college or a university. If you are also dealing with personal challenges like those previously mentioned, living at home and attending a community college will save money and allow you to provide assistance to your family. What is important is that no matter how many obstacles you come up with, they can all be overcome. So don't get discouraged. Press onward.

Paths to College: Which Path Are You On?

Each one of us is on a different path or life journey shaped by our family's history, expectations, economic status, education, and other life circumstances and by our own beliefs, decisions, and choices. These factors do not predetermine the final destination of your path but may be important in guiding the decisions you need to make about college and identifying the supports you need along the way to be successful. So which path are you on? Are you currently in high school but not thinking of college because you have been told by too many and for too long that you are not college material (path 1)? Or, are you still in high school but considering community college because you do not have the money or academic preparation to apply to a four-year college or university (path 2)? Are you in high school and plan to attend a four-year college or a university because you are a straight-A student and your family has the financial resources to pay for college (path 3)? Or, have you graduated from high school, are currently in the workforce and married, or getting out of the military but do not feel college is for you because you're too old (path 4)? Or, did you drop out of school and are working but have ruled college out because you lack a high school degree (path 5)? Regardless of the path you are on, college is still possible.

If you are on life paths 1, 2, 4, or 5, one of the best ways to continue your education is to start at a community college and then transfer to a four-year institution. Even if you have not taken college preparation courses or have a low GPA, community colleges have open admissions policies, which means they are required to accept almost every student who applies. This is not the case for four-year colleges or universities. Since so many students apply to these institutions, and enrollment is limited, they use scores on college admissions exams such as the ACT and the SAT and high school GPAs along with other items such as student essays, and participation in extracurricular activities to screen out students from the applicant pool. If you did not score well on your college admission exams (or did not take them), graduated with an average to low GPA, and did not participate in extracurricular activities, your chances of being accepted to these institutions are very low. In contrast, community colleges do not require SAT or ACT scores or a high GPA and participation in extracurricular activities, but upon admission, assess applicants' academic skills and preparation to determine if additional courses should be taken. So if you're writing skills need improvement, you might have to take a writing course along with other required basic courses but you will get in.

Registration costs for community colleges are also significantly less in comparison to a four-year institution with the average per-year tuition and fees at approximately $2,800 for a community college compared to $8,000 for a four-year institution. And since most cities have a community college, you can live at home and save money on room and boarding. You can also work and take courses in the evening because community colleges cater to working students as well as to those who are full time and attend classes during the day. This is not necessarily the case at a four-year institution where classes are usually offered mostly during the day at the bachelor level. In addition, once you complete the first two years of required course work, improve your academic skills, and raise your GPA, you will be able to easily transfer to a four-year institution because many community colleges have guaranteed admissions programs with four-year colleges or universities. So there are a number of benefits to attending a community college first.

Also if you're older, don't worry because the average age of a community college student is 29 (American Association of Community Colleges, 2011). Students range in age from 18 to 65 years of age.

Another option, which has recently become more available, is online programs. This option seems to work well for students who have to stay close to home, do not have access to a local community college or university, and want to work full time in order to pay for college. However, be very careful when choosing an online program. It must be accredited (i.e., meets an acceptable level of quality), have a positive reputation in the field, and credits must transfer to other institutions if a bachelor or an advanced degree is pursued. Otherwise, you may pay for courses only to discover the credits you earned are not accepted at a four-year college or a university or to a law or medical school.

Online programs can be very alluring because in some cases they cost less, little to no travel is required, and course work can be done in pajamas at your convenience but there are some factors to seriously consider before committing to virtual education. If you prefer to learn through class activities and discussions with others, require structure to meet course deadlines, have limited technology skills, and your field of study requires hands on practice (i.e., biology, counseling), pursuing online education is probably not the best choice for you. Taking courses online requires a lot of self-discipline and work at a computer, which can be tedious and seem like drudgery, especially when it's not your preferred learning style. In addition, when you need assistance with difficult content, access to instructors is limited. So before taking courses online consider your computer skills, study habits, learning style, field of study (i.e., requires hands-on practice), and instructor accessibility because any one of these factors might make the difference between success and failure.

It is also important to know (although online programs don't tell you) that currently many employers do not consider bachelor and advanced degrees from virtual universities as prestigious as those earned from a reputable, face-to-face institution. In other words, if two college graduates apply for the same job and both have identical qualifications, with the exception of where their degree was earned, it's highly likely that the graduate from a face-to-face institution will be hired over the one with an online degree. This perception may eventually change once online education is adopted widely by face-to-face institutions but for now it is an unspoken reality. So if at all possible, *do not* earn a degree from an online program. Take only a few online courses and make sure the credits transfer to a four-year institution. For a list of accredited online programs and courses offered across the country along with tuition costs and student reviews, see http://www.distance-education.org/.

Strategies That Will Help You Earn Your First Degree

Due to the fact that many Latino students are first in their family to go to college, they are often unaware of valuable strategies that many middle-class students use to successfully manage the college experience and graduate. Because many middle-class parents are college graduates, they share valuable information and insight with their children to facilitate admission to college, make the transition from high school to college less traumatic, and increase chances of academic success. Therefore, the purpose of this section is to share some of these important strategies with you.

Attending college regardless of whether the college is located close to home or out of state can be a scary experience, especially when you have little knowledge of what to expect. There are many forms and steps to complete, decisions to make, procedures to learn, and buildings to find your way around. Not only is the campus usually larger than your high school, but there are also many more people who may not look and act like you. All of these factors combined can make going to college lonely and overwhelming at times. To prevent this situation from occurring to you, initiate the following strategies.

Strategy 1. During your senior year find people like you who have been accepted to the same college and go together to reduce anxiety and isolation. You can attend orientation, take the same courses, study, and socialize together, and if the college is out of town, you can room together in the same dorm or apartment. Sharing the experience with others like you makes it less intimidating, more manageable, and fun.

Strategy 2. Once you and your friends start college, in classes and at other campus activities make it a point to meet other people like you and add them to your group. Your group can range from 4 to 5 people to as large as 20.

Strategy 3. Meet regularly to develop relationships with and among these friends to build a network that provides emotional support, study groups, advice and information on college-related topics, and emphasizes group success and cooperative work. The primary goal is to provide guidance, support, and encouragement to each other in order for everyone in the group to successfully manage college and graduate. In other words, this is your college family and family members are responsible for each other's success.

Strategy 4. In classes, befriend others who are different from you, do academically well, and seem to be very knowledgeable of the college system. Although you may choose not to invite these different friends into your group, befriending them is important because they usually have information, contacts, and resources you are unaware of and unavailable to you. Thus, if each individual in your group were to make a friend of this nature, your group's knowledge and access to these resources and contacts would exponentially increase, making your college experience easier. In addition, once you graduate, this large network of friends will be very useful when searching for a job. They can inform you of job opportunities, write references, and serve as a contact to a prospective supervisor.

Strategy 5. Identify a good mentor in the community who you respect, shares your background, has graduated from college, and can provide guidance and support. A good mentor is someone who believes in you and puts forth additional assistance to ensure you are successful.

He or she will get to know you (i.e., strengths, challenges, capabilities, dreams), allay your fears, build your confidence, provide insight and advice, and give constructive feedback when needed. And, if your mentor is in the career that you want to be, he or she can also share stories about successes, challenges faced, and lessons learned.

There are several ways to find mentors. First ask your parents, extended family members and friends, and have them also ask their coworkers. They might know someone who would be interested in serving in this role. Second, look for someone at your place of employment. Third, contact your college (i.e., admissions, minority affairs) because faculty and graduate students working in the field often volunteer to mentor entering college freshmen. Fourth, contact local businesses because they often encourage their employees to mentor high school and college students as service to the community. Fifth, go to churches, community-based organizations, and other nonprofit organizations and ask if they know of professionals in the community who you could approach. Finally, in this age of technology, do not restrict your search by city limits. Use the Internet to identify and email people who may live across the country but would be willing to serve as a mentor.

Using these five major strategies will promote academic success, make the college experience enjoyable, and facilitate graduation as well as counteract the effects from other negative forces. Regrettably, you will encounter some of the same myths and misperceptions in college as you did in high school. They may not be as widespread as they were in high school but they will be there. Therefore, it is important to be prepared and implement these strategies starting in high school and throughout college.

First-Hand Practical Advice

Many high school students believe they have to be smart to get into college and graduate. It is true that some degree of intelligence is needed to get into college and graduate, but it does *not* guarantee success. Persistence, self-discipline, time management, organizational skills, and self-confidence often play a bigger role in leading to graduation. In fact, many college students with average intelligence do well because they understand college is more of a series of hoops to jump through or tasks to complete (e.g., college applications, financial paperwork, projects, etc.) than a test of intelligence. They understand successful completion of college requires tenacity, time, and effort. Consequently, they spend their time studying rather than partying with friends. When a problem like a difficult course (e.g., physics) is encountered, they don't give up, study the same amount of time as usual, or study in the same way. Instead, they commit even more time to studying and in some cases seek the help of others like a classmate, a study group, or a teaching assistant (TA) in order to learn the material. They know if they devote the time to it they will pass.

If you don't currently have qualities like self-discipline, time management, organization skills, and so forth, then you should work on developing them now while in high school because intelligence alone will not ensure your success at college. Talk to friends and teachers who have these qualities and find out the actions they entail. Then develop an improvement plan for yourself and stick with it until these qualities are acquired. If you have these qualities but are concerned about whether you're smart enough to go to college, rest assured that if you're an average student, you can do well in college. You may have to put in more study time but given that you're tenacious and self-disciplined, you can do it.

Considering Graduate School

Now fast forward, thinking of long term after four or five years of college. You've almost completed the bachelor's degree and are ready to graduate. Why consider graduate school? Whether you consider attending graduate school immediately after earning your bachelor's degree or waiting a few years, earning a graduate degree opens the door to so many more possibilities. First, some majors like psychology and sociology require advanced degrees in order to practice professionally in the field and make sizeable incomes. For example, to be a psychologist or to teach psychology as a college professor a PhD is required. Without this, advanced degree individuals, particularly with bachelor's degrees, are often limited to working as attendants at psychiatric hospitals or as houseparents at residential schools and make minimum wages. To avoid graduating with a degree that results in a job with minimal income and little upward advancement, it is important to know in the third year of your undergraduate degree if you will need to attend graduate school.

Second, a graduate degree opens doors to career advancement and other job opportunities that pay significantly more, for example, from teacher to principal, nurse to doctor, and businessperson to lawyer. Perhaps you're thinking, "I will never want to be . . . so why go to graduate school?" You may currently not want to be a principal, a doctor, or a lawyer, but once you mature and gain years of experience at your job, you may want to advance or switch careers. Without the necessary graduate education, you may not be able to take advantage of available opportunities that come your way.

Finally, by getting an advanced degree you pave the way for others in your family to go to college and graduate school and you become a model for your own children. They will learn higher education is important for them and for their future children. As a result, your family and generations to come will improve their economic status and give back to the Latino community.

Perhaps you're already considering graduate school but have heard that you need a high Graduate Record Exam (GRE) score to be accepted and you have to be really smart to go to graduate school. Neither of these myths is true. You will have to take the GRE, but if you graduated at the undergraduate level with a good GPA, many colleges and universities will place less importance on your GRE score and allow you to come in on probationary status. Once you demonstrate that you can do college work and make A's and B's, probationary status will terminate at the end of the first semester.

Like the advice given about going to college, you don't have to be extremely smart to go to graduate school but you do have to be very disciplined, driven, persistent, organized, and should manage your time well. Because graduate school is another series of hoops to jump through, only many more than what you encountered in the undergraduate program. Some degree of intelligence is required but a far greater degree of self-discipline and tenacity are required in graduate school. People don't usually fail because they're not smart enough. They fail because they do not dedicate adequate time and effort to studying and completing course assignments, but instead spend their time at work and at play. So don't let these myths stop you from going to graduate school. Once you enter college, you can and will succeed, if you decide to do it. *Si Se Puede.*

Summary

The following list provides a number of steps for facilitating your admission to college, particularly if you are an average student, your GPA is low, your family has no money for college, you are an English language learner, no one in your family has gone to college, or you have dropped out of school. This list is not intended to be exhaustive but delineates essential steps you and your family need to know. For a comprehensive list of steps for getting into a four-year university or a college directly upon high school graduation go to: http://www.collegeprep101.com. There you will find four checklists created by Lance Millis (2007). Each list details a number of important steps to be taken during the freshman, sophomore, junior, and senior years to facilitate admission into a four-year institution.

9th–12th Grade

The following steps should be implemented each year of high school:

- Commit to going to college by turning your dream into a goal. Print this goal on a large piece of paper or tag board and post it in a location where you see it every day and *believe it.*
- Identify a good mentor in the community who you respect, shares your background, has graduated from college, believes in you, and can provide guidance and support.
- Develop a strong relationship with your mentor and meet him or her at least twice a month for advice, guidance, and assistance with education-related matters and to develop self-confidence.
- Disregard the myths and misperceptions teachers, counselors, and administrators at school tell you about going to college because they are likely untrue. If you are unsure as to whether the information an educator gives you is a myth or not, seek counsel from your mentor to determine the truth.
- Take stock of your challenges and develop a plan of action. For example, if you're weak in math, don't avoid it; take more math classes and obtain tutoring from teachers or classmates. Identifying these challenges and the supports you need to be successful in high school will facilitate getting into college.
- Study every day even if you have to work or take care of younger siblings.
- Practice self-discipline, time management, and organization skills and if you don't have these skills, find a teacher or a friend who can help you develop them.
- Build a network of friends who share your background and dream of going to college and meet regularly. Provide emotional support to each other, study together, and share information and resources on getting into college. Also invite counselors and teachers who do *not* believe in the myths about Latino students to share information on topics like dealing with educators who do believe in the myths, courses to take in high school, the importance of taking challenging curriculum and studying daily, students' rights, methods for developing self-discipline, time management, and organizational skills, and so forth.
- Have the parents of the friends in your network build relationships with each other and meet regularly. Ask your mentor(s) and others from your

community with a college education to come to talk to the group about how important it is to get a good high school and college education, parental rights, the obstacles families are likely to face along the way and how to deal with them such as how to deal with educators who believe in the myths about Latino families, and how a college degree will economically benefit the family and not just the student. In addition to helping parents realize they have common concerns, your mentor should encourage them to share resources, assistance, and support. This step is very important because a group of parents is much more powerful than one lone individual, when advocating for students' needs.

- Ask a counselor(s) who does not believe in the myths to meet with the network of parents to share information on the importance of children studying daily, helping your child study, college readiness tracks versus, regular, remedial, and vocational education, parents' rights, completing college applications, and financial paperwork, and so forth. If you can't find a counselor to do this, ask your mentor, others in your community who have a college degree, outreach groups, or staff from local colleges.

- Befriend others in classes who do academically well and seem to be very knowledgeable about getting good grades and into college because they may have information, contacts, and resources you may be unaware of.

- Tell your parents that you want to go to college and there will be times during high school when they will have to go to school and advocate on your behalf.

- Have your parent(s), another family member, or mentor attend all meetings at school and request a translator if needed.

- Learn to advocate for yourself. When you believe educators have made a decision or action that is not in your best interest, like being placed in special education when you don't have a disability, or don't allow you to take regular or advanced classes, speak up, ask questions, and express your concerns to school personnel. If they disregard your objections, go home and tell your parents and have them go to school to advocate for you. Educators are not always right. You and your parents must question their decisions, and when it doesn't feel right, tell educators, "no." Your parents have legal rights so they must speak up on your behalf. If your parents do not speak English or do not feel confident about their ability to advocate, ask your mentor to accompany your parents to school and have him or her represent your interests.

- Stop by your counselor's office and introduce yourself. Make it a point to get to know the counselor and have the counselor get to know you. Let the counselor know that you *are* going to college regardless of academic and financial challenges and ask for his or her assistance.

- Inform your teachers that you *are* going to college so they will facilitate your success rather than impede it.

- Become familiar with resources (i.e., financial aid information, college visits) in your school and in the community that will facilitate getting to college and actively pursue them otherwise you may not be informed of them. Teachers, counselors, and administrators who believe in the myths about Latino students may never seek you out to give you the necessary information for going to college, such as notices about college visits and scholarships, college application forms, and financial-aid information.

- Develop your English reading and writing skills by working on them daily with a teacher, a friend, or a family member.

- Seek tutoring from teachers, classmates, or your network of friends when you encounter difficult subject matter in class.

- Seek challenging assignments and classes to improve your academic skills rather than avoiding them.

- Take and pass as many higher level math, science, language, arts, and social studies courses as possible.

- Ask to be placed in honors and advanced classes when you feel you can do the work.

- If possible, participate in extracurricular activities at school like sports, drama, choir, clubs, student council, ROTC, and so forth. Or, volunteer in your community at a homeless shelter, food bank, library, and church.

- Take two years of a foreign language in school, such as Spanish, even though you may already speak it or are told by school personnel that you don't need it to go to college.

- Don't ever give up in high school; persist even in difficult times.

11th Grade

The following steps should be done during the junior year:

- Take stock of your assets by identifying your values, skills, abilities, talents, interests, and constraints like finances. This information will help guide your decisions about a possible career and college major. Additionally, it will help determine whether you should apply to a community college, a four-year college or a university or to an out-of-state institution.

- Have the counselor(s) who do not believe the myths about Latino families meet with your network of friends and their parents to share information on college websites and tools and how to use them, financial assistance options

such as scholarships and grant and how to use them, the processes for applying to college and financial aid, developing contacts who can facilitate college
admission, and so forth.

- Surf the Internet for websites such as the following to obtain detailed information and advice on preparing for college, applying for admission, searching for scholarships and financial aid, and making the move from high school
to college.
  - wwwcollegeboard.org
  - http://studentaid.ed.gov/students/attachments/siteresources/CollPrep.
  pdf
  - http://csopportunityscholars.org/
  - http://www.fafsaonline.com/
  - http://www.hsf.net/
- Explore different colleges using Internet, including online programs, and select a few that you are interested in attending and with availability of financial assistance such as scholarships, grants, and work-study programs. Be
sure to visit the community college in your city.
- Make visits to college campuses with your family and select a college to
attend.
- Sit down with your family and consider your academic record, your family's
financial situation, available financial aid, and identify the most feasible path
to college (i.e., community college, local college, or out-of-state university)
and select a college to attend.

12th Grade

The following steps should be taken during the senior year:

- Search the Internet for sites such as Scholarships.com and the Hispanic College Fund Scholarships.com, which lists various types of state and federal
grant programs and scholarships offered by foundations, corporations, and
community organizations (such as the Rotary Club) and apply for those that
you qualify.
- Identify siblings, cousins, friends, your parents' coworkers, people at church,
and other individuals who have attended college and ask for assistance in
completing college applications and financial-aid forms. Or, look for outreach programs sponsored by your city's chamber of commerce or the local
community college to get assistance with the paperwork.
- Prepare and submit college applications.

- Complete financial-aid forms and apply for all types of financial assistance, such as scholarships, grants, and work-study programs and not just loans.

- Identify peers with your background or friends in your network who have been accepted to the same college and go together to reduce anxiety and isolation.

References

American Association of Community Colleges. *Students at Community Colleges.* Washington, DC: Author, 2011, http://www.aacc.nche.edu/AboutCC/Trends/Pages/studentsatcommunitycolleges.aspx.

Education-Portal.com. "How to Get a GED: A Step-by-Step Process to Earn a GED," 2011, http://education-portal.com/articles/How_to_get_a_GED%3A_a_Step-by-Step_Process_to_Earn_a_GED.html.

Millis, L. "Comprehensive College Planning Checklists." *College Prep-101,* 2007, http://www.collegeprep101.com/college_planning_checklist.htm.

Pew Hispanic Center. "Latino Teens Staying in High School: A Challenge for All Generations." In *Fact Sheet.* Washington, DC: Author, 2010, http://pewhispanic.org/category/publications.

What Does College Cost and Where Can I Find Financial Aid?

Jacob Fraire

Learning What It Costs to Go to College

Nearly everyone is concerned about the cost of a college education. Yet, understanding how much college actually costs is not easy, especially when we hear countless news reports of rising college tuition compared to the rate of inflation and read about the wide differences in cost between one college and another college. The actual cost of a college education can be determined as the published cost (what colleges publish, usually on their websites, as their total cost in tuition and fees), plus other educational expenses, minus student financial aid, tuition discounts, and federal tax credits provided to individual students. The result is known as the college's net price. The net price is the amount that a student will actually pay.

Generally, colleges will only publish the cost of tuition and fees, which you pay directly to the institution. Actual costs also include books, supplies, transportation, room and board, and personal expenses. Today, personal computers have become a common learning tool for students; so, colleges have begun to include computers in their calculation of a student's cost of attendance.

One way of reviewing college cost is to compare cost by the type of institution. For example, for four-year public universities, the published in-state average tuition and fees charged during academic year 2010–2011 is $7,605, or about $555 more than the previous year (Baum and Ma, 2010, 10). The average total expenses (including room and board, transportation, and other expenses) for the same year was $16,140. Another method of comparing cost is to look for regional differences in college costs. The average published tuition and fees for four-year institutions in the Southwest is $7,105 compared to $9,857 for four-year public universities in New England, northeast region. When you add room and board, the average costs are $14,236 and $19,444 for the Southwest and New England regions, respectively (Baum and Ma, 2010, 14).

Today, colleges are required to provide a method for students and families to determine their college's net price. The result is that several websites have been developed to do just that. A good place to visit is the Net Price Calculator website hosted by The College Board at: http://www.collegeboard.com/html/npc/index.html.

Financial Aid and Its Role in Helping Pay for College

Student financial aid is the term used to describe monies provided by federal and state governments, individual colleges, and private foundations and donors to help students pay for college. There are two main categories of financial aid: *grants and scholarships* (monies that students do not have to pay back) and *self-help aid* (monies that students either must earn, such as work-study, or repay such as loans).

The federal government is the largest single provider of student financial aid, annually providing nearly $160 billion in financial aid (inclusive of student loans and tax credits). The U.S. Department of Education (ED) provides funding for the Federal Pell Grant Program—the largest grant program for low-and-moderate income undergraduate students. For the academic year 2010–2011, the federal government provided more than $36 billion for Pell grants to nearly 9 million students; the average Pell grant award amount was $4,115 (U.S. Department of Education, 2011).

There is a misconception that student loans are not a form of financial aid. They are. The difference is that unlike grants, student loans must be repaid. During 2010–2011, students and parents borrowed an estimated $116 billion as federal student loans to help pay for college (U.S. Department of Education, 2011). State-supported student loans and private (nongovernment) loans are available for eligible students in addition to federal student loans. Many colleges also offer *tuition discounts and waivers*, which lower a student's total cost. Tuition discounts, when they are offered, are specific to each college; *students should contact the financial-aid office of the college of their choice to ask whether they offer tuition discounts and waivers.*

A College Education Is the Best Investment for a Promising Future

The concern over college cost is serious. However, it sometimes overshadows another important consideration: the economic and personal benefits from earning a college degree. It is true that earning a bachelor's degree requires a commitment of money, time, and personal sacrifice (time away from family and work, as examples). However, these sacrifices and expenditures can also be seen as investments in a student's future and their potential for higher incomes. According to the U.S. Census Bureau people who receive a bachelor's degree, on average earn *more than $1 million in income* over the course of their work life, compared to high school graduates with no postsecondary education (Day and Newburger, 2002, 4). The potential for increased income earnings, again on average, grows as individuals increase their level of education: from high school diploma, to a bachelor's degree, to a graduate or first-professional degree. Simply, the more you learn, the more you're likely to earn over a lifetime of work.

A Closer Look at Cost of Attendance

Colleges use the term "cost of attendance" (COA) to help families understand all the actual expenses for attending their institution. COA includes tuition, fees, books and supplies, transportation, housing (room and board), and other education-related expenses. A college's COA may affect how much financial aid may be awarded to students.

The COA may and typically do differ among institutions, depending on their type (two-year community colleges or four-year universities, as examples). More expensive universities tend to have a higher COA. A student's personal choices (e.g., living in a college dormitory or an apartment versus living at home with their parents) will also affect the COA.

What Is the Difference between Attending Part-Time versus Full-Time?

Students seeking a college degree generally attend either full-time or part-time. Full-time students enroll in at least 12 credit hours per semester term, which is equal to four classes, each counting for three credit hours. Part-time students enroll in less than 12 credit hours per semester term. For students to receive financial aid, they must enroll in no less than six credit hours, or two courses per semester term.

Creating a Student Budget (Sample Budget Provided as an Appendix)

College financial-aid counselors can help students develop a student budget that is specific to their situation. While the student budget may vary from one type of student to another, in general, the student budget provides an account of a student's available monetary resources (including financial aid) compared to expected expenses during the school year. Remember, that a student's personal situation may change from one year to another; so, it is important to monitor the student budget and update it as needed, at least once annually. A sample copy of a student budget is located in the Financial Aid Appendix.

What Is the Purpose of Financial Aid, How Much Is Available, and Who Is Eligible?

The general rule is that a student's family is expected to have primary responsibility for paying for their child's college education. However, federal and state governments and individual colleges recognize that many families need some assistance to afford college. The purpose of student financial aid is to help students pay for college. Some form of financial aid is available to all students, regardless of financial need, so long as the student is enrolled in at least a part-time basis and maintains a good academic standing with the college. How much and what type of financial aid is ultimately awarded to students depend on a student's individual situation, and to some extent, the type of college he or she attends. Let's take a closer look to see how much you as a student can get.

What Is Need-Based Financial Aid?

There are two major types of student financial aid: those based on a student's financial need (*need-based aid*) and those based on a student's academic achievements, artistic, athletic, or other types of personal talents (*merit-based aid*). Need-based financial aid is the most common form of government-supported aid for undergraduate students without a bachelor's degree. Students do not have to identify themselves as in-need for financial aid. Colleges use a federal formula, and in some cases state-required criteria, for determining a student's eligibility for need-based financial aid.

Understanding the Expected Family Contribution (EFC)

The first step in establishing eligibility for financial aid is to determine a student's Expected Family Contribution (EFC). The EFC is an amount, which the federal government determines that a student (and their family) is expected to contribute toward college expenses. The EFC is a student's share of paying for college. The EFC is calculated by the U.S. Department of Education when a student completes the Free Application for Federal Student Aid (FAFSA). A student's EFC will not change regardless of what type of college or university the student attends even if there are differences in their cost of attendance.

- Dependency status

A student's EFC and financial-aid eligibility are based, in part, on their dependency status. There are two types of dependency statuses: students who are dependent on their parents or legal guardians for financial support are dependent students. Students who are self-supportive or meet a certain criteria (see following text) are independent students. A student's dependency status will determine whose financial information, including income, should be included on the FAFSA. Dependent students must enter their and their parents or legal guardians' financial information while independent students are only required to provide their (and that of their spouse if the student is married) financial information on the FAFSA. For the detailed criteria in determining a student's dependency status, visit http://www.aie.org/paying-for-college/FAFSA-info-center/dependency-status.cfm.

- Eligibility criteria

The U.S. Department of Education uses information provided in the FAFSA to determine the amount and types of financial aid available for the student. One of the primary criterion is the family's financial potential, such as their adjusted gross income from the previous year, savings and related education accounts, and certain available financial assets not including the value of the primary home of residence. Some of the additional criteria include: the number of dependents in the household, number of family members who will be enrolled in college during the school year for which the student is seeking aid, and whether the student will be enrolled in a full-time or part-time basis.

- Special circumstances

Colleges recognize that when a student's family situation changes, it might affect their ability to pay for college expenses. For example, when a parent or legal guardian loses his or her job, or an illness in the family creates an unexpected financial obligation, students may no longer have the financial resources they expected to have for college expenses. Students should discuss these special circumstances with the college financial-aid office to determine whether the amount of financial aid awarded to them might be increased in light of the most current information. For these special circumstances, the college will request students to present documentation to show evidence of the circumstance and demonstrate how it has affected the family's financial ability.

What Types of Financial Aids Are Available?

There are three specific types of financial aids available for undergraduate students: (A) grants and scholarships, (B) employment opportunities, and (C) student loans. Grants and scholarships are also known as free money because students do not have to repay the money awarded to them.

A. How Are Grants and Scholarships Alike? How Are They Different?

Grants and scholarships are similar in two ways: they are free money available to help students pay for college and they require good academic standing to continue receiving the aid. However, they may have very different eligibility criteria (e.g., need-based vs. merit-based), different application forms and processes, and the scholarships may be limited to certain academic areas, such as science, technology, engineering, and math, whereas grants are generally available to students regardless of degree type or major.

• Where can I find scholarships?

There are many scholarship search websites and services available to students. Most of the search websites are free, whereas others provide their services for a fee. Both can be good resources, but remember that scholarship providers (foundations, private companies, institutions, etc.) offer their scholarships to help students pay for college with no expectation that a student will repay the scholarship amount; so, they are likely to use reputable no-cost websites to promote their scholarships. Suggested places to begin a scholarship search include the following websites:

Hispanic Scholarship Fund

http://www.hsf.net/innercontent.aspx?id=34

Hispanic Association of Colleges and Universities

http://www.hacu.net/hacu/Scholarships_EN.asp?SnID=1728290173

The College Board

http://apps.collegeboard.com/cbsearch_ss/welcome.jsp

Adventures in Education

http://www.aie.org/Scholarships/

Fastweb

http://www.fastweb.com/college-scholarships

B. Employment Opportunities

• What is a work-study program?

Students can also work during the school year to earn money to help pay for college. The largest federal program designed to provide students an employment opportunity is the Federal Work-Study program. Work-study program provides funding for colleges to offer eligible students part-time work in on-campus jobs or help place students in jobs with off-campus employers. For example, a college may award a student $1,000 for an academic semester; the student will need to work to earn the $1,000. While students actually work for their money, work-study program is considered a part of a student's financial-aid package because the funding provided for their wages comes from the federal government, college, and in some cases state government.

• How much should I expect to work while in college?

Whether a student is in work-study program or finds a job on his or her own, colleges will generally advise students to limit their work to no more than 15 hours per week. Research has shown that students who work in excess of 15 hours per week are less likely to stay in college and ultimately less likely to complete college. A Texas-based study showed that students who worked between 1 and 14 hours per week had a 57 percent degree attainment rate compared to 26 percent for students who worked between 15 and 24 hours per week.

Ideally, a student should keep a full-time course schedule and work only part-time. If a student must work full-time, then close consideration should be given to whether they also want to study on a full-time basis. Remember, the general rule for college-level courses is that a student will have to study three hours outside the classroom for every one hour of classroom instruction.

• Working in on-campus versus off-campus jobs

There are many advantages to working in an on-campus job: students do not need transportation to and from work, students are more efficient with their time, the jobs available may be related to a student's field of study, and campus supervisors may be more flexible in scheduling work hours around a student's course schedule because they recognize that academic performance is the first priority for the student. Off-campus jobs may offer students different options for career-related work, may pay higher wages (per hour) and provide an opportunity to work beyond the semester.

C. Student Loans

Student loans can be complex and are often misunderstood, especially given that they may come from several sources (see types of student loans) and their terms and conditions will vary from one loan program to another. However, students should not avoid borrowing altogether; student loans can be a helpful tool for helping students and families afford college. When used correctly, student loan can be a good investment in a student's future and can be helpful in accelerating time-to-degree for some students.

In the past decade, student loans have become the primary source of student financial aid. In academic year 2010–2011, approximately $110 billion in federal student loans was borrowed by students and parents nationally to help pay for college. Government-supported student loans usually have the best terms, such as interest rates and loan repayment options, and unlike private bank-based loans, are generally made available to students without a minimum credit requirement. Unlike grants and scholarships, student loans must be paid to the lender, or in the case of the Federal Direct Student Loan Program, to the U.S. Department of Education.

Since Most Students Have to Borrow to Pay for College, Borrow Wisely

Student loans can be a difficult topic for many families. There are two common and competing approaches (attitudes) toward student loans: (1) avoid them even if you have to work more hours to pay for college and (2) borrow as much as you can so that you can afford everything you want while in college. College financial-aid counselors are not likely to recommend either of these approaches. The first tactic (working more hours) may affect a student's ability to concentrate on school and study on a full-time basis. Students may be tempted to take a semester off from college to work so they can pay for college later. This action can increase a student's time to graduation and the risk of not completing his or her college education. Remember, the goal of attending college is to graduate with a degree.

The second approach (maximize borrowing) also may not be a wise choice. Students may borrow the maximum allowable by law even before they graduate, or they may borrow unmanageable amounts as undergraduates, which may affect their choices or affordability of graduate school. Student loans make up the primary form of financial aid for graduate and professional education. Since Pell Grants and other need-based grants are generally limited to undergraduate students, graduate students must rely on loans and fellowships to pay for their studies.

There is a third perspective on student loans: borrow, but borrow wisely. Student loans can help lower a student's need to work long hours while in college. Student who work fewer hours are more likely to graduate than those who work long hours. A Texas study found that students who worked between 1 and 14 hours per week had a 57 percent chance of graduating compared to 8 percent for students who worked more than 35 hours per week while in college (Barone, Creusere, Fletcher, and Shook, 2011, 81). Similarly, students should borrow the amount recommended by their college's financial-aid office and the loan funds should only be used for educational expenses, as outlined in the student's budget. Developing a borrowing plan aligned with a degree plan affords students an ability to monitor their progress on both, and use loans as a tool for degree completion, rather than having loans hinder graduation.

Financial-aid counselors also frequently advice students to borrow government-supported loans first, before accepting loan offers from private (nongovernment) banks and lenders. Private loans may be a viable source for some students attending higher-cost universities, but remember these loans may charge higher interest rates and loan origination fees and may not offer flexible repayment terms.

• How much should I expect to borrow to help pay for college?

How much students borrow depends on several factors, including type of institution (public or private university), the degree a student is seeking (associate degree or bachelor degree), and the number of years enrolled before graduation (four, five, or six years). The Project on Student Debt estimates that college seniors who graduated in 2009 did so with an average debt of $24,000 (Cheng and Reed, 2010, 2). Of the 2008–2009 public college graduates who earned a degree, 55 percent also had an educational debt (Baum, Payea, and Cardenas-Elliott, 2010, 19). Students enrolled in two-year community colleges will likely borrow less than those in four-year universities. Generally, the longer a student is enrolled, the higher balance in student loans they will borrow.

What Are the Different Types of Student Loans?

There are three major types of loans available for undergraduate students: (A) federal student loans, (B) state loans, and (C) private bank-based loans. Some families are also able to borrow home-equity loans for college expenses.

A. Federal Student Loans

For undergraduate students, the Federal Direct Student Loan Program has three types of loans: subsidized Stafford loans, unsubsidized Stafford loans, and parent loans for undergraduate students (PLUS). Subsidized loans are need-based and awarded to students with a demonstrated financial need. The federal government pays the interest on these loans while the student is in college and for up to six months after graduation or after the student is no longer enrolled in at least a part-time basis.

For unsubsidized Stafford loans, a student is responsible for interest payments immediately after the loan is made. For both of these loans, students do not have to begin repayment of the loan until six months after they graduate or cease to enroll in at least a part-time basis.

PLUS loans are the only federally supported loans with a credit requirement for parents. The payment period for the loan principal and interest begins when the loan is made.

B. State-Supported and Private Loans

There are two other types of student loans: state-supported loans and private-bank loans. Many states have an education agency, such as the Texas Higher Education Coordinating Board, which issues tax-exempt bonds in order to generate funds to offer student loans. In general, state-supported loans have more favorable interest rates and repayment terms than bank loans. While state loan eligibility will vary from one state to another state, these loans are not necessarily limited to students attending public colleges and universities. To find what state loans might be available for you, contact the financial-aid office of the college you will attend. They can help.

C. Private Bank-Based Loans

Private banks, credit unions, and other financial institutions also make loans for students and parents to help pay college expenses. There are countless types of private loans (sometimes referred to as loan products), with varying interest rates and payment terms and each with specific credit requirements. Finding a private-bank loan can be tricky. Some universities are involved in helping students identify available private loans, whereas others prefer to have the student find the loan themselves before they become involved. In either case, the college's financial-aid office needs to certify all private loan applications for their students. This means that after you have selected a private loan, the bank provides you a loan verification form that you need to take to your college or university to certify before you can complete the loan application process. A new website was launched in 2010 to help students and parents find, compare, and choose from several private loan products.

The Student Loan Marketplace website can be located at http://www.overturemarketplace.com/.

- How can I manage my loans while in college and after I graduate?

Student loans can be a good investment, but they are also a big responsibility. Remember, student loans have to be repaid. Students should begin to manage their loans as soon as they take out their first loan. Key steps for managing student loans include: read carefully all loan documents, keep all loan records in a safe location, get a report on the total amount borrowed after each semester, borrow from a single source (if possible) to simplify your repayments, and contact the lender or U.S. Department of Education once annually to determine the estimated monthly payment amount due based on the total amount borrowed so far and provide them current contact information. Finally, whether you are still in college or are about to graduate, it is important to determine how much you might be expected to pay, on a monthly basis, on your student loans. Adventures in Education provides a simple and useful online calculator to determine the monthly amount you'll need to pay on your student loans. You can find the College Loan Calculator at: http://www.aie.org/paying-for-college/finance-tools/college-loan-calculator.cfm.

What Is the Application Process for Financial Aid?

To apply for all federal student financial aid and most state student aid programs, start by completing the *Free Application for Federal Student Aid (FAFSA)*. The form is available online, www.fafsa.ed.gov and usually takes between 30 and 45 minutes to complete. The FAFSA must be completed during the senior year of high school and then updated annually every spring until graduation. To begin the process, students and parents (in the case of dependent students) must sign up for a Personal Identification Number (PIN). The PIN is needed to create a student's personal file for completing and submitting the FAFSA online. The PIN serves as the student's and parent's electronic signature.

To complete the FAFSA, students will need their or their parents' (see Dependency status) income tax information from the previous tax year. For example, students completing the FAFSA in the spring 2012 must use information from tax year 2011.

The FAFSA online is located at: http://www.fafsa.ed.gov/.

- What other forms, beyond the FAFSA, will I need to complete?

All colleges use information resulting from the FAFSA (see SAR section) to determine a student's financial-aid eligibility for all federal and most state programs. Institutions may also require another form, in addition to the FAFSA, which they will use to award certain private grants and scholarships or institutional aid. Once students complete the FAFSA, they should contact the financial-aid office of the college they intend to enroll to ask whether a separate financial-aid form is required.

• When should I apply?

The FAFSA can be completed after January 1 of the senior year of high school. Students should complete the FAFSA as early as possible. For students enrolling in the fall semester, many colleges have a priority application deadline in early spring, usually between March and April. The financial-aid application deadline for each university is posted on its website. Remember, to complete the FAFSA, students will need information from the previous year's federal income tax form.

• What happens after I apply?

The U.S. Department of Education processes the FAFSA usually within one week after it is completed online. Students should monitor the status of their FAFSA to make sure that it has been fully accepted and processed by the federal government. If there are errors on the FAFSA form, the student will have to correct the errors or provide the missing information before the FAFSA is fully processed.

Students receive an electronic Student Aid Report (SAR), if they provide an e-mail when they submit the FAFSA. The SAR provides a summary of the information provided in the FAFSA and the student's EFC amount. Remember the EFC is used to determine student aid eligibility, especially for need-based aid.

• What happens after I receive the SAR?

The college(s) included in the FAFSA—where the student intends to enroll—receives a report providing the student's information and EFC amount. The institution uses that information to develop a financial-aid award offer for the student. Many institutions do not make a financial-aid award until the student has been officially admitted for enrollment. It is important to complete the admission application and process in addition to the financial-aid application. If the college the student will be attending is not listed on the SAR, students should add that college to their SAR and submit the data to the college.

To make corrections on the SAR online, students must visit www.fafsa.ed.gov and select "Make Corrections to a Processed FAFSA." Remember, students will need to use their PIN.

• Understanding your financial-aid award letter (sample award letter in the appendix)

Once the college has determined that a student is eligible for financial aid, the college sends the student a financial-aid award letter. The letter details the types and amounts of financial aids offered to the student. The student is asked to accept or decline the different types of financial aids offered. The financial-aid award letter also describes the information used by the college to determine how much financial aid to award the student. For example, the letter describes the expenses included in the college's cost of attendance, such as tuition and fees, housing, meals, books and supplies, and transportation. Remember, students have to accept the financial-aid offer as stated in the award letter.

FinAid, an established website on student financial aid, provides a free guide on understanding financial-aid award letters, at http://www.finaid.org/fafsa/awardletters.phtml.

What Do I Need to Know Once I Start College?

• Get to know your financial-aid counselor

Once enrolled, students should become acquainted with the college's financial-aid office. The financial-aid process is ongoing. *Students will need to apply for financial aid every year until graduation, and in some special circumstance, may need additional assistance during the year in which they have already received aid.* Alert—As students progress in their academic studies, new scholarship opportunities may become available. *Warning*—if a student is not making academic progress, their financial aid may be reduced or eliminated. Staying in contact with the financial-aid office may help avoid unexpected interruption of a student's financial aid.

• How do I retain eligibility for financial aid?

Student financial aid is awarded on an academic year basis. To keep their financial aid, students must complete a FAFSA renewal application every spring until they graduate. The renewal application is online and relatively simple, but it must be completed and early completion is recommended.

Stay in good academic standing. Once in college, students must maintain good academic standing to keep their financial aid. Every college defines its own Satisfactory Academic Progress (SAP) policy. For example, a college might require students to maintain at least a 2.0 GPA and pass at least 75 percent of the courses attempted. Students should get to know the policy. Remember, students who fail to meet that policy are at risk of losing their financial aid.

• What happens if I transfer to another college or university?

When students transfer from a college to university, their financial-aid award does not follow them to the new university. Students must complete the FAFSA the spring before the transfer (in the case of traditional fall transfer students) and indicate on the form the name of the university in which they expect to enroll that fall. A similar process follows for determining how much financial aid is available for the student at the new university and the university will issue the student its own financial-aid award.

When students transfer from a community college to a four-year university, they are often surprised by the higher cost at university. However, students might expect that their financial-aid award at the university may increase. It is also likely that a large part of the increase in financial aid may be in the form of student loans. Students should contact the university's financial-aid office because there may be financial-aid programs specifically available for transfer students.

Summary

More than likely you will need to get financial assistance to pay for college. The good news is that federal and state governments, colleges, and private scholarship providers have funds to help. When it comes to getting financial help, here are things to do, terms to know, deadlines to keep, sources to look up.

• Talk to a college financial-aid officer as soon as possible to learn about—
  • Grants and scholarships (these are free money)
  • Federal student loans (to be paid back)
  • State and bank loans (to be paid back)
• Reducing the real cost: by college work-study programs, institutional waivers, and tax credits.
• What are these FAFSA, EFC, and SAR?
• Where on the Internet can I find sources to apply for grants, scholarships, financial aid, and private loans?
• You will need to apply after January 1 of your senior year in high school, and remember that you also have to be accepted into a college before you can receive a financial-aid award letter.
• Once you get financial aid, you will have to continue to apply every year for continuation, and new scholarship opportunities may develop; so, continue your scholarship search actions every year.
• Each year you will need to comply with the satisfactory academic progress to keep your financial aid.

Financial Aid Appendix

- Sample Student Budget. Go to www.aie.org/Paying-for-college/finance-tools/budgeting-while-in-school.cfm.
- Sample Financial Aid Award Letter. See Appendix 3.A.
- Sample Screen Shots of FAFSA on the Web. Go to www.fafsa.edu.gov.

References

Barone, S., Marlena Creusere, Carla Fletcher, and Melissa Shook. "State of Student Aid and Higher Education in Texas." Texas Guaranteed Student Loan Corporation, 2011, http://www.tgslc.org/research/.

Baum, S., and Jennifer Ma. "Trends in College Pricing 2010." The College Board, 2010, http://trends.collegeboard.org/college_pricing/.

Baum, S., Kathleen Payea, and Diane Cardenas-Elliott. "Trends in Student Aid 2010." The College Board, 2010, http://trends.collegeboard.org/student_aid/.

Cheng, D., and Matthew Reed. "Student Debt and the Class of 2009." The Project on Student Debt, 2010, http://projectonstudentdebt.org/state_by_state-data.php.

Day, J.C., and Eric C. Newburger. "The Big Payoff: Educational Attainment and Synthetic Estimates of Work-Life Earnings." U.S. Census Bureau, 2002, http://www.census.gov/prod/2002pubs/p23–210.pdf.

U.S. Department of Education. "Fiscal Year 2012 Budget Summary—February 14, 2011 Section II.D. Student Financial Assistance," 2011, http://www2.ed.gov/about/overview/budget/budget12/summary/edlite-section1.html.

Appendix 3.A

The University of Anywhere
Financial Aid Award Letter

March 2012

Student name
Address
Anywhere, USA

Dear Student:

We are pleased to inform you that you are eligible to receive financial assistance for the 2011–2012 academic year while attending The University of Anywhere. Your financial aid is based on your current estimated Cost of Attendance.

Tuition and Fees	4,990.00
Room and Meals	7,400.00
Books and Supplies	1,000.00
Transportation	1,500.00
Miscellaneous	2,250.00
Total:	$17,140.00

Based on your Free Application for Federal Student Aid (FAFSA), you plan to live on campus, and will enroll in 12 credits in Fall and Spring. The University of Anywhere has classified you as a Resident for tuition purposes.

Visit http://financialaid.universityofanywhere.edu/award for more information. This webpage lists the steps you must follow to receive your awarded financial aid and other useful resources. If you will be receiving any financial aid that is not listed below, you are required to report each source and amount to our offices at askaid@universityofanywhere.edu or call our office. If any of your information changes, your financial aid may be adjusted.

Your Financial Aid:	Fall 2011	Spring 2012	Total
Federal Direct Subsidized Loan	1,750.00	1,750.00	3,500.00
Federal PLUS	5,820.00	5,820.00	11,640.00
University Anywhere Grant	1,000.00	1,000.00	2,000.00
Total:	$8,570.00	8,570.00	17,140.00

We look forward to assisting you in the pursuit of your educational goals!

Managing Your Time
and Services on Campus

"You have to be a WISE Latina."

Sonia Sotomayor
Associate Justice, U.S. Supreme Court
Law School Graduate, Yale University

Your First Year of College: Using the Services on Campus to Help You Succeed

Silas H. Abrego with assistance from Juan Valdez

Your high school or community college graduation celebrations have quickly faded into the past and you anxiously wait for the first day of four-year college. You are looking forward to it, but you are not entirely sure what to expect. As a result, you are rather apprehensive about college life. Everything appears intimidating: immense buildings, thousands of other students, the pressure to excel academically, and your newfound freedom. You realize that very few of your friends will be with you. In fact, everyone has moved forward onto different directions and new priorities. The only thing you are certain about is your desire to prepare for a career and set new academic goals. You want to succeed because of your family's high expectations as the first one to attend college and your community's concern to establish a solid sense of direction for its young people.

You have certainly heard stories about students who did not succeed in college. You may be one of only a small number of Latinos on campus, and the institution you will be attending may be unfamiliar with your educational needs. You know that college relates to new ways of thinking and different learning styles. You wonder if you have the financial resources or the academic readiness necessary to compete at a new level. You can rest assured that college life will be challenging and classrooms will turn into open arenas where knowledge uncovers itself. Your experience becomes the most valuable asset to best explain your views as Latino. On the way to achieving your goals, you may face many disappointments and contradictions. You will need plenty of courage to rebound from each setback or crisis. Your success will require personal sacrifices, unfailing determination, and an ability to recognize obstacles as temporary opportunities to formulate solutions.

How you manage the first year and, more specifically, the first semester—the study habits you develop, the attitudes you cultivate, and the support networks you nurture—will establish a foundation on which you will base multiple academic and personal achievements. Start an early quest by taking advantage of your summer, preparing for the first semester, and becoming familiar with your future alma mater. The more you know about the university and its procedures, polices, and resources, the better prepared you will be to achieve your goals.

Preparing for Day One

Your apprehension about attending college will be greatly diminished if you do some homework during the summer or before transferring to your four-year college or university. Most fears can be attributed to a lack of knowledge about the college experience. This is particularly true if you are a first-generation college student. You may have had very little or no exposure to higher education. Remember that many of your fears can be addressed prior to the first day of classes. Anticipation plays an important role when it comes to college success. So, with a college catalog in hand, you will be ready and feel safe to navigate away from fearing college or university.

College Catalogs

Universities and community colleges print the general undergraduate student catalog every new semester. Catalogs take the form and size of a magazine and have a fancy colorful cover design that stands out from regular textbooks. These are sold in the universities and sometimes given for free at the community colleges' bookstores. You can browse a copy of the catalog at the university's admissions office or library front desk for quick references. There should also be a copy of the catalog available in the university's website that you can print at home.

Once you know where to get your copy of the catalog, *do* not be discouraged by their intimidating sizes and pages. Remember, they contain a wealth of information that help you plot a survival strategy and aid you as you negotiate the institutional maze. As a matter of fact, everything you read in a catalog serves you well because it is the school's contract with its students. But why does the university or college want to have a written statement regarding your obligations?

Institutions of higher education are complex and multifaceted. The curricula are often not presented in a manner that is easily understood. Nevertheless, it is imperative that you have a proper understanding of the purpose of higher education and, in particular, the mission of your college or university. On one of the first pages of the catalog, you will find the institution's mission statement. This statement describes the primary goals the university is striving to achieve. Virtually all curricula and administrative policies are developed with the intent of meeting the institution's mission. Pay particular attention to the goals concerning you as a learner. By doing so, you will understand how the sequence of your courses and the degree requirements and objectives relate to the mission. Moreover, this activity will broaden your viewpoint and help you focus on accomplishing your personal and academic goals. Do not just concentrate on earning a bachelor's degree. Be sure to consider all your educational options.

Other important topics concern university policies and regulations, especially those dealing with enrollment, attendance, and grading. Here, you will find a variety of information that may affect you during registration periods:

- What does it mean to attend college full-time? Remember that most financial-aid awards require full-time attendance.

- When can a class be dropped? Is there a deadline for changing class schedules without penalty, or can classes be dropped at any time during the semester? Bear in mind that many students carry F's on their transcripts because they were not aware of deadlines for permissible course changes.

- What is an "incomplete"? If you overextend yourself during the semester, you may want to use this option for your own benefit.

- What happens when you receive a final grade of an F? Will you be able to eventually have that grade removed from your transcript? Bear in mind that classes may be repeated for credit.

- Can low GPA place your enrollment in jeopardy? Remember that continued college enrollment depends on meeting a minimum GPA required by the university.

Be certain not to omit the critical section describing academic dishonesty, paying special attention to the discussion of plagiarism (copying someone else's work and passing it off as your own). Regardless of your major, you will most definitely be required to write academic papers, and plagiarism (intentional or unintentional) carries severe penalties.

When you turn 18, you acquire a new set of rights. As a college student you have rights as well. The catalog section dedicated to student rights contains useful information. You will learn about appeal procedures (especially useful when you need to appeal a semester grade). You will also find a discussion of your rights concerning sexual harassment and racial discrimination. Finally, you may have questions regarding privacy of personal information or academic records. The section on student rights will have a statement concerning the privacy rights of students. Read it and you will know what course of action to take if your privacy rights are jeopardized.

There are many other issues of interest covered in the general catalog, so be sure to sit down and devote time to look it over. The time you spend reading the catalog will pay off in the future. Every page answers a specific question you may have. Do not wait until the first day of class to get your catalog because chances are these will be gone.

Financial Aid

Financial aid is a frequent concern for many Latino students, be they low income or otherwise. Lack of financial resources is perhaps the single most prevalent reason for leaving school before you graduate. So, learn as much as you can on how to finance your education. Read the catalog section dedicated to financial aid and do not forget to fill out your FAFSA form. Visit the website at www.fafsa.gov to sign up for a PIN and start the application process. Also, each college and university has an office of financial aid primarily to provide students with access to funds and ease the burden of funding your education. These offices deal with many types of assistance ranging from scholarships to grants and loan programs to employment. Become familiar with all your options.

An important step involves making an appointment to see a financial-aid counselor. He or she will help determine your eligibility for assistance in available aid programs. Aside from understanding federal and state aid requirements, it is very useful to be aware of the many scholarships offered by individual universities. Also, it is important to cultivate a long-term relationship with your financial-aid counselor. Your financial needs will most likely change over the course of your college career. A personal contact in the financial-aid office proves valuable when you suddenly find that your financial circumstances have changed. To learn more about financial aid, refer to Step 3 in this book.

Part-Time Employment

Statistics indicate that 80 percent of undergraduate students work at some point while attending college. Working part-time, while completing college, can yield many benefits, especially if you are employed on campus. Most universities have career planning and placement offices. These centers post employment openings for each school year and summer. At the first available opportunity, visit the university student employment office and look over the job postings.

As a new student, you may need to start near the bottom of the pay scale. Don't let this discourage you from accepting on-campus employment. There are many advantages to working for your university.

Campus employers understand that because you are a student your top priority is your education. That realization translates into flexibility. Most on-campus employers are happy to work around your class schedule. Keep in mind that class schedules change with every term. When you have an important test conflicting with your job schedule, you will find a better chance of arranging for time off with an on-campus employer. This is something off-campus businesses are less willing to accommodate. On-campus employment eliminates commute time because you can work directly before or after classes. Before applying for any job, be sure to consider the number of hours you will be able to devote to employment. As a full-time student, you should not work more than 15 hours per week. Your education should always be your priority.

Perhaps the greatest benefit of on-campus employment for Latino students is getting further connected with campus life: meeting other students, networking with staff and faculty, and developing relationships with those who know the university experience firsthand. Many benefits will emerge from relationships you foster with the members of your network. Over time, your colleagues and peers may even become a part of your extended family. Good work supervisors will take an interest in you as a student and as a person and will help you develop work-related skills. Your supervisors may discuss your classes with you and keep track of your academic progress. When you need someone to cut through administrative red tape that may be slowing your progress, contact your supervisor. He or she may know the right person to assist you. Your supervisor can also act as your mentor: someone with whom you can discuss personal issues, goals, and aspirations; someone who can provide you with guidance. Do not forget that recommendations can open doors. Positive recommendations are a result of diligent effort and high-quality work performed while attending college. Being a productive employee and nurturing a positive work relationship with your work supervisors will pay off. So, be sure to weigh the benefits of university employment before you accept a job off-campus.

Academic Advisement

As your registration date approaches, whether it is early in the summer or just before classes begin, be sure to schedule an appointment with an academic advisor. Some schools require all new students to meet with an advisor to ensure that all students have access to experienced assistance in planning their class schedules. If you are not obligated to meet with a counselor, do so anyway—especially if you are a first-generation college student. Such meetings are crucial in developing long-term learning goals by personalizing your individual career goals, needs, and objectives.

It is a good idea to get in the habit of meeting with an academic counselor before every registration period each semester or quarter. Some students change their majors at least once during their academic career. Your advisor will guide you through these changes, so that you will not delay your graduation by accumulating unnecessary credits. However, keep in mind that identifying a major early enhances your academic progress and stability.

Advisement offices have access to a variety of resources that can aid students in search of a major. If your high school provided limited exposure to career and educational opportunities, be sure to visit the college's student advisement center, which may also be known as the career planning and placement center. The office will have information sheets with descriptions of each major including suggested course patterns, information about professors, potential job opportunities, and job demand outlook for the future. Advisement centers can also provide counseling and testing services to help you evaluate your own interests, skills, and life goals. You can find out how a career fits your personal interests by completing a Carl Jung and Briggs Myers test (a short version can be found at http://www.humanmetrics.com/cgi-win/JTypes2.asp). Once you find out your personal interests and how these fit a desired career, the staff will often be able to connect you with someone in your chosen profession. This will give you firsthand experience regarding your chosen career. Again, remember that one of your goals during your academic career should involve building a support network consisting of students, staff, faculty, and the community at large.

Campus Tour and Orientation

Latino students, especially those who are first in their families to attend college, may find it difficult to adjust to university life, so attending a campus orientation is a practical way to begin your first academic year. Make sure to arrange a visit to your campus prior to the beginning of classes, so that you can participate in an orientation meeting along with a campus tour. You will most likely meet in a large classroom, which will give you the opportunity to become accustomed to rooms that accommodate more than 100 students. During the orientation you will also have a chance to walk around the campus and hear about various services offered by your university. It will be helpful for you to bring a family member along or a close friend.

The orientation meeting will introduce you to the history and mission of the institution. You are likely to learn more about university learning goals, registration procedures, financial assistance, and campus resources such as the library. You will be given many opportunities to attend workshops addressing these and other topics, such as student clubs, government, and activities. You will certainly meet other students who are just as apprehensive as you about their new college careers. If you have not yet had an opportunity to speak with an academic advisor, you will be able to schedule an appointment at this time.

Many students do not place enough value on participating in new student orientations. Many do not realize that attending campus tours and orientations plays an essential role in adjusting to new surroundings. During the first week or two of classes, every student encounters issues that require visiting specific departments or knowing what department to contact. You may want to inquire about financial aid, support services, or health insurance. Consider this most frustrating question: Where do I go for guidance when I do not know who can help me? Take the time to attend a new student orientation and become familiar with the geography, buildings, and culture of your new university.

It is always a good idea to have your parents attend a campus orientation, particularly if you are a first-generation college student. It is crucial that they have a sense of the demands you will be facing. The more they understand about the challenges you will come up against, the stronger their support will be, especially if you are still residing at home. Even though you are an adult now, your parents should still be at the top of your support group. Be sure to consult them frequently; they are a source of strength and one of your greatest assets. Also, you may be the one that helps them to understand why college is important and how they can be helpful to you and younger brothers and sisters.

The First Semester—Finally

You made it! You are no longer a high school graduate. You are now a new college student. How exhilarating, liberating, and . . . frightening! So many people are wandering around looking at registration receipts and campus maps. Where am I going? Will I make it to my class on time? Will I have to buy all the books required for each course? Where can I get lunch? Did I park in the right place or will I get a ticket? Are there still on-campus jobs available? There will be so many questions requiring immediate answers. But, unlike some of the other students, you will be able to focus your energy on academic endeavors because you attended the campus orientation. You have already obtained most of the information necessary to make your first college days successful. You will feel extremely confident about your first day of class. Remember to be a proactive leader and share your confidence with other new students.

Becoming a Successful Student

To get the most out of a class, you have to prepare for it. This means preparing beforehand. Do not put a good grade at risk by falling behind. Completing assignments before class will enable you to gain much more from class materials. Having read and prepared assigned homework will enable you to ask questions in class, thereby participating in discussions and making yourself known by coming to the instructor's attention. Completing assignments prior to attending class will also reinforce your new found knowledge, which will improve your understanding and retention of class materials.

To get the most out of a class, you have to attend it. Instructors spend lecture time explaining, expanding on, and highlighting the content of class materials. Do not think that you can be a successful student merely by relying on assigned textbooks. Attending class is an integral part of your education. During your college career you will often come across professors whose excitement and enthusiasm for a class will motivate and inspire you. You can only benefit by attending all your classes.

Attending class is not like watching television. Interactivity and lively exchange, rather than passivity, should characterize your classroom behavior. You will learn faster and retain more when your mind is actively engaged in a class lecture or discussion. Ask questions, answer questions, request clarification and illustrations, and challenge the instructor. All these activities make class time exciting and rewarding. If you are not critically working with and manipulating your newfound knowledge, creating links between concepts and comparing ideas, class time will become like a chore rather than an opportunity to learn.

An excellent way to engage with course content and reinforce concepts is to take notes during class and then review them afterwards (you should also take notes on your reading). Doing so is an effective way to integrate what you hear in class with what you read in your textbooks. You will improve your memory, create links between concepts, and develop questions. Furthermore, when you prepare for final exams your notes will help you remember things the instructor said weeks or months earlier.

Another method by which to process new learning is to supplement your instruction. Do not depend on your textbooks and assignments alone. Supplement your instruction by reading other books and pertinent articles. If you can, join student study groups. By studying with others you can share opinions, test out ideas, and clarify points with which you are having difficulty. You have to take the responsibility for your own learning.

Sometime during your first semester, you should consider participating in a workshop on note taking. Every student has taken notes at some point in his or her academic career, but few know how to do it efficiently. Contact your learning center advisor and request attendance in such a workshop. Being a successful student in college is much more difficult than it was in high school. Take the time to refine and upgrade your study skills, and by doing so you will acquire the tools needed to succeed.

Tracking Your Academic Progress

Many college classes have mid-term and final exams, which often determine your course grade. In addition, on a periodic basis throughout the term you are likely to receive grades on assignments, such as homework, chapter tests, and book reports. At the end of the term, your instructor will give you a grade that is meant to represent your overall performance for the semester. Considering the importance of receiving good grades, it is unfortunate that many students hamper their own success by relying on the instructors to track their progress and by focusing only on the mid-term and final exams.

Make sure that you are aware of your academic standing throughout the semester. For example, you need to know that by week four you have taken one test and turned in six assignments. What if you know that you have completed all the assignments, but you do not know your grade? This should lead you straight to that most important of all class documents, the syllabus.

On the first day of class, every instructor distributes a copy of the course syllabus. You may think the syllabus is something to stash away in the back of your notebook. Do not make that mistake! Keep the syllabus handy at all times during the semester. In it you will find indispensable information: course schedule, reading assignments, exam dates, the instructor's office hours, and his or her grading policy. Some instructors may inundate students with multiple assignments: daily quizzes, weekly book reports, monthly tests, a mid-term and a final, as well as a term paper. Others may only have a mid-term and a final. Some students have a tendency to focus on only the two major assignments. Make sure that you give your time and attention to the small assignments as well. They are equally important.

The professor may count quiz grades as a mere 10 percent of your grade and participation as another 10 percent. If you are quiet and do not participate in class and you tend not to prepare for quizzes, you may discover before you have even taken your first exam that obtaining an A in the class is already impossible. Now the best you can hope for is a B, assuming that you ace, everything else. Imagine that you are sick one day and miss a test, then you get a C on a couple of book reports, and then B's and C's on a couple of quizzes. Suddenly, all your assignments point to a final grade of C. Do not ignore small tasks. And remember that instructors appreciate students who make a good effort, who complete all assignments on time, and who show an active interest in the class.

Become familiar with the instructor's grading policy, so that you can calculate your grade and immediately know your academic standing. By computing individual grades on a periodic basis, you will always know what needs to be done to achieve your academic goals. By being aware of your standing and by tracking your progress, you will be able to recognize when you need assistance. You will be ready to seek help and instructors usually have an open-door policy to give you feedback on assignments and tests. Engaging in class usually pays with gaining good references from your instructors. These could be used for scholarships, jobs, and transferring out to graduate school.

Updating Your Academic Toolbox

Over the past 12 years or prior to college, you have spent countless classroom hours listening to teachers and memorizing information. How much time have you spent acquiring skills necessary to be an independent learner? What about techniques to reduce tension brought on by an upcoming test? How are your typing and word processing skills? What about research skills? Do you know how to use the library for research? Can you efficiently produce high-quality work by using presentation software? Would you like to improve your ability to retain information? Would you like to upgrade your writing skills? How about learning to efficiently manage time? As you know, many high schools attended by Latino students face multiple financial challenges and, as a result, can provide only limited learning opportunities. If you haven't acquired the necessary skills in high school, it is essential that you do so now to avoid falling behind in your academic studies.

Most universities have learning centers or academic student support services that can help you become a more competent, efficient, and resourceful student. You will find workshops on note taking, test taking, reducing anxiety, time management, improving computer skills, study skills, critical thinking, research skills, and instruction in basic computer applications. You will also find group or individual tutoring and study sessions. The typical learning assistance center provides you with a variety of diagnostic tools to help you identify your academic strengths as well as possible obstacles to learning.

At some point in his or her college career, everyone encounters a deficiency in academic skills. Do not hesitate to take advantage of campus resources to help you overcome learning difficulties. *Too many students wait until they are at risk of being put on academic probation (when your GPA falls below a certain point set by the college, usually 2.0) before they seek help. Take the initiative, be proactive, and ask for assistance early.* In fact, if you want to increase your level of achievement, use the campus learning center regardless of your academic circumstances. When you use the learning center, you strengthen your skills, thereby creating opportunities that might otherwise be unavailable. If you are a low-income, first-generation college student, enroll in retention programs such as the Educational Opportunity Program and Student Support Services.

Developing a Support Network

As a Latino or a Latina college student, you may sometimes feel alienated, discouraged, or overwhelmed. In fact, you may feel that you don't belong in college because you haven't had many educational or financial advantages. The first year of college can also be a very lonely time, particularly if you are reserved or reticent about meeting people. Be open-minded and make an effort to always introduce yourself. You will realize that success comes in groups and having the right connections in the beginning of the semester could minimize workloads. Attempting to handle multiple pressures of attending college on your own can become a heavy burden. If you cannot avoid these pressures, be prepared for them by proactively identifying peers and mentors who can become part of your support network. Learning to network is a valuable skill. It will serve you well not only in college but also in your future career.

While in college, you will need friends on campus with whom you can share concerns and socialize. On every campus there are individuals who are dedicated to guiding and assisting you. Some of these people have already had similar experiences, so they know firsthand about the obstacles and challenges you face. They can help you identify solutions.

At some campuses, particularly those that welcome students of diverse backgrounds, it will be fairly easy to identify these peers; for example, in ethnic studies departments, student clubs, and so on. At other schools, it may be more difficult because they might work outside of your major or in a non-mainstream office. Regardless of where they are located, seek them out because they have the experience and knowledge you will need during the first year of college. Your mentors will become crucial links between your very first day on campus and your last day—your graduation.

Scanning the college catalog for programs designed to assist students of diverse backgrounds is a good way to identify potential members of your support network. Check to see if the campus has an ethnic studies department or program. Staff and faculty members in ethnic studies departments are well aware of programs and services that may be of interest to you. Moreover, these professors teach courses that will familiarize you further with Latino history and culture. Many of these classes may count toward the general education requirements. These departments also hire student assistants who can inform you about student activities and groups. Determine if your campus offers a mentoring program, peer mentoring, and/or tutoring labs. There, you will find staff and experienced students willing to assist you.

Many of these offices are staffed year round, so take the initiative and make an appointment to visit them during the summer. Introduce yourself to staff members and let them know that you are a new student. Ask about financial aid and student employment counselors. Inquire about faculty members, tutoring programs, student organizations, and support networks. Having a variety of information about the institution and its players will most likely reduce your anxiety.

Other channels for building a support network include joining Latino student organizations, participating in campus multicultural centers, and becoming involved with student government. Your connections to any of these groups will give you the strength to achieve and the belief that you belong on campus. Do not get so caught up in your academic pursuits that you omit forming a support network that will aid you while on campus and smooth your transition out of the university once you graduate.

Understanding That There Is More to College than Academics

As a college student your first priority is to address each course, regardless of the quality of teaching or its perceived relevance to your future. You will get the opportunity to choose your favorite class topics and receive credit under the general education curriculum. Knowing your alternatives will help you to narrow down your interests. Performing well in your course work is critical to your future success. Do not regard your college classes as a set of hoops through which you quickly jump. Each course and each year of study builds a foundation for the next class or phase of life. Academic success can be a guarantee for lifelong success. The combination of natural talent, desire, hard work, and a good education is difficult to duplicate. Your life will be forever changed for the better when you succeed academically. In order to make your education more rounded, participate in extracurricular activities. A well-rounded and fulfilling college experience should be punctuated with complementary pursuits. Seek them out, enjoy them, and learn from them as if you were already working in a real-life situation.

Participate in student organizations, leadership institutes, intercollegiate and athletic competitions, student government, and retreats or internships. You should make these events an integral part of your college experience. At any college, you are bound to find at least one organization that will spark your interest. By joining one, you will meet great people, learn new skills, and have fun.

Participating in student government is an excellent way to develop leadership skills and experience. You will learn how institutions work, practice the art of politics, run meetings, and campaign for office. There are few better or more enjoyable ways to prepare for a career, and student organizations will help you build a résumé.

If you are taking a full load of classes, working 10 to 20 hours per week, and studying two hours for every hour of class time, you will definitely be a very busy person. However, after participating in a time management workshop, you will have the skills and discipline to free up the time necessary to pursue extracurricular activities sponsored by your college.

Encountering and Overcoming Discrimination

You will experience mixed emotions when faced with racism or discrimination for the first time in college. Latina women may encounter both gender and ethnic discrimination. Even though colleges and universities are committed to providing an institutional climate conducive to learning, discrimination still exists. If you encounter it, let's hope your encounter will be an isolated event or an expression of individual ignorance, rather than a reflection of institutional culture.

There is no doubt that some faculty will think you have been admitted because of your ethnicity rather than your academic achievements. In classroom discussions concerning Latino topics, others may assume that you are an expert. There is no denying that racial slurs and stereotypes exist on college campuses. If you think that remarks are made out of ignorance, bring it to the attention of the involved person. If racial slurs are frequent and you are certain you are being discriminated against, bring the matter to the attention of the appropriate campus administrator who is responsible for diversity programs. In addition, to help you handle any hostile feelings of your own, seek out a minority faculty or staff member who will listen to you or who can refer you to helpful counsel. Most important, always remember that you belong in an educational setting. Regardless of any hostile and racist attitudes you may encounter, you will achieve your goals.

Giving Back to the Community

Finally, as you complete your higher education, which prepares you for the world of work and your dream career, remember you have a responsibility to give back to your community. Formal education and the desire to support the general community allow you to blend academics and personal desire, which produces a social change agent.

Certainly your immediate family has contributed significantly to your success. However, someone special made a difference in your life and influenced you to persist despite adversity. It could have been a teacher, a coach, a minister, or someone who saw in you potential and desire to succeed. Furthermore, there were others who came before you and sacrificed to maintain access into higher education. The important components of the educational experience financial aid, academic support services, and student development programs are the results of long-term advocacy by those who knew the importance of social change.

Reaching back to others like you to pursue higher education is critical. Inspiring and motivating younger Latino persons to prepare and succeed in college is now one of your tasks. For instance, you can mentor young children in your community and make them understand how college was possible for you. The community will have a positive outlook for the future when children cultivate ideas such as attending college.

You must improve the quality of life in your community and advocate for the right to live with dignity. You can start by making a difference and providing a clear path for future generations to come. It is due to Latino contributions from the past that today's opportunities are accessible. Just the way they opened the doors for you, the support for future generations lies in your hands today.

Summary

How you approach and negotiate your first year of college will indicate much about your success during subsequent years. Following the advice of this chapter will provide you with a strong foundation for success. Achieving success is never easy, but proper planning will go a long way in making your educational journey a rewarding one. Always appreciate that you, as a Latino or a Latina student, add richness to the university. Also, never fail to appreciate the diversity of students you encounter, especially those from different cultures and those holding different value systems. Do not lose sight of your purpose, and do not be deterred from achieving your educational goals. Rely on your support group to help you move beyond your baccalaureate degree and into graduate schools or programs. Also, remember and appreciate the support of your family and community.

Eleven things as must dos:

1. Read the college catalog as soon as possible.
2. Find and visit the financial-aid office each year.
3. Visit the work-study office.
4. Seek out academic advice at the beginning of each semester.

5. Go to the career center early in your college experience.

6. Attend campus tour and orientation.

7. Attend and be active with each of your classes every semester.

8. Know the course syllabus for each of your classes.

9. Update your academic study skills as often as you can.

10. Start to network immediately.

11. Participate in extracurricular activities.

References

Flores, Judith Le Blanc. "Facilitating Postsecondary Outcomes for Mexican Americans." 1994. ERIC ED 372903.

Isaac, Alicia. *The African American Student's Guide to Surviving Graduate School.* Thousand Oaks, CA: Sage Publications, 1998.

Lopez, Edward M. "Challenges and Resources of Mexican American Students within the Family, Peer Group, and University: Age and Gender Patterns." *Hispanic Journal of Behavioral Sciences* 17 (1995): 499–508.

Velasquez, Patrick M. "The Integration and Persistence of Chicano Students in Higher Education: Student and Institutional Characteristics." 1996. ERIC ED 394423.

Getting Off to a Good First Start: Strategies for Academic and Personal Success

Shernaz B. García

The focus of this chapter is on preparing you to have a successful college experience, beginning with your very first semester. The suggestions address two main areas: academic supports and psychological safeguards. Both of these areas are vital for you to know. Whether you're reading this while waiting to hear from the colleges to which you've applied, or if you've already been admitted and know where you'll be going to college, you may have mixed feelings about your decision. For some of us, this is the first time we're moving away, leaving behind our family, friends, and community. Some of us may have decided to stay closer to home (for many reasons, including finances, family ties, or cultural expectations), in order to juggle school, family, and work responsibilities. And for some, going to college was always part of the plan for the future, and there is only excitement about taking the first step in this direction. No matter what your situation is, it is a good idea to be prepared for what lies ahead so that you have a successful college experience.

Going to college is a big step for *all* students. But for many of us in the Latino or Latina community, going to college may require new knowledge, skills, and strategies that are very familiar to other students whose families and communities have traditionally experienced college life and know how to navigate the higher education system. You may find that college administrators, advisors, and faculty, or even other students, can and do assume that everyone knows how to do college. In reality, though, as you may have discovered in high school, or during the college admissions process, there are things you are expected to know. But no one talked about them, and you wished later that someone had told you about them! Think of this as the hidden curriculum, because that's what it is—it is invisible to us because we have lived and grown up in communities where we didn't need to know these things in order to be successful. But when we get to college, knowing these expectations, procedures, and ways of thinking about college life can help you to more easily achieve your academic and personal goals. Although the focus of this chapter is to provide you with a broad selection of strategies for academic success, many of them will also make these hidden expectations more visible and accessible to you.

Part I: Academic

Clarifying Expectations—What Do I Want from College or Why Am I Going to College?

Thinking about this question will help you to identify strategies in this chapter (among others) that can help you to achieve your goals. Although no one fits neatly in just one category, it's important to know what you want, because your goals will influence how you plan, what you experience, and even how much it will cost in time and money! It is also helpful to know what motivates you as a college student. Here are a few examples of how students think about going to college:

- *I'm here to major in computer science so I can get a job as a software engineer.* If your reasons for going to college sound similar, you will likely see a college degree as a means to an end and are planning to finish your program as quickly as possible so you can get a job.

- *I want to take courses at my community college to raise my GPA and then transfer to a four-year college.* Some of you may need to take this step before you can reach the goal in the earlier example. If you are one of these students, then your short-term objectives may include taking enough courses to raise your GPA, doing well, in order to transfer to a four-year college or a university. As in the first example, you are likely to be concerned with getting what you need in the most efficient way possible.

- *I'm here to learn and experience what the college or the university has to offer, I like to learn new things and have many interests.* Some students are drawn to college for the new academic opportunities and experiences available. They may not have a clear idea yet, of what they want to do after college, but see college as providing them with options, and helping them to decide on a career. If you are one of these students, you may be more interested in taking more electives, and discovering new career and degree options. Unlike students in the earlier two examples, who want the most efficient degree plan (fastest way to finish college), you may even change majors, and are still searching for what suits you best.

- *College is an exciting place where I can meet new people and have new experiences.* If you are one of these students, you may be drawn to college for the opportunities it offers for meeting new people and for the social events available to you on campus. Yes, you want to get a degree, but you don't see this as your only or primary goal. Although college life has much to offer, and your extracurricular and social experiences will be valuable, you will have to be careful not to be swept away by these social activities or this could have a negative impact on your academic performance. If the college or university that you will be attending has a reputation for being a party school, you may have to work harder at balancing your social demands and academic responsibilities!

Preparing for the College Experience and Your Classes

Planning ahead helps you to have a successful academic experience with fewer unexpected challenges, avoiding problems, and reducing stress. Anticipating possible difficulties also allows you to take preventive steps so that you will have few or no regrets later. As the saying goes, "don't close the gate after the horse has bolted!" or, as we say in Spanish, "¡no vale la pena llorar sobre leche perdido!" (It's no use crying over spilt milk!) The following steps can be helpful.

Develop a Degree Plan

- Soon after you begin your program, find and meet with your advisor and become familiar with the requirements of your degree plan.
- If you took advanced placement and dual credit courses in high school, find out if your college or university has received this information and given you credit for all those that apply. Be aware that not all colleges and university will accept these courses, and there are minimum GPA or score requirements associated with them. But it is important to find out if your college does, so you can receive credit.
- If you are planning to transfer to a four-year college or a university in the future, make sure you know which specific courses or sections of a course at your community college will be accepted by the college or university you are planning to attend. Equally important, find out if these transfer credits will count toward your degree plan later: getting transfer credit is not the same as meeting a degree requirement, because programs and colleges even at the same university can require different courses for their major or degree plan. You can avoid disappointment, frustration, added costs, and a longer program if you plan ahead. Be aware that this information is not always easily

available, so you may have to be persistent to obtain it. The following strategies may be helpful:

- Contact (by phone, Internet, or in person, when possible) an academic advisor at the university to which you want to transfer and obtain copies of the degree plan for your major.
- Obtain a copy of the transfer credits policies and courses for the university to which you plan to transfer.
- Compare your community college course options with degree requirements to find courses that can count for both academic programs. Ideally, you will be able to take courses that will count toward your community college program, *and* apply to your major when you transfer.

See Your Advisor Regularly

Once you have been assigned an academic advisor, it is important to meet this individual on a regular basis. At minimum, you should schedule a meeting once a semester, but may find it beneficial to meet more often when you have questions or need more information, especially during your first semester, when you are still finding your way on campus. Here are some reasons why you should become acquainted with your advisor:

- You get a realistic map for what you need to accomplish, number of credit hours per semester, and time required to complete your degree.
- Your advisor can help you to plan the course sequence; for example, you will learn about prerequisite courses that must be taken first or before others.
- Early advising can make sure you get into the courses you need, especially if they fill up quickly.
- Ongoing advising is a valuable tool to monitor your academic progress. Your advisor can also direct you to resources on campus to support your academic growth.
- Your advisor can often be the first point of contact if you need help with courses, degree information, policies, registration procedures, and so forth. Because he or she knows you better than other university officials or administrators, the guidance you receive will be more personally relevant to your situation.

Know Your Schedule

Taking the time to study your course schedule before the semester begins will help you to avoid conflicts, to get to class on time, and to be prepared to participate as an active learner when you get there. Before the semester starts:

- Make sure you know the location of your classrooms and allow yourself enough time to get to class punctually. This is particularly helpful when your classes are scheduled to meet one right after the other. If they are not held in the same building or part of your college campus, calculate the amount of time you will need to get to the next class. If necessary, alert your instructors about your situation so that you are not misperceived as being unmotivated because you may be a few minutes late to class.

- If you have a job (on or off campus), coordinate your class schedule with your work schedule, and make sure you are allowing enough time to commute back and forth, and to study.

- Balance demands of course work with other personal, family responsibilities. Although your academic advisor can help you to design a degree plan that will meet your needs, only you can determine if the generally recommended plan will work for you. For example, what will it mean for you to be a full-time student? Many full-time students tend to take more than the minimum number of hours required to be in full-time status (e.g., 15–17 hours instead of 12) because the college may offer flat-rate tuition. Only later do some of these students realize that the course work or demands are too high and cannot be met. If you have job-related or family responsibilities, or personal circumstances that will require your time and attention, consider carefully what will work for you.

Come Prepared with Your Textbooks and Other Required Materials (e.g., Calculators, Laptops, Software)

Textbooks may be only one of several different requirements associated with a course. Depending on your major and field of study, you may be expected to have a graphing or scientific calculator, laptop (or access to one), specific software applications, or other materials and equipments. Once you find out what these requirements are you can determine the most effective ways to get what you need at the lowest cost. The option of buying used books and materials can reduce the costs of going to college, but ask yourself the following questions to help you decide:

- If I buy a used book, can I get a copy that has not been marked up too much? Avoid purchasing a copy in which the previous user's notes could prevent you from using the text in ways that match your study habits and preferences.

- Can I get the same books at a lower cost from a different bookstore or from the Internet? In addition to the local college or university bookstore, other bookstores, or websites (e.g., Amazon.com or half.com) may offer very attractive offers, especially for students.

- If I purchase a used copy or buy the book online, will I be able to get the right edition? Books are revised very frequently in some subjects or disciplines where information is changing rapidly, and although the option you are considering may look very attractive (e.g., it is being sold at a very low price), you may get a text that does not contain information you will need, or the information may have been reorganized such that the chapters in the old and new versions no longer correspond to each other, making hard for you to track what the instructor is teaching or referring to.

- If I order the books and other materials online, will they arrive on time? Generally, you can get expedited shipping for an additional cost. However, if this is not an option, or if you need the books right away, consider other temporary sources such as your college library, from which you can borrow them. If you already know some of the students who will be taking the course, it may also be possible to borrow their copy to make a photocopy of the chapters until yours arrives. If all else fails, consider asking your course instructor for assistance—you may find that he or she is willing to loan you a copy for a short time, and an additional benefit to you is that he or she will realize that you are a serious and dedicated student!

Make Note of Deadlines for Adding or Dropping Courses, in Case You Need to Change Your Schedule

Missing a deadline to drop a course can sometimes result in an F on your transcript, so it is best to learn what to do before this happens.

- Know where the deadline information is published, in case you need it. A great deal of information is now available online, in addition to print materials such as student catalogs, policies, and procedures in colleges and departments. Your department's or college's advising office can also be a very helpful resource for this information.

- Make a note of these deadlines, even if you don't think you'll need it.

- Find out if you will need your professor's or advisor's approval to drop a course.

- Many colleges or universities have refund policies that reduce the amount of the refund after specific dates. Meeting these deadlines may mean you can get a full refund.

Become Familiar with the Academic Resources Available at Your College Campus

A college or a university campus offers many resources to support your academic, social, and personal success. If you are the first member of your family to attend college, as is often the case for many Latino or Latina students, you may need to allow yourself the time to explore what's available and how you can use them. Here are a few suggestions to help you to become familiar with these opportunities.

Libraries—Not Just for Books Any More!

Although you may be tempted to rely on the Internet for information and sources for research papers and other assignments, a great deal of professional and academic information isn't yet available electronically, or must be purchased when online. However, a print copy may be available at the library at no cost to you. Besides, libraries offer many other services that you will find helpful.

- Attend orientation sessions offered each semester by the library; sign up for a tour.
  - Learn how to find the resources for your courses and major.
  - Learn strategies for using the Internet.
  - Learn how to conduct searches for research projects and reports.
- Get to know your reference librarian—he or she can really help you with your library research for assignments and locate other materials.
- Libraries often provide access to computers, printers, copy machines at a relatively low cost; some services may be free for students.
  - Computer labs are often available on a sign-up basis.
  - In large universities, more computer labs are being added to various colleges, such as natural sciences, engineering, law, business, and education.
- The library can offer you a quiet place to study.
- Last but not least, there are study rooms that allow a place to meet with your study group, or with other students to work on projects, or prepare for the next exam.

Learning Centers

Learning centers offer valuable resources that every student—not only Latina or Latino—should know and use. Many students find that what they have been taught in high school about writing papers and doing research doesn't take them far enough when they get to college. College writing requires all of us (including native English-speaking students) to learn new ways of thinking and expressing our ideas, using the writing and speaking styles of our academic majors and disciplines (e.g., in textbooks, professional books and journals, and in the classroom). For those of us who have learned English as a second language, this goes beyond grammar, vocabulary, and pronunciation. *Just as our first language gives us ways to expresses ourselves as members of our cultural community, being proficient in academic English requires us to become familiar with the ways of thinking and expressing ideas that are being used by members of our academic community.* Remember:

- Even if you were studying college-level materials in Spanish, this would still be true. So, think of learning academic, college-related writing, and speaking styles as becoming bilingual or bicultural in the many ways that any language is used across settings.

- Like you, native English-speaking peers of English dialects that are different from Standard English may have experiences that are very similar to yours.

- Some of your professors and advisors may not understand that you are not a poor writer or a weak student. Language policies are a controversial issue, and you are likely to meet people with many different views about language.

You will find that learning centers provide services that are free or at reduced costs, including (but not limited to):

- Understanding your assignments.
- Writing a good research report or paper.
- Tutoring for academic subjects, including math, physics, chemistry, or psychology.
- Managing your test anxiety, or stress about classes and/or assignments.
- Support and resources for students who speak English as a second language.
- Study skills and time management, including preparing for tests and exams.

University and College Administration (e.g., Registrar, Dean of Students, Student Services)

Occasionally, you may find it necessary to visit an administrative office at your college or university, beyond your advisor's or department's office.

- Make copies of any documents you are asked to submit.
- Keep note of the person(s) you contacted, and contact information, in case you need to follow up.
- Keep a file with all information and correspondence related to important academic decisions. Ask for copies of documents, when necessary.

- If you are at a large college or a university, remember that administrative staff must work with many students. You may find them to appear impersonal at first, until they get to know you personally.

- It is to your benefit to get to know the key staff in offices you visit often or regularly; be friendly and express your appreciation for the assistance you receive. This will also help them to remember you personally, which can be helpful for future visits.

Becoming a Member of the College Learning Community (or, Being an Active Learner)

What does it mean to be an active learner? This means more than speaking up in class, and turning in assignments on time. Active learners think about ways to study that will give them a thorough understanding of the material, and they find ways to connect what they are learning to their lives and future goals. They ask questions, are curious about the information they are expected to learn, and continue to expand their learning outside class time and beyond class requirements. You may already be an active learner, in which case some of the following strategies may already be familiar to you. Hopefully, you will still find a few new ideas to consider.

Be Prepared for Class (Before, In, and After)

- Come to class prepared—read the chapter, review previous material, complete all homework assignments on time.

- Attendance is important. In many courses, it will count as part of your course grade. Even when it doesn't, being in class gives you opportunities to participate in discussions, and to learn directly from your professor, who may point out what's important to know, what to study for the next test, or may explain new concepts in a way that makes it easier for you to understand them. In some courses, there are small group discussions and learning activities that will expand your learning beyond what is covered in the textbook. In these types of courses, missing these learning activities can also impact your overall understanding of the material, and result in a lower grade.

- Note taking helps you to remember the important parts of the lecture. Effective study skills are important: for example, does taking notes or creating outlines help you to remember what you read or hear in a lecture? Or, do you prefer to highlight key concepts directly in the text? Whatever method you choose, it's important that it works for you. The learning center at your college may also have useful ideas for developing study skills.

- Contribute to class discussions; participate in small and large group discussions. As mentioned earlier, some courses are very interactive and you will be expected to contribute to group discussions. This can be challenging for many reasons: some of us are shy or self-conscious about speaking up in groups, some may not be accustomed to speaking up and sharing their ideas, whereas others may have been taught by teachers who used lecture formats to teach and did not expect student input. In addition, you may notice that the expected conversation rules and styles are quite different from what you were taught at home or at school, including turn-taking, direct and indirect ways of conveying messages, and roles for listeners and speakers (i.e., who may speak, when, where, and why). If you are hesitant about speaking up in class, remember that this is a skill that improves with practice, even if it doesn't come naturally at first! Here are some ways to get started:
    - If you are not comfortable speaking in large groups, find other ways to let your professors and peers know that you are prepared, have ideas to contribute.
    - If you are not used to participating in the ways that are being used in your classes, discuss this with your advisor, and others who will understand and help you to develop strategies to balance your own style with the demands of the classroom. Think of this as learning a different way to communicate that will make you bicultural, and therefore increase your success in a variety of settings.
- Go to review sessions offered to prepare for tests and exams. In addition to information that is often shared during class, professors and teaching assistants (TAs) often provide study hints and strategies to prepare you for an upcoming test or exam. These hints can help you to focus on the material and to study more effectively. They also provide a better understanding of the professors' expectations and will therefore increase your chances of doing well.
- Consider joining a study group. Study groups are helpful because group members can help each other to learn the material. In addition, there is shared responsibility (interdependence) for learning together, with each member contributing to the group. Group members can also provide emotional support in the learning process.
- Review your study skills and prior academic preparation for the course. If you feel you may be under-prepared, or need to learn new ways of studying, make an appointment at the learning center.

Get to Know Your Professors and Give Them a Chance to Know You

Your professors are an important part of your educational experience in college, and some of them can become mentors who play a vital role in your success.

Just as you may have had some teachers in middle or high school who believed in you, who encouraged you, and who inspired you, some professors will play a similar role during your college years and beyond. At the very least, you will be asking some of them for letters of recommendation as you are applying to transfer to a four-year college or a university, or as you are getting ready to graduate and look for a job. But that is not all—you may develop a lifelong relationship with one or two of these individuals, who will not only support you while you are in school, but also will continue to advise you, listen to you, and encourage you for many years to come. In general, there are many good reasons to get better acquainted with your professors and other instructors.

- Know what each professor's expectations are, for the courses they teach.
- Use office hours to clarify expectations, have your questions answered.
- Think of them as sources of academic support for the courses they teach.
- If you need to drop the course, discuss your options with your professor. Some may be willing to consider taking an incomplete as an alternative. This allows you extra time to complete course requirements, could save you from having to pay for course again, and avoids the possibility of getting a failing grade.
- Learn more about your professors' research and academic interests and volunteer to work on a research project that relates to a topic of interest to you. Often, these volunteer opportunities can develop into paid research assistantships, which will help you financially while also giving you a valuable educational experience. For those of you who are still exploring options, this can be a wonderful way to get exposure to career options that you may not have considered before, simply because you were not aware of them!

Find Others Who Share Your Interests

- Join student organizations and clubs.
- Expand your learning beyond the classroom or laboratory walls.
- Both are important for graduate school admissions and employment in the future.

Part II: Psychological

As mentioned before, going to college can be thought of as a new and different cultural experience. Students who are the first in their family to go to college, as you and many other Latino or Latina students may be, should be prepared for these culture bumps. Hopefully, you will not encounter many and can prevent them altogether with some advance preparation.

What Should I Know and Do If . . . (Some Common Trouble Areas for Many Students)

My Professor Thinks I May Have Plagiarized

As a member of the academic community, it is critical for you to know and understand the policies and expectations for academic integrity. As a student, you will be expected to abide by these policies personally, but also to uphold them with others (e.g., if you are a TA, or working in a research lab with other students and faculty). An important expectation for maintaining integrity is that we give others credit for their ideas, including concepts we are using from texts and other publications, Internet sources, and other media. *There are many factors that may lead to a professor's conclusion that a student has plagiarized.* These include:

- A student's inability to paraphrase ideas in his or her own words. This can happen when the language of the text is difficult or beyond the student's current level of understanding. Students who are nonnative speakers of English (including international students) are at a higher risk for being misunderstood.

- The student does not know the expectations and format for citing academic sources appropriately, for his or her academic discipline.

What should you do if this happens to you? The best approach is to prevent this from occurring, by taking the following steps:

- Become familiar with college or university policies related to academic integrity.
  - Know what is considered to be academic dishonesty.
  - Understand that the consequences of dishonesty are serious and can range from failing the course to being dismissed from the university.
- Make sure you are familiar with style requirements in your academic field, and know how to use them effectively and appropriately.
  - Always document all your print sources.
  - Find Internet resources that may also be available in addition to, or instead of print materials.
  - Seek out peer mentors in your major or discipline, who can guide you to the most effective resources and share strategies that have worked for them.
- If you are unsure whether you have adequately paraphrased material, make an appointment at the learning center to get editorial assistance, and/or to get tutoring with difficult and complete vocabulary, terms, or ideas.

- Ask your professor (or the TA) if he or she would be willing to review a draft of your work and give you feedback. Ask for specific guidance regarding word choices, the expectations related to citations and references, and so forth.

- Find out which professors offer students options to check their work by using Internet resources through Blackboard (an online course management tool). One such option currently available is Turnitin. Students can submit a draft of their paper through Blackboard and get feedback that helps them to identify passages that have not been sufficiently paraphrased in their own words.

I Have a Disability or Chronic Health Condition for Which I Will Need Accommodations

Because this may be the first time that you are responsible for managing your needs related to a disability or chronic health condition, knowing what resources are available for you will help you to successfully advocate for the accommodations you need to ensure your academic success. This can be difficult, especially if your condition is invisible. But as more students with disabilities are successfully graduating from high school and entering college, there are several resources available to support you, and an increased awareness in general that traditional methods of teaching may need to be modified for you. But gaining access to these services requires you to take the first steps:

- Register with the campus office that provides services to students with disabilities. When you do, you will be eligible to access the accommodations and supports that you need, with the assistance of the staff in this office. This may include notification to all your professors each semester, regarding your specific needs and ways in which course requirements may need to be modified for you.

- Make sure your professors understand the impact of the disability on your performance, and accommodations you will need to meet their expectations. Meet with them at the beginning of the semester to go over the specific accommodations listed in your accommodations letter, and discuss which options are most relevant, given the requirements of the course. Because these will vary, and you may not need all the accommodations in every course you take, this conversation can be very helpful for your professor to understand his or her role in ensuring your success.

- Keep professors updated on your progress, and if you need to adjust any of your accommodations.

I Don't Think I Can Complete All My Course Requirements on Time Due to Illness, Other Emergencies

Occasionally, you may find yourself struggling to meet all your academic obligations for a variety of reasons. For some, the demands related to school may be conflicting with other responsibilities at work or at home. Others may experience a personal emergency, or you may simply realize that your course load is very demanding in a given semester. If you find yourself in any of these, or similar situations, make sure to approach your advisor for options, which may include dropping a course or taking a pass or fail, adjusting your course sequence, or, in more urgent situations, withdrawing from the college or the university for the semester. There are several options for you to consider to determine which one is the most suitable for your circumstances.

- Consult with your advisor—this should always be the first step you take, no matter which following option is best for you. Advisors are often aware of campus supports and resources that may be available and related to the reasons for your concern. They can also direct you to the right people, to process any paperwork that may be required.

- Taking an incomplete in the course—this option is often effective if you need to temporarily reduce the academic demands on your time, but feel that you could complete all requirements with an extension beyond the usual end of the semester. These extensions can vary from a few weeks up to one semester and in some universities up to a year.

- Dropping a course—this option allows you to continue to be enrolled, but with a lower course load. It may be preferred if you do not think you can complete the requirements even with an incomplete.

- Withdrawing from the college or university—usually, this option should be reserved for situations when the earlier options are not feasible or realistic and you will need to be away from college for the rest of the semester. College procedures for withdrawing may vary, so make sure you know what steps to follow. Dropping all your courses may not be sufficient.

- Taking a leave of absence—this option allows you to take a break from being in college, and to be readmitted at a later time (after one or two semesters). Although any student can decide not to return to college for any reason, submitting a formal letter or request has its advantages: some colleges and universities will waive the readmission fee if you have completed this process.

At all times, consider talking with your family members about any family-related responsibilities that may be affecting your schoolwork. They may not be aware of the demands placed on you by your academic activities or of any conflicts that you are experiencing. They also may not have considered options that will allow you to remain in school while simultaneously caring for their needs.

Navigating Culture and Language—Becoming Successful Border Crossers

You feel like an outsider, wonder if you belong in college. Latina or Latino students (as well as other nonwhite students or students from working-class families) may be in the numerical minority on some campuses, and their experiences are not reflected in the expectations and activities that are available to them. This may create feelings of isolation and can create emotional and psychological stress. Some common incidents reported by other Latino or Latina students that you may encounter are listed as follows:

- Following something you shared in a class discussion, a fellow student may comment, "You don't say much in class; I didn't think you knew much about chemistry!" (based on anecdote shared by colleague)
- A professor may comment, "You're doing really well in this course, for a Latina or Latino student!" (based on a personal experience)
- You're on a field trip to Mexico as part of your anthropology course. You are often called to be your group's interpreter because you speak Spanish, yet your cultural knowledge and understandings may not be valued, understood, or appreciated. You begin to wonder if that's the reason why you were selected to go on the trip and resent your fellow students or professors for not recognizing or appreciating your academic contributions to the project.
- The discussions about immigrants and immigration reforms in the news media have generated heated debates on campus. This makes you very uncomfortable to be around your peers—some of them don't think you belong in the United States, even though you were born here, just like them. You are tired of having to explain and just want to be left alone.
- You want to share what you have learned at school with your friends and family at home, but some of them react by saying that you've changed or may comment that you're acting white. You begin to wonder if you did the right thing by going to college and if you'll ever feel as connected with these friends or family members as you once did.

What You Can Do

These types of experiences reflect societal and attitudinal barriers that are mirrored on college campuses and in local communities. Do not allow them to keep you from following your dreams and meeting your goals! (Refer back to Step 2 for a more detailed discussion of these barriers to learning and how to overcome them.) In addition, here are a few more suggestions:

- Join student organizations or clubs focused on equity and access for all students.
  - You will find that many of the students here share your dreams and can support you in confronting and navigating through these difficult experiences.
  - Faculty mentors of these clubs are more likely to understand the barriers you may be faced with and can suggest strategies for dealing with them, especially related to your courses, advising, and degree plan. Because they are familiar with campus policies, they often also know college and department administrators who will be responsive to your situation.
- Find other faculty mentors, including Latinas or Latinos who have overcome similar experiences, who are willing to advise and support your efforts.
- Become familiar with your college's policy on harassment, and check with the office of the student ombudsperson to see how they can help you. This is usually the last resort, when other options have not worked. Although we are often hesitant to take this approach, and may see it as too confrontational, it is important to protect yourself. Besides, you have the right to a safe learning environment!

Developing your Academic Support System (or, Who Is Going to Be There for You If You Need Anything?)

Being in school and juggling academic and personal responsibilities is difficult to achieve without the support and encouragement of those who are close to us. Even when we have the tools for academic success, we may feel overwhelmed, frustrated, or challenged by the path we have chosen. In addition, some of us will face barriers to success because of assumptions, perceptions, or expectations placed on us by others (e.g., stereotypes, low expectations, lack of supports). For this reason, it is important to know who's in your corner: Who are the people or groups that will be able to provide you with the reassurance, guidance, and encouragement when you most need it? What are the sources of the cultural comforts that will sustain you in your moments of difficulty? Being academically successful should not require you to give up everything else you enjoy doing, or giving up connections with family and friends. Balancing study time with leisure and stress-reduction activities can relieve stress and will increase your productivity when you are studying.

Know Who Your Community Supports Are Likely to Be
(Family and Friends, Other Supports in Your Community
Such as Church, Social Groups)

- Make sure your family, friends, and others who are important to you understand what you are doing and why.

- Explore ways that they can help you in navigating cultural, linguistic, and social boundaries: many of us find that our college experiences change the way we think and how we see ourselves, as well as how we are perceived by others. These changes can make us feel like outsiders when we are at home even while we may continue to feel we're on the outside looking in at college. You are not alone in experiencing these feelings, and not only Latino or Latina students experience this. Do you know others in your community and possibly in your family who can share their stories and tell you how they faced these challenges? What might you learn from them? (Read the stories of real Latinas or Latinos in section three of the book titled, *How I Made It in College*.)

- When necessary, and if possible, talk with your family and friends about any conflicts you are experiencing so that you can find mutually agreeable ways to balance home and school responsibilities.

- When you have to make important decisions that affect your college life and work, make them with the support of family and/or others who are important to you. This allows them to support you in ways that will also help you achieve your goals.

- When you go home, make sure to pick up the foods, other items to take back with you, that will make your college environment a little more familiar and reassuring (culture comforts).

- Explore different ways of staying in touch. If you can't go home as often as you or your family would like, do you have other ways to be connected? Occasionally, could they come up to visit you, especially if you have a busy weekend coming up and do not think you will have the time to drive home and back? In today's rapidly advancing technological society, many new options are becoming available some of which may work for you. For instance, do you have a family plan for your cell phone that would allow you to call or send text messages more frequently, at no additional cost? Does your family or do your friends have relatively easy access to the Internet, and could you use videoconferencing tools such as Skype to chat with them more often? This gives you both a chance to see each other during times when you cannot go home to see them.

On-Campus and Professional Networks

Finally, remember that some of your support systems may be on campus, in the form of new friendships, relationships with your advisors, mentors, and other social organizations of which you are now a member. As mentioned earlier in this chapter, these networks may include your study groups, peers, student organizations and clubs, and ethnic studies units or organizations. As you advance in your program and have made decisions about your major and future career, the professional organizations in your discipline can become another important source of support. Many organizations offer student memberships at a discounted rate, making it easier to join. This is an excellent way to make friends, connect with others who share your academic and professional interests, join networks and, in the future, find a job.

Important Things to Remember So You Can Meet Your Academic Responsibilities

Part I—Academic

- If you are going to transfer from a community college to a four-year college or a university later, find out which courses will also meet degree requirements for your major.

- Develop a relationship with your academic advisor and professors, who can help you to develop your degree plan, plan ahead for each semester, monitor your progress, and be your first point of contact if you need guidance.

- Be an active, curious, and empowered learner—know what's expected, be prepared for class, attend regularly, make sure your professors know you have ideas to contribute, become part of a learning community with your peers and others.

- Don't hesitate to use campus resources such as the library, learning center, to meet academic expectations such as writing papers. Many requirements involve learning new ways of thinking and expressing ideas and will vary based on the academic major and discipline.

- Last but not least, seek out others who share your academic interests—join clubs or student organizations, volunteer on a professor's research project, or in the community. This will expand your learning beyond the classroom walls and enrich your college experience!

Part II—Psychological Safeguards

- Remember that culture bumps may not be avoidable, and you may occasionally feel isolated or discouraged. You are walking the footsteps of many others who have faced similar challenges. Listening to or reading their stories may inspire you, offer ideas for how you can prepare yourself, and may help you to feel more connected with your community.

- Take the time to develop your academic, social, family, and community support systems. This will nurture you in the many ways that you may need along the way.
  - Keep your family and friends in the loop—make sure they understand what you're doing, why it's important to you, and how they can support you.
  - Look for mentors on campus and in your community—including Latino or Latina students, professors, and others—who are willing to share their success stories and support your efforts.
  - Every college or university has an office for students with disabilities, in case you need these accommodations. Be sure to register so you can access these services.
- Remember that there are many options available if you are concerned about being able to complete your courses or assignments on time due to a personal, family, or medical emergency.
- Don't forget the little things that can mean so much—foods, photographs, other cultural or personal comforts that will make you feel more at home!

What is offered in this chapter will not only make you a successful undergraduate student at college, but also help you to get employed, go on to a graduate school of your choosing, and help you become a leader in your community. Congratulations on having taken the first step in this direction!

Technology Questions and Answers: Using Computer and Internet Technologies to Learn and Succeed

Henry T. Ingle

Setting the Context for Learning Technologies and Expected Student Mastery Levels

Organized around eight critical points of advice and guidance to first-time college or university Latino or Latina students, this chapter is focused on the growing role these computer-based tools can play in your educational success today and into the future for communication, information exchange, and gaining access to the evolving electronic knowledge base on the Internet and other digital technology media. However, without the expertise in the effective use of these technological tools, you as a student may run the risk of losing out on some valuable student learning outcomes of a college or a university education and subsequent life success.

At the same time, I hasten to add that there is nothing better in this day and age than to keep in mind that a healthy dose of skepticism about technology marketing hype is also a very good thing to have. Individuals such as Kevin Kelly, author of *What Technology Wants* (2010), reminds us all that "the fancy technology supposedly crucial to an up-to-the-minute education often is not the major factor in a person's success" (Kelly, 2010, 22). Kelly persuasively argues that students need to acquire "technology smartness" as opposed to "technology absorption," as exemplified in the day-to-day life of so many young people today who have become reliant on mobile technological handheld communication devices. Smartness, in this context, translates into learning to use technology appropriately and effectively as a tool, as contrasted with the phenomenon of "technology addiction".

You as a college or a university student, therefore, need to recognize the fact that in today's business of learning in higher education, a variety of technologies are playing a major role in shaping the requirements for success in the 21st-century educational and workplace settings. Technology in this context is primarily helping students accomplish their work assignments and maintain currency in all that is happening in their field of study, while staying in touch with changes in the larger society. It is a tool for communication, accessing information, and knowledge exchange. As a result, it is now expected—and in some cases required—that all students in higher education arrive on campus with at least a laptop computer and be able to work with technology as one of several key ingredients for achieving success with their learning agenda. It is a tool for college-educated individuals to conveniently and more effectively connect their worlds of schooling, home, personal and family life, and work. Furthermore, as your level of literacy and expertise with these learning technologies progresses, you need to keep in mind that the technology indeed is not the embodiment of success, but rather a device for accessing and shaping answers to critical questions that are part of your desire for learning. As such, you as a student need to learn to use the tool both appropriately and effectively in search of answers to critical questions and the expression or sharing of what you are thinking, discovering, and as a result, learning.

Often simply referred to as technology, these tools have their genesis in the growth and evolution of both micro and new handheld portable wireless computerized devices, as an outgrowth of the Internet, the World Wide Web, Wi-Fi or wireless telecommunications connecting services, and a growing digital and web-based media arsenal. Also included today under the term technology are a series of networks fueling the growth and use of media for interpersonal social and organizational information-seeking purposes, such as Facebook, MySpace, YouTube, e-Harmony, Google, Twitter, the iApple Apps, iPods, iPads, the Kindle, and similar other electronic book reading devices, and a whole host of Smartphones, including iPhones, BlackBerry, and the related android phone models as reflected in the new Motorola Droid X and Droid 2. Illustrative of the learning potential of such technologies is the iPad application entitled "Discovering Ancient Pompeii," which has been extensively cited in the best practices literature. Pompeii, in ancient Greece, is the longest continuously excavated archaeological site in the world, where university professors and their students are today revolutionizing how scientists work in the field as a result of using iPad technology. Rather than recording notes and sketches on a paper tablet or piece of paper with a pen or pencil, researchers at the site use the iPad and its companion Apps to capture invaluable historical data faster, more easily, and with far better accuracy and the ability to quickly share with others in their learning group or with scholars working at a distance. This is an example of smart thinking when it comes to technology for teaching and learning.

This evolving buffet offering of technological devices, coupled with the digital communication software they use to operate, play a strategic role in how you access, organize, and use information. More importantly, the technology can connect you to other people and ideas in a matter of seconds on diverse and multiple content topics and subjects across the globe and bridge distances, both near and far, on an anytime, anywhere, and any subject basis. What's more, this can happen regardless of boundaries and geographical distances, as well as different time zones and life-operating conditions. But, it does require the appropriate use of the tools and a level of proficiency or technology literacy for their effective use. Thus, along with the hardware and software products you as a student will soon learn that to use these technologies effectively, it is really the *people-ware component* (meaning people like you or faculty using the tools) that can make the major difference in becoming a 21st-century educated citizen. This is the process of thinking smart about technology and the multiple roles it can play as part of your own evolution as a human being and the success you are seeking in obtaining a college education.

In terms of Latino or Latina students who, more frequently than not, come to higher education with limited technology user experience, as well as the need for some form of remedial instruction in selected college success skills and abilities, as well as in subject areas important to their academic success, it is clear that the use of this new learning technology now offers a range of possibilities. That said, you need to recognize the fact that, technology like other subjects that shape a college study program, requires a certain level of proficiency on your part that may, in turn, be a stimulus to seek technology remediation or skills upgrading instruction. Thus, in addition to the short high-quality tutorials online in such high-demand areas for remediation instruction, such as English, writing, the language arts field, math, algebra, calculus, the sciences, history, economics, and other business topics, there is also need for online technology literacy at a level of sophistication important for success in a college or a university setting. This increasingly is calling for experience in navigating the modality of Internet-based online instructional courses available to you, as well as the use of the computer for electronic e-mail, presentations, and the crafting and editing of assigned essays, papers and reports. For this purpose, you need to be aware that there are now numerous online resources available on the Internet in different university and college settings through the use of course learning management software, such as Blackboard, Web CT, Desire-2Learn, Moodle, Sakai, Pearson Learning Studio, or e-College, which facilitate important instructional functions such as online chat and discussion sessions, communicating on an anytime basis with your instructor, and delivering papers and reports electronically to a faculty member's drop-off mail box for assignments of this nature. A perceived byproduct of the growing availability of these materials is the action of putting technology in the hands of learners and allowing them to take direct responsibility for their own learning and progress with the learning at their own pace and in areas where they sense the need to correct deficiencies hindering aspirations for college success.

Profiling the Critical Areas of Technology Proficiency Linked to College Success

There are eight critical technology-for-student-proficiency actions I am suggesting students need to undertake in a seriously committed manner. These eight considerations are drawn from my own personal experience in working with university technology programs over the past 25 years and the vantage points I have gained by these years of experience. Many of these concerns may possibly highlight what you, as a Latino or Latina student, already sense are lacking in your own background and as a result, you will need to improve or upgrade as you take the necessary steps to bring your own personal levels of smartness with technology to the appropriate stage. To this end, you will need to invest concentrated time, effort, and energy to successfully master and confidently adopt and use technology as a learning tool for success. This mind-set will need to be part of your everyday life as you progress through your college and university studies, to the workforce, life, and beyond.

I will briefly share these eight stepping stones with you in the pages that follow, and where appropriate, provide you concrete, practical examples of what to do as you prepare your own personal to do list for moving from the state of being a technology novice or newbie to a smart and proficient technology fashionista. This concretely translates today into being able to compose, send, and receive e-mail messages, transmit electronic documents and attachments, or put together visual displays and data spreadsheets, shaping up a PowerPoint presentation, store, display and integrate photos, video clips, graphics and artwork, or perhaps download audio, video, and simulation files in digital formats from the Internet. It may also require that you gain expertise in working with the online course learning management systems, such as Blackboard, Web CT, Desire2Learn, e-College, Moodle, or any of the earlier referenced course learning management platforms, to access learning modules, participate in online discussion groups, or send documents electronically to the instructor's e-learning student projects mail box.

As part of these online teaching–learning methods, some college and university faculty members, experienced in web-design work, have more recently started developing Wikis for use with student teams in and out of the classroom and with other community stakeholders in learning activities of an entrepreneurial, scientific, artistic and humanistic, or public policy nature. This is a collaborative, faculty-moderated software-based technology, which allows instructors to selectively set up pre-identified websites with learning curriculum resources off the Internet and other self-created materials. Wikis are a growing part of a collaborative Web 2.0 innovation that links students to other online groups and significant others across the country or close by in their communities on specific projects. A Wiki, therefore, allows for the easy creation and editing of a multiple set of interlinked website pages to facilitate various types of people and ideas interaction with different online communities. Increasingly, in college and university settings, this also means researching, finding, and critically evaluating the best of the best on the Internet and the World Wide Web from a variety of electronic databases and information available at governmental websites, those from commercial and private sector organizations, and other nonprofit groups and research agencies. In addition, this may also mean that you develop proficiency and comfort levels for active participation in online or hybrid instruction (partly face-to-face and partially online) in a distance delivery format requiring high levels of expertise in navigating these virtual learning media, methods, and approaches.

Let us take time to look at these *eight technology actions steps* I am recommending and the important learning outcomes that I think you need to take away to enhance your chances for success in the day-to-day campus working environment with technology, where more often than not, you may be the first in your family to experience. So, do not think of yourself as a technology under-resourced student, but rather as a student who will be persistent in reaching out for the right resources to achieve success and become technology empowered. To get an overview of the steps in this process, you may find it useful at the onset to refer to the following list, "Achieving Technology Smartness and Proficiency: A Suggested 8-Step Process," which follows and profiles the collective cluster of the eight steps involved in deciding what actions you may need to take as you proceed on your technology learning journey on a college or a university campus, and thereafter, in your life as you move into the workforce.

Achieving Technology Smartness and Proficiency: A Suggested Eight-Step Process for College Students

Step 1: Ask the troublesome questions to resolve your technology don't knows and can't do's.

Step 2: Take immediate steps to get started with technology for your success.

Step 3: Connect the hardware with software and important people-ware linkages in your technology visions.

Step 4: Develop your base of technology expertise on a routine and continuous basis.

Step 5: Challenge yourself to do more with technology than what others expect.

Step 6: Expand your horizons by learning to critically evaluate online information.

Step 7: Participate in the new college learning environment: anytime, anywhere, any subject distance education.

Step 8: Become both a consumer and a generator-creator of knowledge through technology.

Technology Step 1: Ask the Troublesome Questions: Resolve Any of Your Technology Don't Knows and Can't Do's

Asking questions is not stupid. There are no stupid technology questions. Don't be afraid to speak up and ask the questions that are troublesome to you in the technology arena. It is the right thing to do as you seek to become comfortable with technology and successfully meet the expectations for the use of these tools in your campus learning agenda. Getting answers to the unknowns and puzzling areas of concern swimming around in your brain is the first, ever so important step in becoming technology savvy and literate. We learn about technology by asking others, seeing, being shown, observing others doing it, and doing it ourselves. It is a combination of these cognitive, affective, and psychomotor skills that can facilitate the optimum comprehension and learning mastery with any innovation, and in particular, in the information technology and computer field.

Let me first put forth the major pros and cons for the use of technology in teaching and learning, as well as in your own personal journey to develop the necessary proficiency levels. The guidance provided is derived from a collective base of best practices from across colleges and universities and other students like you who previously have undertaken the journey to better understand, value, and take ownership for using technology in their lives and visions for success.

The process will equip you as a student to be able to request from the campus IT or Information Technology department the necessary campus support for technology, which often begins with setting up an e-mail account and your own personal e-mail password, knowing where computer labs and facilities are situated on the campus and their operating hours, as well as understanding the dynamics, policies, security practices, and services that are in place on college and university campuses to help you make the right decisions in gaining access to technology in a relevant and a cost-effective manner. This process requires students to go beyond the machine or technology hardware to also tap technology user support and the help desk services on campus, becoming familiar with the policies and requirements set up by the campus and faculty in terms of technology opportunities that make sense for a variety of campus applications. Part of this educational experience is signing up and participating in the workshops, seminars, and the other ongoing set of activities you must undertake and perfect in the use of selective commonplace software products, such as PowerPoint presentations, website development, spreadsheets, Microsoft Office or AppleWorks, graphics, and visualization design programs. It also includes introductory training sessions in the use of browser technology for gaining access to the Internet, e-mail, digital library resources, databases, and information from the vast set of information resources available on the so-called super information highway in cyberspace.

Also included in this stage of asking basic questions about technology is the need to become readily familiarized with the policies, ethical, legal, and expected behavioral requirements, including password protocols and security protections, as well as what kinds of communication behaviors are allowed or not allowed when engaged in the use of the technology. You will be required to respect and abide by the protocols and procedures of the campus community in terms of using the technology resources, and be aware of the sanctions and penalties when you do not.

It also allows you to become comfortable with the available campus facilities such as computer labs, software, best practices, and policies that contribute in significant ways to your own advancement as a student in successfully meeting instructional requirements important to the learning outcomes you and your instructors have established to help you successfully complete your college education. This is a particularly important challenge for students from diverse backgrounds, such as is often the case with first-generation college-going Latinos or Latinas, who may not have had consistent previous experience in technology mastery important to meeting the rigor and qualitative dimensions of college and university-level instructional expectations. As a result, I strongly recommend that as soon as you are on a college or a university campus before you begin your classes, by all means clear your schedule on a daily basis, to become well-informed about the technology resources and introductory training sessions to help you gain appropriate access to these tools and in the process, be aware of the rules and regulations for the use of technology and the information they facilitate for you both on and off campus.

Technology Step 2: Take the Necessary Immediate Steps
to Get Started with Technology for Your Success Plans

There is a much-quoted Chinese saying that a journey of a thousand miles begin with the very first step you take and then followed by countless other careful steps. I think this is equally as valid an observation to make for students moving to become more proficient and literate in their quest for technology smartness. The top concern here often starts first is answering the question of what hardware and software configuration do I need to get.

Specifically, you will need information and guidance about very basic technology necessities, such as a minimum computer hardware setup, printer, and software installation package (Windows 7 or Mac Operating system) to purchase and work with, which includes the questions of laptop versus a desktop unit, the necessary computer memory and storage capacity, wireless service capabilities, and if working both on and off campus, a computer storage stick or device to easily carry your work products from one place to another for accessing. In addition, most of colleges and universities are now using course learning management systems, such as I earlier referenced, which include Blackboard, Web CT, Desire2Learn, Moodle, Sakai, the Pearson Learning Studio, and so forth, to facilitate electronic online computer communication for faculty and students to use in both face-to-face, fully delivered online, or in a combination mix known as hybrid classes, where technology functions as enhancement to supplement their contact with students through e-mails, discussion groups, virtual faculty office hours, and related functions. This includes, as I earlier referenced, such functions as an electronic online drop box for virtually sending in assignments, downloading classroom teaching–learning and presentation materials, the course syllabus, convening online discussion groups at a distance both in *synchronous* (gathering in real time with the students and faculty all present) and *asynchronous* (at your convenience depending on your own schedule) time periods. Therefore, as a student, you need to be prepared for these procedures and processes involving the use of computers and information technologies so there is little or no confusion and surprises when you are called on to participate in these computer-based and digital technology instructional activities.

Furthermore, today, one of the primary ways in which colleges and universities communicate with students is through e-mail accounts, online web postings, and the new course management platforms for distributed learning opportunities for either hybrid or fully online instructions, operating via the Internet and on the web directly on your computer and at the campus websites. The use of these technologies not only gives students access to updated just-in-time and recurring critical information, oftentimes including the course catalog and class schedule they cannot frequently obtain in other formats, but it also provides students and faculty access to online library and research publications and journals.

Therefore, to assist you in your getting-started-with-technology plans, I suggest you first do some basic reading of student primer and guidebook publications on computers for education, the Internet, handy tips in choosing your computer configuration, all of which are to be found in the reference section of the campus library. In addition, take time to visit the technology corner at the campus bookstore, seek the advice of the designated academic technology staff specialists in your campus IT department, and sign up to take the mini-workshops and seminars regularly offered on your campus computer labs and the library for this purpose. They provide programs and services to familiarize you with the recommended hardware and software configurations for students to purchase, the expected costs, and convenient ways of purchasing them, as well as helping you gain the necessary technology skills, and familiarizing you with the important campus rules, policies, and acceptable practices you must observe, as well as evolving resources for your use.

In terms of purchasing the appropriate computer and accessorized equipment for your own personal use—over and beyond accessing the campus computer lab facilities available to all students—the best advice is to consider your particular needs and assignments, and in the process, make a determination of what your primary uses will be. Most likely it will initially be such functions as word processing, editing, accessing the Internet for class research assignments, sending and receiving e-mail messages and attachments, or perhaps, in some cases developing PowerPoint presentations, websites, and web-based art and graphics design works, or gaming and simulation activities. Such thinking will guide you in determining basic consumer decisions as PC or Macintosh computer, desktop or laptop or both, and the price range. Generally speaking, the Apple Mac computer is more expensive than a PC, and the basic price range for such technology is within the reach of about $400 to $1,200 (but continuously dropping in price on an annual basis). To this, you most likely will need to include some additional costs for the computer screen size, printer configuration, auxiliary connector tools and software products, and the recurrent costs of paper and ink cartridges for the printer. In addition, there are the costs of Internet connectivity resulting in monthly services provider charges for your home installation and hookup. Most, if not all campuses, however, are wireless-connected.

Most likely, your initial technology configuration purchase will take you through your university career for about five years before you have to either replace or upgrade to a new, improved computer configuration for your own personal use. As mentioned earlier in this chapter, the most recurrent issue with technology is continued adjustment to change and new developments emanating from the engineering and software design industry.

Recently, campuses in California and elsewhere have started to move away from the traditional Microsoft-based e-mail exchange services to new e-mail access services on Google, which may well become prevalent in the educational sector. By moving to Google Apps for this purpose, there is an overriding interest to provide more storage and other much-in-demand user features with an "edu" or educational institutional online e-mail address. More importantly, when Google is used as the campus telecommunications platforms for technology advancement, student and faculty are given more than seven gigabytes of storage and there are no distracting advertisements on the site. This makes for less cumbersome connectivity.

Technology Step 3: Connect the Important Hardware, Software, and People-Ware Linkages in Your Technology Vision

The strongest rationale for technology in your life as a student and college-educated individual is that it will connect you with people. Also, this view requires that you give concentrated attention to the people-ware ingredients, and that of your own human intelligence and will to master and improve your technology skills and abilities.

Technology on college and university campuses will most definitely *change the manner in which you as a student learn,* as well as *what, how where and when you learn.* It is a major shift in the way in which you will be expected to think, to use your intellect, and to act in classes you take and the people you meet and interact with as part of teams your professors and instructors will ask you to join for this purpose. Technology as a tool also requires students to work with time and information in a variety of new ways that may not be as familiar to you, such as real-time (synchronous) and virtual-time (asynchronous) learning, adherence to copyright rules and regulations for using information off the Internet, and verifying references and other sources of information from electronic digital databases. The campus library can guide you in this respect in a quick and easy-to-understand manner. So, make it a point to spend time with the librarians and ask for guidance and direction in terms of the use and accessing of digital and web-based information sources and references.

Uppermost, the way in which teaching and learning takes place changes as a result of technology. Memorization and routine remedial teaching–learning approaches are de-emphasized in favor of critical learning skills emphasizing higher-order thinking and information processing skills of synthesis, analysis, and evaluation of knowledge and its value to the different problem-solving venues required of you by your professors and teachers. Technology, in this context, becomes a means to an end that goes beyond the mere properties that define it as a technological innovation or hardware tool. It helps students create a new mind-set valuing access to information and communication in a timely and effective manner as a strategic competitive advantage for success throughout the changing stages of your life.

As a result, in your role as student and learner, you are encouraged to acquire these higher-order thinking, speaking, and related skills of expression or people-ware attributes that are strategically enhanced by ever-changing and improving technological resources, such as the integration of computer software PowerPoint presentations in class assignments or even a web presence to profile your work. The one constant condition you will face is technological change and innovation in *what* you communicate, *how* you communicate, and with *whom* and *when* you communicate. This will be a major adjustment throughout your professional and personal life, and technology will continue to play a critical role in how you best handle these challenges for communication and information exchange.

Increasingly, technology tools also are taking on more human, people-like characteristics that make the user, or people-ware component, a most important consideration for you in terms of becoming part of a technology users' group on your campus. User groups allow you to teach and learn from each other and also troubleshoot problems that need to be resolved, to progress to more advanced levels of technology proficiency or literacy to tackle different assignments you are required to undertake and complete without the hurdles of a major learning curve.

Technology Step 4: Develop Your Base of Technology Expertise on a Routine and Continuing Basis

You will have to invest concentrated time, energy, and level of effort upfront to develop both a new mind-set and proficiency skills set to enhance your effectiveness with technology and to continue to stay current in new developments. Technology in the new digital economy in which higher education today functions relies on a variety of ever-changing software products and conditions for teaching and learning, as well as rules and regulations for using information digitally taken off the Internet in terms of such areas as copyright and plagiarism considerations (i.e., appropriately identifying and using other people's ideas and words that you find on the Internet). These concerns reflect the content differences of the various university programs of studies, as well as the specific requirements of given technology tools for unique software configuration applications and user know-how to be successful in their use. This, in turn, shapes up the set of expectations for proficiency in the use of these tools of instruction that will challenge you and the kinds of class papers and presentations you will be required to produce in a creative and professional manner.

Effective use of the technology is critical to student success in terms of meeting established learning outcomes in a timely and effective manner, as well as subsequent success in the workplace once you graduate with your college degree. Illustrative of these considerations is the use of statistical software programs for research assignments or a particular type of accounting software for students in accounting, business, and financial planning courses, or graphic design programs in engineering courses. The use of telecommunication media and related digital media and technology are now an everyday, commonplace reality of modern-day life and their presence will only increase and expand as new innovations take hold and the society becomes more technology literate and technology-reliant. Your future employers will expect that you have acquired this knowledge and skills as part of your college and university studies.

Therefore, you as a student, early on in your college career, need to create almost a fearless attitude toward the handling and use of these technological tools, which contrary to popular fears are almost break proof no matter what you do with them, and increasingly more able to handle a variety of tasks and functions in a human-like manner. They are becoming more people friendly and ever so essential to all that we do. And while society as a whole may not have an automatic love affair with technology, it most surely has a fascination and a need to determine what the human being can do or not do with it.

It is said that practice makes perfect and that is precisely what I have discovered in my own life as I have both fooled around or played with technology in my unstructured free time and challenged myself with the arsenal of available technological communication tools and gadgets in a variety of price ranges. These tools continue to be routinely introduced and adopted for more widespread use in working with the teaching–learning demands of a modern college and university setting. You need to prepare yourself for the progressively higher levels of skills and abilities you will need to be able to use in your the major and minor areas of study you finally select to pursue for the completion of a university or a college degree at the undergraduate level and subsequently at the graduate school level if you pursue advanced study options. And such determination becomes doubly important as you move into graduate education and eventually for professional or doctoral degree studies for unique areas of specialization in career fields that often have not yet been identified, such as the green technology, GPS, and sustainability fields.

Technology Step 5: Challenge Yourself to Do More with Technology than What Others Expect

You must think of technology as a strategic set of ingredients made available to you for experimenting and creating multiple lifelong success recipes. As a result, you most likely will learn best by pushing the envelope to do more than you expected you could do. Similar to the ability to write and express yourself in increasingly more effective ways, the ownership you need to take is to pursue new technology in a life-journey activity where you will always be learning more and new things. The mastery of a diverse set of technology software products and technological tools pushes the outer boundaries of where the teaching and learning processes can take you as a learner under the tutoring of your teachers and fellow students. This mastery journey is never-ending given the variety and diverse kinds of new resources that come into place annually as you become a consistent user and owner of the evolving media products, services, and methods.

It makes for a lifelong journey of continual learning as an evolution of a new teaching–learning method focused on a learner-centered approach, which is growing in popularity to make the student at once both a consumer and a developer and creator of information and technology approaches. This in turn creates the type of workforce that the society is now in critical need and is asking colleges and university to produce. For Latino or Latina students who at times come to the college or university learning experience with a bit of trepidation and uneasiness, or lack of experience with the working environment, technology allows you to customize your learning requirements to focus both on your strengths and areas in need of improvement. Technology approached in this manner can allow you to work on a tailor-made approach to better guide you in the mastery of learning areas where you feel a bit deficient or underprepared.

In the experimental learning environment of colleges and universities, technology allows you to stretch yourself and master new skills and abilities that are often enduring and important to success in all of your life's peaks and valleys. As a result, at some point in time, you will also be knowledgeable to determine which technologies you will need to own by purchasing them for your consistent use both on and off campus. Your college or university bookstore can often assist you in these purchasing efforts and guide you in the right direction for financing the purchase and various licensing, software, security, and repair-servicing and upgrading options.

Technology Step 6: Expand Your Horizons by Learning to Critically Evaluate Online Information

You will need to progress from the four walls of the traditional brick and mortar classroom, a book or two, and the professor to a virtually limitless world of learning resources, people, places, and ideas that now define you as a learned person. In short, you will now be dealing with multiple sources, perspectives, and points of view that will require you as a student to develop your own critical thinking and analysis skills.

Technology facilitates access to a seemingly endless, diverse, and far-reaching, almost limitless set of retrospective, historical, current, and yet-to-be discovered digital and human resources across the multiple pathways that technology can take you as the learner in a relative short period of time. It stretches the learner's curiosity and helps faculty work with more realistic student-centered and collaborative learning approaches. These efforts, more likely than not, will require you as a student to participate in online or partnership teams that can optimize the reach of education on an anytime, anywhere, any subject basis. This is a major boom for the dream of lifelong learning and new career development opportunities spawn by the almost omnipotent presence of these new computer and information technologies.

As a result, one of the most critical skills you will need to master in navigating this new technological world is the act of critically evaluating the validity, accuracy, and truthfulness of the information that gets transported on this super information highway. This is particularly critical in the online modality because of the vast resources available at your fingertips with the convenience of a click of a mouse or a keystroke, as well as the other individuals with whom you exchange messages, and the types of messages that you yourself will communicate. You need to remember that once information is on the web and Internet, it is very difficult to change or totally delete, and even much more challenging to validate its accuracy and truthfulness. These information literacy skills, therefore, represent a critical part of your preparation to use technology tools in an effective and appropriate manner.

Access to this vast array of resources, therefore, carries the need for special information review and evaluation skills that you will be expected to employ in separating the wheat from the shaft in terms of credible, factual, and useful information, as opposed to fluff and unsubstantiated assertions found on countless websites on the Internet. Today, most colleges and universities now offer media literacy courses that equip you to more effectively evaluate information resources on the Internet and how best to reference and cite them in any product you are creating on the basis of this information. There also are a variety of published primers guiding students in what to do and what not to do in this new digital communication environment, as well as the combination of computer configurations that might be most appropriate to purchase.

I encourage you to register and take such classes early on, and throughout your college and university career. Take advantage of the learning you will gain to help you become more technology savvy and as a result, more effective in your future life roles and progressively more responsible career development opportunities as a result of this level of technology smartness and knowledge.

Technology Step 7: Participate in New College Learning Environments: Learning Anytime, Anywhere, Any Subject through Distance Learning

Perhaps more important to you than anything else I share with you about technology is the fact that you must prepare yourself for a new learning environment. A college education now and in the future will be organized for anytime, anywhere, any subject teaching–learning. With the advent of the Internet, wireless communication networks, and sophisticated learning course management systems, such as Blackboard, Web CT, and e-College, faculty and students will be permitted with fully online delivered instruction or a strategic combination of face-to-face classroom and an online presence to more conveniently access information in a variety of formats that today is commonly referred to as hybrid instruction. As a result, the geographic location where you live need no longer be the determinant of what you can learn and how you enhance your life opportunities with these learning opportunities.

For many reasons you may be a student who enrolls in a college that uses online learning as its main way of teaching, like the University of Phoenix, Kaplan, and other private, for-profit educational institutions. More and more, two- and four-year colleges are adding Internet-based teaching and learning programs, which bring about the rapid growth and staying power of online and distributed learning opportunities. In some cases, it is through such systems as Blackboard, e-College, Web CT, Open Source, and so forth that some students are afforded the only opportunity to pursue and complete a college education as a result of the geographic location where they live or the life family responsibilities they have, which prevent the more traditional and regular on-campus college attendance.

This learning alternative or option also requires that you as a student assume a stronger, more direct responsibility for your own learning, while also engaging in a stronger participatory role in the learning activities. It requires a more rigorous level of discipline and stick-to-it-ness on your part. As they say in the distance education virtual reality teaching field, there are no back seats in an online classroom and everyone quickly learns who you are and whether you are participating or not. As a result, you have to be in the driver's seat and gain the skill and ability to log in and out of the online course or use selective aspects of the online course platform in hybrid settings to deliver your assignments to your teacher or professor in their electronic drop box for assignment via the Internet.

Skills and abilities acquired in the use of these technology-based instructional delivery systems can give you a competitive advantage in the workplace. The process equips you for subsequent continuing learning you will no doubt have to pursue to be on the cutting edge of your profession and the ever-changing nature of the workplace economy. Today, and for the foreseeable future, this will include virtual telecommunications working teams collaborating at a distance and in virtual space that many employers now use with great frequency, both for training and for staff development, as well as for meetings, and developing team assignments. It will also play into your life schedule to more easily engage in continued learning throughout life at different stages and in settings that are convenient to the different lifestyles and obligations to balance your home and family, schooling and work responsibilities amidst the constraints of time, money, and schedules.

As a student, therefore, it moves you away from the concept of being stranded as the one and only person on an island to that of having to participate in many other human spheres. You cannot shut yourself off from the diversity of others in an online teaching and learning environment. You are forced to come to grips, therefore, with both your cognitive abilities and also develop the attributes of the array of emotional intelligences to deal effectively with other individuals from diverse backgrounds and conditions in a virtual working environment at your desktop or laptop computer at a distance.

There is also the matter of convenience in the dramatic increase in online and distance education opportunities via the Internet, the World Wide Web, modularized web seminars and workshops at your fingertips, and other virtual telecommunications environments accessible from the comfort of your desk at work, your car, or an armchair at home. In is an environment where the learning comes to the learner, as opposed to the learners needing to transport themselves at a predetermined time to a certain physical space on a college campus site. This is what is called the anytime, anywhere, any subject learning environment.

As a result, I think you need the experience of taking an online hybrid or technology-enhanced course (i.e., instruction offered partially face-to-face and partially over the web and Internet) while still in the campus setting so you develop proficiency in working and succeeding in these new virtual environments. You can develop collaborative learning abilities and skills in working with team members from diverse backgrounds and experience to complete important assignments, and even make them better than if you had just been working alone. Both great interpersonal communication skills and new technology expertise can be simultaneously acquired in these new virtual online settings, but it does require greater discipline, commitment, and consistency of effort on the part of the student.

Technology Step 8: Become Both a Consumer and a Generator-Creator of Knowledge through Technology

Technology requires you to assume greater responsibility for your own learning both as a consumer of other people's knowledge and as a generator-inventor of new knowledge as you progress in your college education over the years. Indeed, one of the most significant byproducts in mastering the use of technology in your own learning is that the teacher and student roles are at times reversed in such a manner that students will need to move from just consuming the information provided by the faculty to one of generating new content and knowledge, and as a result, become teachers to others by drawing on their own life experiences.

This incredible characteristic of the new virtual educational environments affords Latino or Latina students strategic opportunities to effectively integrate highly relevant cultural, language, and background life differences into the teaching and learning settings and gain an appreciation for what others can teach you as well as what you can teach others. Technology can facilitate this process because of the vast resources of information and options for packaging it to communicate with a diversity of others, which it facilitates. In the process, you as a student can take ownership and greater responsibility for mastery of your own learning to meet the particular instructional needs and conditions you have set for yourself to move the future taking shape in your mind into a work-life reality.

Simultaneously, technology used in this manner can make a major difference in college and university curricula and what students consider important to learn, as well as how they learn it. It is in this area of technology use that you also need to develop critical skills important to later life assignments. This no doubt may include the requirement that you make sense of information in terms of evaluating and summarizing the major points and communicating the significance of the information to others in an appropriate, culturally sensitive, relevant, and easy-to-understand manner. This type of ability is particularly relevant to a world that increasingly is becoming globally oriented and interdependent, in terms of both an individual's future professional areas of work and the achievement of the socioeconomic well-being of a person, which a college and university education often provides. It underscores the adage attributed to the late president of the United States, John F. Kennedy, that "much is expected of those who much is given." This increasingly is the perspective of Latinos or Latinas as the youngest and fastest growing population in the United States and rapidly becoming a critical ingredient for shaping the future of the United States as a society of future teachers, learners, and doers in the world.

Summary of Important Points

There is no denying that the Internet, digital media, and technology are playing a pivotal role in our world today. I trust, therefore, that you find some level of agreement with this perspective, and that in your own metamorphosis to become technology savvy, you will also pinpoint other critical steps, over and beyond the handful of eight I have flagged, to achieve technology smartness and proficiency for your own well-being and success. Keep in mind that throughout our life we are all likely to be students in what is being termed the new learning economy and as such, we all need to think and act within the context of the new knowledge-based and information-abundant 21st-century world in which we are now living. It is important, therefore, that you keep an open mind to change and seek answers to your questions about today's technological tools as well as those that may be on the horizon for tomorrow and thereafter. Working to cultivate this mind-set in your college and university studies will most assuredly prepare you for effectively realizing your aspirations. Hopefully, in the process, you will be able to live a purposeful life that measures up to the education you will be working hard to receive to make a difference in society and in your own life.

References

Arum, Richard, and Josipa Roksa. *Academically Adrift: Limited Learning on College Campuses.* Chicago, IL: University of Chicago Press, 2011.

Chenoweth, Karin. *"IT'S BEING DONE": Academic Success in Unexpected Schools.* Cambridge, MA: Harvard Education Press, 2008.

Ingle, Henry T., and Yolanda R. Ingle. "Pathways to a Better Future: Reconfiguring the Educational Context for Change." In *Latino Change Agents in Higher Education: Shaping a System That Works for All,* edited by Leonard A. Valverde and Associates, 23–38. Chapter 2. San Francisco, CA: Jossey-Bass Publishers of John Wiley & Sons, Inc., 2009.

Kelly, Kevin. "Achieving Techno-Literacy—Computers Are a Tool, Not a Solution." *New York Times Magazine,* September 10, 2010, 21–24.

Kelly, Kevin. *What Technology Wants.* A Barnes & Noble e-Book. Viking/Penguin Press, October 2010.

Li, Charlene, and Bernoff, Josh. *Groundswell: Winning in a World Transformed by Social Technology.* Cambridge, MA: Harvard Business School Press, 2008.

Mizuko, Ito, Heather A. Horst, Matteo Bittanti, and Donah Boyd. *Living & Learning with New Media: Summary of Findings from the Digital Youth Project.* Kindle Book Edition, June 2009. Available through Amazon.com.

Moursund, D. "A College Student's Guide to Computers in Education." A Working Draft. University of Oregon, May 2007, http://pages.uoregon.edu/Moursund/Books/College Student/Draft%205–16–07.pdf.

Mulholland, Andy, Jon Pyke, and Peter Fingar. *Enterprise Cloud Computing: A Strategy Guide for Business Technology Leaders.* Tampa, FL: Meghan-Kiffer Press, 2010, www.mkpress.com.

Nakamura, Lisa, and Peter Chow-White. *Race after the Internet.* New York: Routledge Press of Taylor & Francis Publishers, 2011.

O'Reilly, Tim, and Sarah Milstein. *The Twitter Book.* Sebastopol, CA: O'Reilly Media, 2009.

Peña, Luis. "Handy Tips to Choose Your Computer." Online Article in YoungMoney. com Newsletter, March 11, 2004. Daily Forty-Niner via U-Wire.

Powell, Carol Lea Clark. *A Student's Guide to the Internet.* Ft. Worth, TX: Hartcourt Brace College Publishers, 1998.

Powell, Carol Lea Clark. *Working the Web: A Student's Research Guide.* Ft. Worth, TX: Hartcourt Brace College Publishers, 2000.

Powell, Carol Lea Clark. *The Hartcourt Brace College Guide to the Internet.* Ft. Worth, TX: Hartcourt Brace College Publishers, 2001.

U.S. Department of Education. *Transforming American Education: Learning Powered by Technology (Technology Plan, 2010).* Washington, DC: Technical Working Group, Office of Educational Technology, March 5, 2010, 114 pp.

Washington, Jesse. "Has the Digital Divide Shifted?: Latinos, Blacks & Other Minorities Access the Internet on Phones, at Higher Rates, But Some Say Trend Isn't All Positive News." *Associated Press. San Diego Union Tribune (Section C: Business News),* January 17, 2011.

Watkins, S. Craig. *The Young and the Digital: What the Migration to Social Network Sites, Games & Anytime, Anywhere Media Means for Our Future.* Boston, MA: Beacon Press, 2010.

Successful Transition from a Community College to a Four-Year College or a University or to the World of Work

Baltazar Arispe y Acevedo Jr.

We all have dreams and hopes of what we want to be in life and how we want our families and friends to think about us. Success is a target that we want in our lives; some of us succeed and some of us do not. If you are successful, then you should work to continue to be so, and if you have been distracted, then you need not give up but rather continue to take corrective actions to get you on the right track to success. Sometimes circumstances change or events take place that alter or change our course in life.

In this chapter you will be introduced to several steps that you may consider as you prepare to map out your future. The focus here will be on the process of enrolling, succeeding, and moving from a community college to a university or a college, employment and/or to continue training in your career choice.

Harvey MacKay, the author of *Swim with the Sharks* (1988, 76), advises business leaders that, "you fail to plan, then you plan to fail." This advice is good to consider no matter what stage of our life you happen to be. Planning is the first step that you need to consider when you are at the crossroads of your life but it requires a reality check to guide your planning.

Find Out Where You Stand

You might be thinking, "What comes next in my life?" This question may be the result of several factors that impact your life, such as:

- Your recent graduation from high school
- Your discharge from the military

THE REALITY CHECK MODEL

- Family Support
- Academic & Career Planning
- Financial Resources Planning
- Sponsors & Advocates
- Transition Plan

VISION

What I Want To Be
Where I Want To Be

© B.A. Acevedo / Graphics: Laura Soria

- You might have been displaced or laid off from your job
- You may have gotten married recently
- You are now a single parent
- You may have dropped out from high school

Every so often we have to get a medical checkup to find out the status of our health. This is a reality check of your body and the information and advice that you receive from your doctor will help you plan a healthy lifestyle. An educational checkup is no different than a medical one except that it involves a review of where you are, who you are now, and what you want to be in the future in terms of your education and career. The following model is provided to guide you during your reality check and assessment as part of your planning process to enroll in a community college.

Applying the Reality Check Model

Each student who is in a community college is there for a different reason; each has distinct goals that are personal and only his or her. Your goals depend on how you plan the steps to take to achieve your vision and this model serves as a guide for what you may consider a map to your vision. This model involves several *action steps* and they all begin at a *baseline* or the starting line as in a race. Let's review these *action steps* so that we may identify the *gaps* that need to be filled with resources or assets that you find within your family, community, social network, the community college, state and federal governments. Yes, there are many resources; it is only a matter of where to look.

Family Support

The Hispanic culture is one that places family relationships at its core: *primero la familia*. The decision to move forward to enroll in a community college is one that should involve your primary and extended family. Hispanic families are very close knit and this relationship offers a network that will support you before and during your pursuit of a college degree or additional career training. It is advisable to involve your parents, if you are living at home, in your plans especially if this is your first step after high school graduation. They may have been able to save some money to assist you with educational expenses, provide you with continued residential space, or support such as an Internet-connected Wi-Fi network for your computer.

The Dallas County Community College District (www.dcccd.edu) has identified some typical questions and concerns for family members as their children begin to consider transferring to a four-year college or a university. These are questions that should be directed at an advisor whom you and your parents may meet with during the planning phase of your transfer to college or university. Some of these questions are: How will my son or daughter organize time for the class? How much money will he or she need? If he or she is going to a campus, will he or she need to drive a car? What if he or she becomes ill? How do I know he or she will be safe on campus? Can I visit him or her on campus? These questions and corresponding resources are addressed in a later section of this chapter.

For those of you who are married you may have question such as these: Who will take care of my young children? How can I take classes around a work schedule? How can I afford it? Will I feel out of place being older than the rest of the students? As a married couple you will have other factors to consider during this phase of your planning since you may have children, and your economic status and available resources are dependent on both having sustainable jobs. It is important that both spouses develop a budget that takes into account all of your related family and educational expenses and the resources that you will have to access or acquire to maintain your family. Also, your children may need day care, and in many instances your parents or other family members, such as brothers, sisters, cousins, aunts, uncles, and grandparents, may be willing and able to lend a hand with child care on an emergency or as-needed basis. There is day care, in many instances, at the college or nearby at a reasonable cost, which you may need to use on a daily basis.

How Will It Affect Our Family?

The counseling and advisement staff at the seven colleges of the Dallas County Community College District (http://www.dcccd.edu) provide these excellent insights about the impact of a college education on your family. What can a degree do for the family? Well by offering more education in a chosen profession, it offers more income and an expanded career pathway for life. Having a degree can open doors for new jobs and more promotions!

What kind of work will need to be done and how much time does it take each week? A full-time student is expected to take around 12–15 credits per semester (typically a four-month period), which is estimated to be around 36 hours of work a week! This combines class time (either in a classroom or on a computer if the student is a distance learner) and homework time, so it is very important to set aside time specifically for schoolwork. However, remember that many classes are offered at multiple times, including evenings and weekends, to help allow for other obligations such as work or family time.

Academic and Career Planning

This is the most crucial step in your planning process once you and your family have decided that going to a community college is a good starting point for you. How you approach this step is determined by where you are at the moment that you decide to apply for admission. The following are some key items that you need to consider depending on whether you are in your education, employment, or military status.

Step 1: Review of Academic Records

If you are still enrolled in your high school then you need to meet with a counselor (preferably 10th grade) and go over your academic transcripts and conduct a review of the courses that you may have already completed or which you will complete within your senior year. A counselor will also provide assistance and guidance about your local community college and provide a list of resources that are available at a campus for you to access. The focus of this review will be on the credits and grades that you made in your high school classes and if you took any advanced placement (AP) courses that may be accepted as college credits by your community college.

Secondly, you need to determine how strong you are in terms of capacity in your reading, writing, and math on the basis of your grades and test scores. This information will assist you to develop a college course schedule that makes use of your skills. *Whatever you do, do not get directed toward all remedial courses as a first option when you apply or during orientation at your college. Remedial courses typically do not count toward your degree and if you are on student loans, the amount of money you are eligible for begins to run out.* Request and take all qualifying exams that may determine your ability to enroll in standard academic courses that have credit that can be applied to your academic transfer plan or to your technical training plan. You need to make sure to make two copies of these documents: one for your personal file and the other to share or to show to the college's offices of the registrar, the admissions office, academic advisement departments, and to support your course selection during your participation in the community college orientation and registration.

These action items will be similar for *veterans* who are returning to an academic transfer program or enrolling to pursue a technical training program. As a veteran you may have accumulated some advanced academic or technical training that may be counted toward your community-college degree or training plan. Upon separation from the military, you will have been provided with a portfolio of your service and the various assignments and specialized training that you acquired during your active duty at various assignments. *A more detailed discussion about military personnel is provided at another section of this chapter since the options available to veterans are very comprehensive and are covered by various federal departments and even law.*

If you have been in the workforce and have been laid off or have decided to change careers, your path will be similar, and in some instances, a bit different. It may have been years since you graduated from high school or maybe left a community college to begin working. You will need to take care of two items before applying for admission to a community college to pursue an academic transfer program of study or enroll in a technical training program. First, contact your high school or prior educational institution and obtain copies of your academic or training program certificate and make sure to request these in a sealed envelope that you can hand over to the office of admissions or advisement staff at the college. Secondly, obtain reference files from your employers that have the titles and job descriptions of positions that you held and also any records about any technical training that you may have completed while employed. You may use these records to request advanced placement exams in certain subjects or technical fields or demonstrated skills as a result of your work experience. The results may provide you with academic or technical training credit that can be applied toward your program of study and qualify as part of your certification, transfer, or graduation requirements.

Some of you may have dropped out of school for reasons that may be rather personal or even out of your control: that does not matter now. What matters is that you have an opportunity to pursue your career goals at a community college. If you do not have a general equivalency diploma (GED), then you can enroll in a community-based organization program, such as those sponsored by SER: Jobs for Progress, LULAC (League of United Latin American Citizens), the county workforce training agency, and in many instances high school districts, and libraries, to get a GED. Community colleges offer GED training at a minimal cost as part of their adult education programs. Upon your successful completion of the GED exam, you will receive a diploma that qualifies you to apply for admission at a community college. When you are ready to do so, then you need to go over the previous action items and also begin to create a reference file to guide your educational and training program of study.

Step 2: Career Planning

Community colleges have excellent resources to guide you in career planning and in preparing a transfer guide to a four-year college or a university. For example, the Maricopa County Community College District in Phoenix, Arizona, has an onsite resource guide (http://www.maricopa.edu/) to assist students in making the right career choices during their exploration of options in both academic transfer and technical training programs. Another site is available at both the Empire State College of the State University of New York (http://suny-empire.esc.edu) and the Dallas County Community College District (http://www.dcccd.edu). There are similar sites at your local community college, and all you have to do is to enter the name of the college in the Google Search Cell and follow along with the information that is often listed by programs and departments at the institution.

In preparation for conducting a career plan, you need to review your educational assets from your high school, your military career, or from training that you received on the job. If you have to, go back to your high school counselor, military training portfolio, or employer training records to get a sense of your skill sets. This evaluation should tell you what your math and reading levels are; what technical skills you have, such as those that are evident in computer or technology literacy; or you may have specific job skills such as drafting, computer-aided design; or leadership skills from your military experience. If you are applying to a community college because of a career change due to a work-related layoff, a downturn in the economy, or because you want to go into a different field, you are also encouraged to develop a career plan. Remember that no one is without assets.

A common career interest inventory that is used by these agencies is the Strong Interest Inventory. You might take time to conduct an online review of the Strong Profile, College Edition (R) (https://www.cpp.com/). According to the developers of this career inventory, "The *Strong* Profile, College Edition, takes the wealth of career interest data provided in the *Strong* Profile one step further. An additional personalized report helps students explore the path that is right for them by identifying specific college courses, jobs or internships, and extracurricular activities that will allow them to express their unique interests and personal style. Step-by-step advice on how to evaluate academic majors that fit their interests and preferences provides extra help for college students beginning to prepare themselves for success in the world of work." You may download a copy of a sample career profile at this website.

In many instances this self-paced career interest inventory is in use at the LULAC Education Outreach Center, SER: Jobs for Progress and the GI Forum. All of these service organizations are committed to the advancement of educational opportunities for Hispanic students throughout the United States. The websites and e-mail contacts for these agencies are provided at the end of this chapter for your reference. (See Appendix A.)

The results from this action item should identify your educational assets, capacities, and training-related skills while also providing you with information about some gaps. These gaps are those challenges that need attention on your part; for example, you might find out, from your academic record that you need to improve your math and reading skills or learn to communicate by working with groups or teams of individuals. You should see these gaps as opportunities for you to improve and develop your capacity to succeed in your academic and training programs as well as your chosen career. These corrective actions are similar to getting back on track, if you were driving and started to lose control of your car. At no time must you view these gaps as weaknesses or deficiencies but rather experience or skills that you need to learn or which you may need to improve such as getting better at math or learning to write or communicate better.

Financial Resource Planning

Step 1: Identify Financial Resources

Do not allow the absence of a financial plan to become the major barrier to enrolling and to get off track in the pursuit of your academic plan or the completion of your certification in a technical or career development program. The availability of resources to pay for college tuition, books, computers, transportation, training supplies, and equipment is there. See Chapter 3 for details. You look into developing a financial plan at the same time you begin the application process to enroll in a college.

In instances when there have been massive layoffs in certain industries, the state's employment and dislocated workers program may be of assistance during your entry to another career field. Community colleges have traditionally been a key provider of workforce and employment preparedness training under the sponsorship of the federal government's Workforce Investment Act, which provides career assessment, counseling, and guidance to identify new careers and also provides training stipends to dislocated workers based on their financial needs and work history. Another consideration here is the unemployment benefits or severance pay that you may be eligible for and which must be made known during your application for financial aid. A more comprehensive review and assessment may be obtained at either the career development center at the college or the regional Workforce Development Board, which is administered by both county and municipal governments. Look up each of your local government services by visiting county offices and city hall.

Step 2: Get to Know Your College's Financial Office's Resources

The starting point for your financial-aid process and application is at the Office of Student Financial Aid that is a part of a typical community college's Division of Student Support Services. So that you may become familiar with the process you may consider the federal government website http://www.fafsa.ed.gov/#, which is the main reference for the various financial-aid opportunities that are sponsored by the U.S. Department of Education and which are administered by your local community college. This website has the necessary information on how to submit your FAFSA, which is then available to all colleges and universities that you may choose to apply to. The Office of Student Financial Aid also has various references for local, regional, and state organizations that also maintain ongoing scholarship and other forms of financial aid. A comprehensive guide to FAFSA is provided in the appendix with a step-by-step process to filling out the application and getting your family's financial situation in the appropriate format.

The following are some recommendations and action items that you may consider as you prepare a budget for the income and expenses that you will have during your college career. The key components of this budget are:

- Determine the sources of income that will be available to you. These may include funds from your parents, student loans, scholarships, work-study, or other types of employment, and if you are a veteran, sources of funds from the government.

- The next step will be to determine all of your expenses, and these will include tuition and fees, books and technology (computers, software, and peripherals such as flash drives and print cartridges), rent, utilities, transportation costs, food, and clothing. These totals may be different if you are married and have children since the cost factors change to include day care costs, medical insurance, and of course, you have to consider that the number to be considered will change based on the fact that you have a spouse to consider and also by the number of children in your family.

- The next step is to take these two financial components and develop a basic income to expense statement. To do this, add up your expenses and subtract those from your income to arrive at what is referred to as a fund balance; the amount of funds that you have left after all expenses are accounted for. The net fund balance must not be a negative number, otherwise you will be living beyond your means.

- Let's assume that you have a negative fund balance. To get back to a balanced budget you must either cut expenses or add more funds to your monthly income. Cutting expenses is difficult since you may come to believe that everything you plan to pay for is a necessity. Of course, the only means to increase your income is to get a part-time job, cut certain expenses such as entertainment, find a less expensive apartment, make greater use of public transportation; but whatever you do, do not get into debt since the interest will not be minimized by the lender.

A budget is only as good as your will to live by it. You must stay on track and not be frivolous or impulsive, otherwise you may begin to live beyond your means, and this may lead to undue stress that affects your academic focus.

Step 3: Maximize Your Military Benefits

Those of you who have served in the military are in a very distinct situation from the other community college applicants. Of course, there is no such individual as a typical college student in today's society and you will stand out. You have been involved in an organization that has nurtured you, taught you to be organized and disciplined, and most of all, attentive to the charge to complete tasks in collaboration with other soldiers whose training and experience is similar to yours. Another example of your development has been training that has prepared you to work to complete complex tasks and responsibilities. Unfortunately, you are entering a world of education that is not as orderly and sometimes seems full of contradictions. You can be sure that your military background has prepared you well to respond to any situation that you may encounter and your leadership skills will enable you to assume this challenge with energy and diligence.

The community college that you are applying is replete with many resources that are designed to serve you as a returning student veteran. It is advisable to always have all of your military records with you as you proceed with the application process, orientation, and registration as well as any advisement that is directed at you as a veteran. A word of caution here: always keep a second set of your military portfolio in a safe place in case any documents are misplaced or lost. The Office of Veterans Affairs at the University of Texas Brownsville and Texas Southmost Community College (www.utb.edu/em/fa/) provides an extensive overview of all the educational programs and benefits that are available at a typical community college. Also, the following is an overview of all of these programs and the documentation that you should have readily access to so that you may submit them as requested for a particular program or service:

- Copy of DD-214 (Member 4)
- Copy of Statement of Discharge (copy per each semester)
- Any approvals from the Veterans Affairs Clinic in case you are applying for medical benefits
- Copy of VA Form 22—1990 or Certificate of Eligibility or VA Form 22—1995 if you are applying for the Reserve Educational Assistance Program (REAP)

Now let's move to steps and the alphabet soup of terms of programs and benefits that have been established by the U.S. Congress to assist you with your post-military education. Upon your exit from your last military duty station, you had an exit interview and had to clear all standard personnel points. At that time you should have received a dossier or portfolio of your military record and your benefits and the types of services that are available to you as a veteran. As mentioned before, make a set and keep it safe at home or in a bank's safety deposit box. Upon your first visit to the college, go to the Office of Student Support Services and ask to see campus Office of Veteran Affairs. These documents will be necessary to apply for the following programs that you may be eligible to receive services and resources from, and a very informative website is maintained by the United States Department of Veterans Affairs at http://www.gibill.va.gov/. Again these programs are described in detail at Texas Southmost Community College website (www.utb.edu/em/fa/) and include the following.

The Post-9/11 GI Bill

The Post-9/11 GI Bill (http://www.us-gibillschools.com; www.armedforcesedu.com) provides financial support for education and housing to individuals with at least 90 days of aggregate service on or after September 11, 2001, or individuals discharged with a service-connected disability after 30 days. You must have received an honorable discharge to be eligible for the Post-9/11 GI Bill.

Montgomery GI Bill

The Montgomery GI Bill (MGIB: http://www.gibill.va.gov/) is available for those who enlist in the U.S. Armed Forces. MGIB encompasses both the Montgomery GI Bill—Active Duty (Chapter 30) and the Montgomery GI Bill—Selected Reserve (Chapter 1606). Under Chapter 30, Active Duty members enroll and pay $100 per month for 12 months and are then entitled to receive a monthly education benefit once they have completed a minimum service obligation. Under Chapter 1606, a reservist must be actively drilling and have a 6-year obligation in the Selected Reserve to be eligible.

Reserve Educational Assistance (REAP)

REAP was established as a part of the Ronald W. Reagan National Defense Authorization Act for fiscal year 2005. It is a Department of Defense education benefit program designed to provide educational assistance to members of the reserve components called or ordered to active duty in response to a war or national emergency (contingency operation) as declared by the president or Congress. This program makes certain reservists who were activated for at least 90 days after September 11, 2001, either eligible for education benefits or eligible for increased benefits.

Survivors' and Dependents' Assistance

Dependents' Educational Assistance program provides education and training opportunities to eligible dependents of certain veterans. The program offers up to 45 months of education benefits. These benefits may be used for degree and certificate programs, apprenticeship, and on-the-job training. If you are a spouse, you may take a correspondence course. Remedial, deficiency, and refresher courses may be approved under certain circumstances.

Eligibility

You must be the son, daughter, or spouse of:

- A veteran who died or is permanently and totally disabled as the result of a service-connected disability. The disability must arise out of active service in the Armed Forces.
- A veteran who died from any cause while such service-connected disability was in existence.
- A service member missing in action or captured in line of duty by a hostile force.
- A service member forcibly detained or interned in line of duty by a foreign government or power.
- A service member who is hospitalized or receiving outpatient treatment for a service-connected permanent and total disability and is likely to be discharged for that disability.

This change took place effective December 23, 2006.

Educational Assistance Test Program

Section 901 is an Educational Assistance Test Program created by the Department of Defense Authorization Act of 1981 (Public Law 96–342) to encourage enlistment and reenlistment in the Armed Forces. Benefits are available to individuals who entered on active duty after September 30, 1980, and before October 1, 1981 (or before October 1, 1982, if entry was under a delayed enlistment contract signed between September 30, 1980, and October 1, 1981).

It is to be noted that although Public Law 96–342 established a beginning date for the test program as October 1, 1980, the military service departments did not start offering the test program to new enlistees until December 1, 1980.

All three of the following criteria must have been met to establish eligibility for Air Force Eligibility Requirements for Section 901:

Must have enlisted between December 1, 1980, and September 30, 1981.

Enlistment must have been in one of the following Air Force Specialties: 20723, 20731, 20830, 46130, 46230A, B, C, D, E, F, G, H, J, or Z, 46430, 81130.

Enlistment must have taken place at one of the following locations: Beckley, WV; Buffalo, NY; Dallas, TX; Fargo, ND; Houston, TX; Jackson, MS; Louisville, KY; Memphis, TN; Omaha, NE; Philadelphia, PA; Seattle, WA; Sioux Falls, SD; Syracuse, NY.

National Call to Service Program

This National Call to Service (NCS) Incentive program requires a participant to perform a period of national service to be eligible for benefits. It is a Department of Defense program that is administered by Veterans Affairs.

Eligibility Requirements for Incentives

There is a three-tiered service requirement to qualify for incentives under the NCS program:

- First, after completion of initial entry training, individuals must serve on active duty in a military occupational specialty designated by the Secretary of Defense for a period of 15 months.
- After this, and without a break in service, these individuals must serve either an additional period of active duty as determined by the Secretary of Defense or a period of 24 months in an active status in the Selected Reserve.

- After completion of this period of service, and also, without a break in service, the remaining period of obligated service specified in the agreement will be served as follows:
  - On active duty in the armed forces
  - In the Selected Reserve
  - In the Individual Ready Reserve
  - AmeriCorps

Any combination of the services referred to in the preceding text may also be approved by the secretary of the military department concerned pursuant to regulations prescribed by the Secretary of Defense and specified in the agreement.

Choice of Incentives

- Individuals who participate in this new program have a choice of incentives as follows:
  - Cash bonus of $5,000
  - Repayment of a qualifying student loan not to exceed $18,000
- Entitlement to allowance equal to the three-year monthly chapter 30 rate for 12 months ($1,034 effective October 1, 2005)
- Entitlement to allowance equal to 50 percent of the less than three-year monthly chapter 30 rate for 36 months (50 percent of $840 effective October 1, 2005)
- Coordination with Montgomery GI Bill benefits

The basic rule is that NCS participants are not entitled to additional assistance under chapter 1606 or chapter 30 benefits. However, if the NCS participant has eligibility under either of these chapters, he or she may be paid the amount of chapter 1606 or chapter 30 benefits minus any amounts paid under the NCS program. The education benefit options will be administered to the extent possible like chapter 1606 of title 10. The effective date of the NCS program was October 1, 2003 (http://www.gibill.va.gov).

Expand Your Base of Sponsors and Advocates

By now you should have completed all those action steps that apply to your situation, and they should have begun to fill in the gaps that impeded your progress to your vision. There is something to consider here, and that is that the development of relationships with other students, faculty, and staff will bode well for you as you share mutual experience and resources. You also need to expand your circles of mentors, sponsors, and advocates so they may supplement those of your immediate family. Be sure to always be your own best friend and advocate by demonstrating the values and work ethic that your family has instilled in you.

Your circle of relationships will be very important as you want to be remembered by your instructors and others who had occasions to interact with you at your college and at other community or work sites. These individuals will serve as references for employment and as advocates for your continued educational endeavors if your goal is to transfer to a college and a university to pursue a bachelor's or a graduate degree. This inventory of relationship can be established by:

- Participating in campus events such as a volunteer in special events or as a member of a club.
- Applying for an internship in a department or with a community-based agency so that you gain experience to supplement your educational curriculum.
- Becoming a work-study student in a department or with a project such as Talent Search, Upward Bound, or with the GEAR-UP Program.
- Volunteering with a research or training program so that you can be seen as a potential protégé and establishing a mentorship relationship with an experienced individual who will provide guidance, support, and advice that is related to your career and academic aspirations.

Develop a Transition Plan

This plan should be the result of all of the prior activities and action steps that you have taken up to now: it is your blueprint to how to move on to the next step of your college or university education or getting back to the workforce. The transition plan consists of several components that reflect both your instructional or training activities at the community college and what needs to be done to transfer to a four-year college or a university or enter the world of work. These components are as follows.

Step 1: Taking the Right Courses

It is important that you always get advised from either your academic or training counselor or the advisors at the college's academic advisement center. At the same time, make an appointment or begin to communicate with the admissions department or the academic advisors at the college(s) that you are considering transferring to. Ask the following questions during your interactions or even better, a site visit:

- May I have a copy of the degree plan for my major?
- How often are degree plans changed or modified?
- What is the website for your department and how often is it updated?
- May I obtain a copy of the articulation plan between your academic department and my community college?
- What are the best times to communicate with your advisors?
- What are some deadlines that I need to always check on as I prepare my transfer application? Missing a deadline may mean having to wait a semester to reapply, and this will cost you both time and money as well as delaying your graduation.
- Do I have to submit a separate application to my academic department even if I am admitted to the college? In many instance it is not assured that you will be automatically admitted to your preferred field of study because you were admitted as a student to the general college or university. Each academic department might have its own entrance or program requirements.

You will do well to keep a log or a portfolio of all your interactions with your community college's counselors and advisors and those at the four-year institution. It is advisable to follow up on a timely basis: every month, at the end of a semester, and when you are preparing to register for your next semester's courses. Do not leave anything to chance since you are the one who needs to be in control of this most important decision.

You are primarily responsible for making sure that your courses are transferable to the four-year institution that you plan to apply to, but most important *is whether it is articulated.* Don Silver (2009, 72) offers this reminder, "courses that you take at a community college that are articulated do more than just transfer to a four-year college." An articulated course is one that you take at a community college and can be transferred and accepted as fulfilling the first two years (lower division) requirements at the college of your choice. The academic advisors at your community college should have a reference of which courses are articulated to which four-year colleges and universities. Silver (2009) also provides some very good advice when he advises that you "don't rely just on online or print catalogs since information [about articulation and transfer requirements] can change at any time."

It is very important that you always double-check whether the courses that you are registering for in any particular semester will be articulated when they are transferred to the four-year institution. *Remember that it is costing you and your family both time and money to attend the community college, and any course work that is not transferrable or articulated means loss of money and time that cannot be recovered.*

Step 2: Visit the Four-Year College or University

This is an important step for several reasons:

First, you get to become familiar with the lay of the land, where everything will impact your ability to get around and be on time to your classes:

- Get a map of the campus and get to know every building and what type of instruction or training takes place there.
- Find the location of the office of the registrar, the admissions office, the advisement centers, and the office of financial aid.
- Get informed about the Office of the Dean of Students since this is the location of all campus orientation activities and also all campus student activities that you will want to join and participate in as part of your college experience.
- Visit the housing office and get information about both on- and off-campus housing options and all costs associated with those residential arrangements.
- Walk the campus and the immediate neighborhoods and determine if you will need to have a car or if there is sufficient public transportation. It is sometimes very difficult and expensive to get on-campus parking, so you may consider not having a car for the first semester unless it is necessary for work or to go home if you are residing at home and attending a college or university within driving distance.
- Take a virtual tour of the campus of your choice if it is too far away for you to visit or located in another state. Appendix A has several websites for you to log in to and take virtual tours of campuses throughout the nation and within your community.

Step 3: Getting Back to the World of Work

When you decided to pursue another career or were involved in an employment situation that resulted in layoffs or reductions-in-force due to the economic downturn, you chose to pursue another training or a different course of study to expand your employability. Your goal was to get back to work so that you can continue to support your family and attend to their quality of life. Just as it was important to have a transition plan for transferring to a four-year college or a university, you must also have such a plan.

The following are some action items that you may consider, as you get involved in your vocational training or advanced career training at your community college:

- Prepare for the workforce on your first date at the campus by enrolling in any career development seminars that are offered by the campus placement office, your specific training program, or the vocational or technical training departments of the different programs in your college. These are usually posted on the website for the individual training division.

- Enroll in available communication seminars or classes that will expand your capacity to work with a group and learn how to negotiate, mediate, or resolve workplace conflict.

- Participate in Toastmasters, which is both a students' club and one that holds weekly meetings at sites within your community. This club engages its members in communication exercises so that they expand their skills in making presentations to large or small audiences. Your ability to communicate will add value to your résumé and to access any additional on-site training that is offered at the workplace.

- Attend a résumé preparation workshop so that you may always have a professionally crafted résumé ready when jobs are posted for your application.

- Attend workshop on how to draft application letters that will get you noticed. These workshops are usually offered as continuing education seminars.

- Find out if there are internships in your career field and participate in those so that you may acquire more awareness of the workplace.

- Develop a three-ring portfolio of all of your courses, the résumé, and letters of recommendation from former employers and faculty.

- Locate the most accessible GI Forum that will provide you referral to scholarship and other volunteer and service organizations such as Hispanic Education Foundation, Veterans Outreach Program, and SER: National Jobs for Progress.

- SER: Jobs for Progress has a mission to serve Hispanics with both training and placement in technical fields and has chapters in nearly every state and large community in the United States.

- Always check the wanted ads and visit the local or regional workforce commission office within proximity of your college or residence on a weekly basis since jobs may be posted and filled quickly. Be first in line for consideration.

- Become skilled with the Internet and its various job search sites and visit those sites on a timely basis for job posting and updates.

Summary

It is important that you conduct an ongoing checkup of your progress toward your stated goals and always start by asking yourself, "how am I doing?" This is a question that you should also ask of your family, friends, and faculty so that you can respond with a corrective action plan to steer yourself back on course if you start to deviate from the main roadway to your future. You must always be your own best advocate and do not hesitate to ask for advice and insights of other individuals within your college and community who have a vested interest in your success.

References

Mackay, Harvey. *Swim with the Sharks without Being Eaten Alive*. New York: Ballantine Books, 1988.

Silver, Don. *Community College Transfer Guide*. Los Angeles, CA: Adams-Hall Publishing, 2009.

Reference Websites

American GI Forum: http://www.agifusa.org/

Dallas County Community College District: www.dcccd.edu

Empire State College of the State University of New York: http://suny-empire.esc.edu

Federal Government Financial Aid: http://www.fafsa.ed.gov/#

League of United Latin American Citizens: http://lulac.org/

Maricopa County Community College District: http://www.maricopa.edu/

Montgomery GI Bill: MGIB: http://www.gibill.va.gov/

National Call to Service program: www.gibill.va.gov

Office of Veterans Affairs at the University of Texas Brownsville and Texas Southmost Community College: www.utb.edu/em/fa

Post-9/11 GI Bill: www.us-gibillschools.com

SER: Jobs for Progress: http://www.ser-national.org/

Strong Profile, College Edition (R): https://www.cpp.com/

U.S. Department of Veterans Affairs: http://www.gibill.va.gov/

Appendix A

Internet Resources

Empire State College of New York: http://subjectguides.esc.edu/content. php?pid=24669&sid=178225

Dallas County Community College District: http://dcccd.edu

Maricopa County Community College District: http://www.maricopa.edu/

The Campus Visit:	http://www.campusvisit.com
The Student Universe:	http://www. studentuniverse.com
Youruniversity TV:	http://www.youuniversitytv.com
Campustours, Inc.:	http://www.ecampustours.com/sitemap

Office of Veterans Affairs. The University of Texas and Texas Southmost Community College, Brownsville, Texas: www.utb.edu/em/fa/

Appendix B

Financial Aid Resources

Financial Aid Information (http://www.dcccd.edu)

What Is a FAFSA?

The Free Application for Federal Student Aid, or FAFSA, asks questions about a family's income and assets to determine an EFC. Each college compares a family's EFC with the total costs of attendance to determine the amount of their financial aid package.

Total Cost of Attendance – EFC = Financial aid amount

When you complete the FAFSA the college reviews your file for additional financial aid. In addition to federal and state grants, you may be eligible for other grants, campus employment, or low-interest student loans. (Remember, scholarships and grants are money that doesn't have to be paid back!)

Four Steps for Filing your FAFSA

Step 1: Get a PIN

What is a PIN? The PIN is a four-digit number issued to you by the U.S. Department of Education that allows you to complete and sign the FAFSA electronically, to check the results of your FAFSA, and to make corrections to your application online.

Getting a PIN

Get your free PIN online from the U.S. Department of Education. If you provide an e-mail address when you register, your PIN information will be sent to you by e-mail within three days of your request.

PIN for Parents

Parents must request their own separate PIN to use as an electronic signature on the FAFSA.

Step 2: Complete the FAFSA on the Web Worksheet

The U.S. Department of Education provides a worksheet that you can use to gather the financial information you'll need to complete the FAFSA before you go online. Download the worksheet now.

Step 3: File your FAFSA

Once you've received your PIN and completed the "FAFSA on the Web" worksheet, log on to www.fafsa.ed.gov to file your FAFSA. Complete each step and write down your confirmation number when you finish entering the form. (You will need the confirmation number in case any problems arise with the processing of your application.)

Step 4: Monitor the Status of your FAFSA

After you've filed your form, you can check the status of your FAFSA online, or you can call the Federal Student Aid Information Center at 1-800-433-3243 and use the automated response system. Schools should receive the results of your application two to three days after it's been processed. If you do not receive a response from the U.S. Department of Education within two weeks after submitting your FAFSA, you should contact the Federal Student Aid Information Center for assistance.

Remember—the FAFSA can cover tuition and living expenses.

Appendix C

Comparison Shopping for Colleges and Universities
http://www.dcccd.edu

Find the Right University

There are many factors to consider when choosing a four-year college. Ask yourself the following questions:

- Do you want to attend a private or a public college?
- Do you prefer a large or small campus?

- Do you want to travel or stay close to home?
- What are your goals and interests? Do you know what you want to major in?
- Does the college you're considering offer a good program in your major?
- Does it offer you career counseling if you don't yet know what field to study?
- What is the reputation of the college you're considering?
- How will that affect your career goals?
- How does the university you want to attend handle transfer students and does it offer financial aid?
- Will you have to retake courses when you transfer?
- Do you want to live on campus?
- Do you want to join a sorority or fraternity, participate in athletics, or learn to be a leader?

Appendix D

Transition Reference Table
http://www.dcccd.edu Revised 4/22/11

The Dallas County Community College District provides an excellent chart to use in evaluating your transition choice. To help narrow down your choices, you might want to use, look at the following, or print a comparison chart to fill out!

Transitions from Community College to University

Admissions

	Community College	University
What are the requirements for admission?	Open door (with requirements for entrance into certain programs)	Requirements based on community college GPA and the number of transfer hours earned for university admission. Many majors within different universities have their own GPA and transfer-hour admission requirements to be admitted to their programs

(Continued)

Admissions (Continued)

	Community College	University
When is the application due?	Before you start taking classes	All universities have deadline dates for submitting an application. Usually, the deadline is at least one semester before you start (check with the university where you want to transfer for specific dates)
Do I need to pay to apply?	There are some community colleges that have an application fee that must be paid when applying	The application fee varies by institution, so contact the university to find out the exact fee. Check on special opportunities for transfer students to have the application fee waived at the university where you want to transfer
Do I need multiple applications?	Just one application for admissions	Some majors require an additional application. Check with the university where you want to transfer for specific dates
Where do I apply?	The state of Texas, for example, has one centralized application site and there may be others for other states as well www.applytexas.org	www.applytexas.org
Who will assist me with application process?	Admission representatives can assist you in completing the application process	Most universities have admission representatives who specialize in working with transfer students. Contact their admission offices and ask for a transfer counselor or a transfer center or unit

Financial Aid

	Community College	*University*
Is financial aid available?	Yes	Yes
When is the financial aid application due?	Typically before you start taking classes	Usually at least one semester before you start (check with the university where you want to transfer for the specific date)
Who do I talk to with financial aid questions?	A representative of the financial aid office	A representative of the financial aid office
Are grants & scholarships available?	Yes	Yes
When is my tuition due?	Before classes start and be sure not to miss the deadline or you may have to register again	Check with the university about payment dates when registering for your classes. Before classes start, check with the university so that you do not miss the deadline
Do you offer scholarships for transfer students? When should I apply for scholarships?		Yes, some universities offer scholarships to transfer students based on overall GPA, PTK membership, and other factors. You should contact the financial or scholarship office for the deadlines, any specialized application procedures, and possible award amounts

Advising and Orientation

	Community College	University
Do I have a specific advisor I need to talk to?	Advising center in student services	Contact transfer specialist is available, a general advisor, or an advisor in the department of your desired major
Must I attend a new student orientation?	New student orientations are available. Check the community college for requirements	Not all universities have orientations for transfer students to attend; please check with your university
What are the expectations for textbooks?	Check with your professor or the college bookstore about textbook requirements	Check with your professor or the university bookstore about textbook expectations
How can I learn more about the university before transferring?	Some colleges offer you an opportunity to meet with an admissions representative at your college during each semester. This person can assist you with transition into the university	Some universities offer prospective student special events or meetings during each semester. Contact the university's admissions office for more information
How do I register for classes?	Some colleges require you attend an orientation, meet with an advisor, or both before you can register for classes. The adviser will assist you in selecting courses and information on registering for classes	Some universities require you to either attend an orientation, meet with an academic adviser, or both before you can register for classes. The academic adviser will assist you with selecting classes, provide information on registering for classes, and determine whether you are meeting degree requirements

Curriculum

	Community College	University
Where can I take my core curriculum classes?	Yes	Yes
Will my core curriculum classes count for my degree?	Yes—if you complete your core at the community college you will meet the core requirements at the university when you transfer	Yes—in most cases, ask a university representative about printed or electronic resources that explain the applicability of your course work to a specific degree program
How do associates of applied science (AAS) degree or career or technical courses transfer?		Some universities offer bachelor of applied arts and science degree that will combine your applied credit with specialized course to create a customized bachelor's degree
What classes can I take that are guaranteed to transfer?	Meet with an academic adviser at the community college your first semester to get started on the core curriculum. Also get information from transfer101.org on whom to contact at universities regarding the transfer process and courses that will meet university degree requirements	Save yourself time and money by contacting the admission office or the academic department at the university you would like to attend at least one semester before you want to transfer. They can recommend a list of both core and major courses you can take at your particular community college that will satisfy the university degree requirements

Preparing for a Graduate and/or Professional Degree While Still an Undergraduate Student

Roberto Haro

Access to graduate education is not new for Latino students. An increasing number of Latino students, especially Latinas, are enrolling and successfully completing graduate degrees. The number of Latinos attending graduate programs to earn a teaching certificate and become teachers continues to increase. A beneficial side to this is that many Latino students are earning master's degrees in conjunction with the teaching certificates. But what about access to selective graduate programs? Yes, it is difficult to enter graduate programs at highly selective universities such as Stanford, Princeton, and Duke, but even here, Latinos are beginning to enroll and complete law degrees, MBAs and PhDs. In this chapter, I will mention some of the strategies Latino students have used to gain admission to selective graduate programs at American universities.

For Latino students attending a two- or a four-year college, access to graduate and professional studies pose some serious challenges; *but none that are insurmountable.* The rewards for doing graduate study are well known and documented. According to The College Board, a national educational association, the median income for a college graduate is $55,700. The median income for those without a college degree is $33,000 (Camara, 2009). A college graduate is less likely to be unemployed than a high school graduate. The median annual salary for Hispanics with a graduate degree is almost 40 percent higher than someone with a BA or a BS. It really pays for a Latina or a Latino to do graduate study and earn a degree such as a master's or a doctorate. These figures keep fluctuating, but the advantage a Hispanic student with a graduate degree enjoys over high school and college graduates is substantial. Moreover, a graduate degree prepares one for leadership roles in society, whether in the private sector, in government service, or in community service careers. The most successful Latino leaders usually have graduate degrees. Therefore, all of the authors of this book and I strongly encourage Latinos to go to graduate schools.

Early Preparation for Graduate Admission

Now let us focus our attention on ways for you to better prepare for and gain access to graduate education. Before discussing how to plan and prepare for a graduate program, some important terms must be mentioned and described.

The term *graduate study* is often used to connote postbaccalaureate enrollment in a program leading to master's or doctoral degrees. Examples include a master's in a field such as political science or sociology, and a PhD in fields such as anthropology, English, history, and zoology, to name but a few. *Professional* programs are those that lead to relevant degrees in fields such as business, law, medicine, nursing, public policy, and public health. Examples of these degrees include masters in business administration (MBA), masters of fine arts (MFA), a law degree (now usually a JD), and a doctorate in medicine (MD).

With the aforementioned as background, some key issues must be foremost in the minds of parents and students attending a two- or a four-year college with an eye toward doing postbaccalaureate study. And, there are some important considerations that affect students currently enrolled at a two-year college. Step 7 or the previous chapter was devoted to Latino students enrolled at community colleges. However, getting high grades, selecting a major, taking and passing critical lower division courses, faculty recommendations, and extracurricular activities apply to all Latino students, regardless of the type of institution they attend. While some of the terms used earlier may sound confusing, I will explain them as they arise.

Postbaccalaureate study means any training or course work taken after a student has earned a bachelor of arts (BA) or bachelor of science (BS). For students planning to become teachers, their graduate course work often leads to a teaching certificate, rather than a graduate degree such as an MA. However, more and more students preparing to become teachers earn master's in a subject field such as math, biology, music, or in an educational specialization, such as English as a second language. This gives them an advantage in finding a job and may result in a higher entering salary.

The four-year college curriculum is divided into two parts. Lower division means courses taken during the first two years of college, often referred to as the freshman and sophomore years. Upper division means the last two years of the curriculum; the junior and senior years. Lower division courses are usually general in nature, where a student is exposed to basic knowledge in a field such as chemistry, mathematics (algebra, calculus, and statistics), physics, English, and history. Many lower division classes are often called survey courses because they provide a general overview of a field or a subject.

There are important distinctions between two- and four-year colleges. It is not my purpose in this chapter to engage in a major discussion regarding those distinctions. Instead, I will focus my comments only to matters that students enrolled at a two-year college should think about and do to get into graduate school, including a few advantages germane to community college attendance, before mentioning things that apply to all students, regardless of the type of campus they attend. I do so because once in college you will soon learn that things you do or don't do a year or two in advance does matter when making applications.

While Enrolled in a Two-Year College

For students enrolled at a two-year college, it is never too early to begin planning for graduate study, even if you think you will be finished with your undergraduate studies in five or six years! (The terms two-year colleges and community colleges will be used interchangeably to avoid repetition.) There are advantages to attending a two-year college. Consider the following. Many Latino students cannot afford to attend a four-year college or a university directly out of high school and opt to stay at home and attend a local community college. Most two-year colleges offer *smaller class sizes* than those at large public universities and allow students to attend part-time. The smaller class size permits regular and direct contact with the instructor. At some of the larger state universities, such as the University of Texas at Austin, the University of New Mexico, and the University of Arizona, lower division students seldom meet with the professor in charge of a class, especially in courses such as organic chemistry and physics. Smaller class sizes, usually with 25 or fewer students, mean the student receives more individual attention from the instructor than at a public university where important lower division courses may enroll well over 100 students.

For students considering careers in the health services, lower division math and science courses are significant. These courses are required for health services majors. For example, organic chemistry, with a laboratory, must be in a student's portfolio if he or she plans to attend medical school. The same is true for calculus. These lower division courses at major research universities such as the University of Michigan, the University of California at Los Angeles, and Texas A&M, for example, are very competitive and have large enrollments. Because they determine whether or not a student will be able to qualify for a science, mathematics, or engineering major, a Latino student must do well in chemistry and calculus. Unfortunately, some Hispanic college students have limited high school backgrounds in science and mathematics. At two-year colleges, Latinos report that their experience with mathematics and key science courses was positive because of smaller class sizes and *regular interactions with the instructor*. It is not unusual, therefore, for Hispanics to earn strong grades in courses such as calculus and chemistry at a two-year college.

Another advantage students have at most two-year colleges is *access to remedial courses*. A remedial course is one that allows a student to compensate for a deficiency in high school. An example is where a Latina student at a two-year college attended a high school where introduction to calculus or algebra was not offered. The college remedial course allows this student to take a class designed to prepare him or her for college calculus and advanced algebra. The same is true in the sciences, where many high schools, because of financial restrictions and limited teaching resources in the sciences, are unable to offer science courses with laboratories. The two-year college is able to help the student develop the skills to do well in these critical fields.

Enrollment at a two-year college has benefits that involve the transfer process. Many *community colleges have agreements with four-year colleges and universities that provide guarantee transfer and admission to a four-year campus*, if the student successfully completes a required set of courses. In essence, it is a contract that says if a Latina or a Latino student successfully completes the required lower division courses at a two-year campus, they are guaranteed enrollment at the four-year institution. And in some cases, the transfer agreement with the community college often waives the admission fee at the four-year campus. An example of such an agreement is the program between Santa Monica College and UCLA (Paredes, 1979). A similar arrangement is in place between Santa Barbara City College and the University of California at Santa Barbara. There are also opportunities for interinstitutional transfers. Consider students who attend the University of Houston Downtown campus. They are part of the University of Houston system and may transfer from the Downtown to the main campus. When they earn the BA or the BS degrees at the main campus, graduate programs at Houston or other major campuses will give added attention to Latino students with a major from the main campus.

While on the topic of transfers from a two- to a four-year campus, another important consideration needs to be mentioned. Not all four-year colleges or universities are the same when it comes to competing for access to the better graduate programs and schools. A four-year degree earned at a small state college or a regional university does not carry the same weight as that of a flagship campus like Arizona State or New Mexico State universities. Before continuing, a few terms need to be explained.

A state college is often a public four-year campus that offers BA and BS degrees, and teaching certificates, as well as a limited number of master's degrees in a few academic majors. Most were once institutions primarily known as teachers' colleges due to their emphasis on teacher preparation. However, as demand for higher education increased, especially in states west of the Mississippi River, teachers' colleges matured and developed into state-supported campuses that provided a wide range of academic degree programs and disciplines. Regional universities are also state-supported institutions, but offer everything a state college does, and more. These universities frequently offer graduate and professional degrees at the master's level. A few even have graduate programs leading to specialized doctorates, for example, doctor in education (EdD). Some state colleges and regional universities are open enrollment institutions. This means that the four-year campus admits all students who have a high school diploma and may not require students to take standardized tests like the SAT or the ACT used for admission screening. However, because of competition for access to many of the regional universities, admission requirements have been put in place, such as a minimum high school B GPA. These institutions are quite different from what are referred to as major research universities, and especially flagship campuses.

A major research university can be private or publicly supported. These are institutions that in addition to offering the bachelor's and master's degrees in various disciplines, also offer PhDs and degrees in law and medicine. Examples of major research universities are the University of California at San Diego, Rice University, and Oregon State University. A flagship campus is usually the premier publicly supported research university in a state, such as the University of Utah, the University of Colorado at Boulder, and the University of Oregon at Eugene. These institutions are very selective about the students they admit. Most require a minimum B+ or A− high school GPA and a high score on either the SAT or the ACT. Access to these institutions at the undergraduate and graduate levels is very competitive.

The best graduate and professional programs often give added attention or weight to student applications from major research and flagship campuses. This is an important consideration for Latino students enrolled at a two-year college. By transferring to a major research institution, rather than a state college or regional university, a Latino student will have a much better chance of gaining admission to a highly regarded graduate or professional program. Latino parents should understand the advantages of their children transferring from a two-year college to a major research university or a flagship campus and plan accordingly.

Planning for Graduate Study

Regardless of the type of undergraduate institution a Latino student is attending, there are critical things that should be done to improve access to graduate study, even at the most selective universities. My comments will be in three broad categories: (1) selecting the proper academic program; (2) ways to improve GPA; and (3) how to draw attention to your academic potential.

A. *Selecting the proper academic program* may seem easy, but there are critical issues that Latino students and their parents should consider. Listing a few will be helpful. What undergraduate majors are considered valuable if a student plans to attend law school? What majors are important for a student interested in becoming a nurse? If a student wants to earn an MBA, what undergraduate majors provide the strongest foundation for a career in business?

Prior to entering your junior year at college, you will have to declare a major that will provide you with the appropriate background to qualify for graduate education. What is a major? Basically, it is a concentration of courses that provide a student with in-depth knowledge about a particular subject field, such as economics.

Selecting a major should involve an interest in the subject matter and knowledge about the teaching department and its instructors. Some students select a major without exploring the rankings of the department and the faculty. Consider the following. Alicia, a young Latina, was told that sociology was a good undergraduate major to prepare her for graduate study in social work. She selected sociology as a major without learning about the sociology department and the faculty within it. Much to her dismay, only three or four of the sociology courses offered in the department at her university appealed to her. She learned that the department focused on existential phenomenology because of the training and interests of the three senior faculties in the department. She was more interested in social psychology, and only three classes were offered by the department. After a year, Alicia changed her major to psychology. However, instead of graduating in five years, she had to take lower division courses that were required for upper division psychology courses. Her graduation was delayed by a year.

"I wish someone would have told me about the sociology program here," she told me. When I asked Alicia to elaborate, she said, "I didn't care for the emphasis the department placed on a particular area of sociology. So, I transferred to the psych department. However, many of the courses I wanted to take in psych required lower division courses that I hadn't taken. I lost a year taking lower division courses required for upper division psych classes." It was a costly and distracting experience for Alicia and her parents, who had to pay for an extra year of schooling. I'm happy to say that Alicia applied for and was admitted to the master's program in social work at the University of Michigan.

There are several ways for a student to learn about a teaching department on their campus. First-hand information may be gained by meeting with some of the senior faculty in the department and taking a lower division course from one or two of them. Another way is to speak to an academic advisor in student affairs area. Each four-year college or university has advisors that help lower division students plan their schedule of courses for the year. These advisors provide information about departments on the campus, including areas of concentration, and faculty background and interests. A third source of information is word of mouth. It is important to talk with other students majoring in the discipline and learn from them about the department and the teaching faculty. Once the major is selected, a student works with a departmental advisor. Most departments assign students to a faculty advisor. However, a student may approach a faculty member in a particular department and ask if he or she will serve as his or her advisor. The advisor is a key link in preparing for graduate study. Once an advisor learns about a student's career plans they can help the student develop an academic program. The best departmental advisors share information with the student about particular courses that should be taken, the order or sequence, and instructors that a student should get to know.

A student's career plans must condition the selection of a major. Suppose a student wants to get an MBA. What is a suitable major? Many top graduate business schools encourage a student to major in economics. Why? In this major, he or she will be exposed to different economic systems, theories, and research methods that will examine and explain, and help to understand economic cycles and conditions on a global, national, and local level. Because of the complexity of economic systems and their impact on national and international businesses, many deans of admission at graduate schools of business encourage students to develop a strong background in economics. It is therefore highly desirable for a student interested in getting an MBA to have a strong background in economics, even if it is just a minor in this discipline.

What about law? So often, students think that majoring in business or criminal justice is the way to prepare for a career in law. This is not necessarily so. Most deans of admissions at law schools say that a student can major in almost any field and successfully enroll in a law school. However, the more informed deans of admission at law schools, especially the selective ones, stress certain skills a student needs to do well in law school. What are they? Critical reading skills, analytical thinking, and well-developed writing abilities. A student majoring in botany will develop certain skill sets unique to botany. However, they may be completely different from what will be needed in a law school. Consider, instead, majoring in philosophy or literature. Why? Philosophy requires extensive reading and textual analysis. Logic is also a fundamental component of philosophy. Are the skill sets and trainings received in philosophy easily transferable to the demands of legal education? The answer is yes.

There are, however, other majors that will provide a Latina or a Latino student the proper preparation to do well in law school. Literature and history are good examples. Both require extensive reading with an eye to contextual analysis and critical reasoning, and insist on strong writing skills. Therefore, the ability to read critically, think analytically, and write clearly, which are integral parts of history and literature, are very helpful for a student who plans to go to law school.

B. *Improving a GPA* is a very significant part of getting to graduate school. While most graduate schools will look carefully at a student's grades at the undergraduate level, the better graduate programs pay considerable attention to the grades a student earns during his or her last two years of study or upper division courses. There are several reasons for this. First, most academic advisors and counselors, and faculty know that good students improve their grades as they learn to negotiate the academic curriculum in college. Second, a student's study skills and learning habits strengthen as they mature and become familiar with the subject matter. And finally, it is assumed that a student selects an academic major because they like the subject matter or have done well in classes that are part of the major.

Several things can be done to attain higher grades. Some of the suggestions include: becoming part of a study group; taking advantage of programs to improve study habits and reading; and finding tutorial assistance. Another strategy that will be discussed later is meeting regularly with a class instructor. I will have more to say about this last point later.

What is a *study group*? Basically, it's a group of students—usually five or six—coming together in a class to cooperate on learning the assigned materials. What a study group does is allow the students to do all of the readings and assignments, but assign specific areas of the materials to individuals in the study group. When the students meet, they have a general knowledge of the assignment, but also benefit from the in-depth analysis that each one of them has done with a specific theme or part of the assignment. By collaborating in this way, students talk through the assignment, ask questions, and fully explore the subject matter. It is a way to foster communication and learn a subject while gaining the perspectives of others. Students who participate in a study group usually earn much higher marks in classes than those who do not. This is also an ideal way to network and to profit from the skills and talents of others. For many Latinos who feel alienated in college and find it hard to earn top scores in a class, joining a study group saves time, improves learning, and leads to higher grades. I cannot underscore too strongly the advantages that a Latino student gains from being part of a study group.

Most colleges and universities, especially the larger ones, have what are called *student learning centers*. These are places where trained campus staff with strong academic credentials work with students to improve their study skills and learning abilities. They also help students improve their GPA, and even offer seminars on standardized test-taking techniques. A good example of this type of service is the student learning center at the University of California, Berkeley. The director of the program has a PhD and is on good terms with the faculty in different disciplines. The center has a staff of advisors, trainers, tutors, and even mentors available to assist students. Students come to the learning center for various reasons. Some, having difficulty with a particular subject, are referred to the learning center by an instructor or a teaching assistant. Others learn about the variety of services offered and make it a point to visit the center.

There are several ways Latino students may find out if their campus has a learning center, and what services it offers. Using a computer to go online and find out about tutorial services or programs to improve study and learning skills is a valuable and easy way to gather information. Checking the campus directory for information on such programs and activities is also a reliable way. And for many students, word of mouth invariably identifies ways to boost grades and learn how to take standardized tests.

For a Latino student interested in applying to graduate school, finding and using the services offered by a learning center will have immediate benefits. Most learning centers work closely with faculty in different disciplines and are skilled in helping students to understand what the instructor expects in the way of student performance. If an instructor's class relies heavily on quantitative measures, such as calculus or statistics, learning center tutors and resource people will know this and determine whether the student has the required background in mathematics or statistics to do well. If a student is tentative or not well prepared to handle the math in the class, learning center personnel will recommend different ways to study or improve a student's quantitative reasoning skills.

Before continuing, I would like to reinforce what was stressed in Step 6, the need for every Latino college student to own, or at least have easy access to a computer, preferably a laptop. The increasing complexity of assignments and course requirements mandates the use of a computer, whether to do research, calculations, or writing. Without a computer, a student must negotiate complex assignments with outmoded and time-consuming methods. If a student does not have the money to purchase a computer, some four-year colleges and universities make them available for a modest fee or for free in either the learning center or the campus library. Most learning centers provide free instructions for students to make optimal use of a computer, especially to do class projects. Moreover, they help students maximize their time on a computer, and help them prepare and print out documents and reports to complete class assignments. On some four-year campuses, especially the more selective ones, professors assume that the students have a computer and access to a reliable printer. Many professors refuse to accept handwritten reports. So, owning or having easy access to a computer and a printer should be a requirement for every Latino student interested in going to graduate school.

Another service provided by most learning centers involves writing. The first impression you make on an instructor or in an application for graduate study is through your submitted written work. I have heard many deans of admission at graduate programs and professional schools comment on how often they receive applications with marginal writing. First impressions are critical, especially in competing for openings at selective graduate programs. Most graduate programs require an example of a student's writing abilities. If a student's essay is not properly focused, cogently written, and well structured, the application will not receive careful review and there will be a high probability of rejection. To avoid this, a Latino student can do two things: take advantage of tutorial or group sessions at a learning center to improve writing abilities; and work closely with an instructor or teaching assistant to become an effective writer. Many faculty, especially at state colleges and regional universities, work with students to pinpoint limitations in written expression. Latino students should take advantage of any assistance that will help them become better writers. And remember, a good written statement requires rewrites, more than one or two. Saving drafts on a computer as a Word document allows you to do rewrites with little effort and print the final draft once. Also at the graduate level, faculty require you to submit written papers of 10 to 20 pages, instead of doing test for class grades.

Test-taking skills should not be overlooked by Latino students. I have already mentioned that some learning centers provide seminars and short-term (a few weeks) classes on how to take different kinds of tests, especially multiple-choice standardized tests. Increasingly, because of larger class sizes at the undergraduate level, many instructors rely exclusively on multiple-choice examinations. Latino college students who have not been exposed to test-taking techniques are at a competitive disadvantage. Learning how to take multiple-choice examinations not only improves a student's GPA, but also helps them with graduate placement examinations such as the Law School Admissions Test (LSAT) and the GRE. There is a double benefit, therefore, in learning how to take multiple-choice examinations and perform well on them.

There are, of course, campuses that do not offer the full range of learning improvement services that many of the larger universities like Texas at Austin, or the University of Utah offer. Where free assistance on a campus is not available, there are companies, such as Kaplan, that for a fee will deliver services to help students improve their scores in basic courses and boost results on standardized tests. Like others that provide services for a fee, Kaplan claims they can raise a student's grade in a class by as much as one level, that is, from a grade of B to either B+ or A−. They tailor study guides for basic courses such as chemistry at a particular campus designed to help students better understand the class, and improve their performance on examinations. Other services that these companies provide include courses to help students increase their scores on standardized tests, such as the GRE and the Graduate Management Aptitude Test. While test makers like the Educational Testing Service deny that such courses, especially the ones offered by Kaplan, make a difference in a student's score, some of the reliable research indicates that taking a Kaplan course to help improve test-taking abilities actually boosts a student's score by between 10 and 15 points. This may be the difference between whether a Latino student is admitted or rejected by a graduate program. The limitation with companies like Kaplan is that they charge a fee, and many Latino students and their parents do not have the extra cash to purchase these services. However, the more adept a Latino student is at test taking, and achieving higher marks in classes, the better will be his or her chances to be admitted to the graduate program of his or her choice.

C. *Latino student profile development for graduate admission.* For want of a better term, it is important for Latino students to "market" themselves in the application process for graduate study. Many Latino students, because of family customs and cultural factors, stress modesty and normative ascription. The later technical term in psychology is a process where people in a culture encourage, if not insist on, their children achieve only at the average attainment of their peer group. A Latino student and his or her parents must understand the need to highlight and celebrate academic accomplishments and personal qualities that are examined carefully by admissions officers at graduate and professional schools. The competition for access to the most selective graduate programs is nothing short of ferocious. Well-to-do parents often pay for a private admissions counselor to help a son or daughter gain admission to a top graduate program or a professional school. While competing against a wealthy and influential family may seem futile for Latinos, especially from modest economic backgrounds or from single-parent families, there are ways to overcome these challenges. Sonia Sotomayor, appointed to the US Supreme Court, by President Obama in 2010, was able to overcome her status of low income family and still get into Yale Law School.

A good friend in a senior educational leadership position in Texas told an audience of Latino parents that no matter the level of competition, there are ways for Latino students to be accepted at the most selective graduate and professional programs. He had some important advice for parents, but underscored one overarching consideration: "Parents must be willing to encourage and support their children to excel, and the student must have the *ganas* (determination) to meet the challenges." Determination and perseverance are critical factors in competing for admission to selective graduate programs. However, there are important tangible ways for a Latino student to present his or her best side to admissions officers at graduate programs and/or professional schools. Five important topics are discussed here. They include: identifying appropriate graduate programs; social networks and support groups; faculty as mentors, sponsors, and references; internships and volunteer activities; and crafting a viable profile.

1. *Finding the right graduate program.* Too often, Latino students do not carefully research the type of graduate programs that mesh with their career interests. Most four-year campuses have a center that helps students with career planning and placement activities. I will not address what these centers do regarding placement. Instead, it is better to look at career planning. A good center helps the student research different career fields and then take aptitude examinations. Aptitude tests are designed to determine whether a student has the right skills, interests, and knowledge appropriate for a particular career or a profession. Students interested in health services often opt to apply for medical school without considering other possibilities, such as becoming a pharmacist, an eye doctor, or a dentist. A good aptitude test provides guidance about a Latino student's suitability for a specific profession. Consider the case of a talented Latina student.

    Marisol, a student in one of my classes, had been encouraged by her parents and close friends to become a doctor. She approached me one afternoon and shared her ambivalence about going to medical school. Marisol was an excellent student with very high marks in math and science. When I asked Marisol to tell me about her career plans, she told me how her parents expected her to go to a medical school. But she also mentioned several things that made her apprehensive about becoming a doctor. I asked her if she had been to the career planning center on the campus to explore different careers in the health fields. She said no. I called the center and spoke with the director. A few days later, Marisol went to the center and took a battery of tests. Several weeks later, a smiling and determined Marisol met me. She had taken the aptitude tests and learned about her strong affinity for work as a pharmacist. Instead of earning an MD, Marisol earned a PhD in pharmacology and is happy working as a researcher for a health maintenance organization. Marisol's story is not unique. Many Latinas and Latinos pursue a career that someone in their family has selected. Taking tests to determine whether or not the selected profession is what the student really wants and can do well is critical.

Latino students should realize that there are many career choices. For example, two of my students wanted to go to law school. However, one of them had an aptitude for advocacy and working with groups. After taking an aptitude test, she learned that one of the most suitable career fields for her was public policy. She attended an Ivy League school, earned a master's in public policy, and is working happily with the Latino community in Denver.

The lesson here for you as an undergraduate student is to be as certain as possible about a profession or career path. Visiting a career center on the campus and learning about aptitudes and related careers is a critical step in planning for graduate school. Once a student is certain about a career choice, the next step is to learn about the different graduate programs and one(s) that provide the most desirable orientation. Again, a career center is very helpful in addressing this concern. Most of the career centers at four-year colleges routinely gather information on different graduate and professional schools. A Latino student should examine carefully the types of graduate programs that best serve him or her. Sometimes, cost is a factor, such as the difference between attending a graduate program at a selective private university with tuition of $35,000 or more per year, or at a highly regarded publicly supported research university where the costs are $15,000 per year. But don't let costs be the determining factor. You can always find money to support your education. You may have to go into debt, but you will earn it all back within a few years and be able to pay off your debt.

2. *Networking and support groups.* Latino students at many large four-year institutions often feel alone and alienated. However, this need not be the case.

There are ways for Latino students to become comfortable on a campus, especially one with an enrollment of more than 20,000 students. Consider the story of Tony, a Latino student in Orange County, California. He was interested in creative writing and wanted to get a graduate degree in literature. He was part of a small group of Latino students at the state university that met often. They would frequently share information about activities on and off the campus that were of interest, and often met at a local pizza parlor. One evening Tony mentioned to a member of the group about his interest in creative writing. The other student asked Tony if he had ever attended one of the readings at a local Latino bookstore. Tony called the bookstore and spoke with the owner, who invited him to a reading. After the reading, the owner of the bookstore introduced Tony to the Latina writer, who was reading that night. The three of them had coffee and discussed Tony's interest in creative writing. Unknown to Tony, the owner of the bookstore was a former MacArthur Fellow (a prestigious award given to highly creative and innovative men and women). The bookstore owner asked Tony for a sample of his writing. He and the Latina writer received a few essays and short stories that Tony had written. A few weeks later, Tony received a letter from the creative writing program at the University of Iowa. The owner of the bookstore and the Latina writer had called the head of the graduate program in creative writing at Iowa and mentioned Tony. Tony eventually attended the University of Iowa and earned a master's in fine arts and is now a successful writer.

The aforementioned is an example of how networking and participating in a support group can be very beneficial for Latinos interested in earning a graduate degree. There are other valuable outcomes that result from networking. Consider the following. A talented Latina professor in the graduate school of education at UCLA created a support group for undergraduate Latina students. The group's purpose was for the Latinas to support each other and share information. Although the Latina professor did not teach any undergraduate courses, she acted as an unofficial advisor to the students and helped several Latinas get into selective graduate programs. Participating in a support group can lead to valuable contacts and information that will help a student qualify for and be admitted to an appropriate graduate program. The Latina professor told me she often called friends and contacts at major graduate programs to inform them about any of the students in her support group. Without her help, many of the Latina members of the support group would not have attended a highly regarded graduate program. What about the faculty at a graduate program or a school? Too many Latino students do not research graduate programs to find out if there are Latino faculty, or if there is a hospitality toward Latinos. At a prestigious private research university, there were two Latino faculties in the graduate school of business. These professors had worked diligently to recruit qualified Latinas and Latinos to the business school. They made contact with instructors at various colleges with large numbers of Latino students. Gradually they were able to share information about their interests in recruiting Latino students. They also lobbied large corporations and businesses to provide scholarships and grants-in-aid for Latinos. They shared with me that not enough Latino students bother to investigate their program and the assistance the university and graduate school of business provides.

"It's a shame when Latinos bypass our MBA program because the university is private and has a high tuition," said one of the professors. He went on to say that there was scholarship money available to cover the two-year graduate MBA program for any Latino student who qualified and did not have the funds to attend. "I just wish more students would look us up online, or contact me. If they call, and have good grades and the potential, then we're definitely interested in them and we'll try to recruit them," he told me. A little bit of research at a career center or online can surface numerous opportunities for Latino students to access a strong graduate program.

3. *Cultivating faculty and mentors* is critical for Latino students. It does not matter if the faculty member is Hispanic or from another ethnic or racial background. One of the most supportive faculty members for Latinas at a major research university was an African American professor in sociology. He helped many Latinas and Latinos improve their grades, select the right graduate program, find scholarship money, and even contacted faculty at graduate programs to lobby for the admission of these students.

    Faculty mentoring is a viable way for a student to get to know a faculty member and talk about career plans. Small liberal arts four-year colleges are known for the rapport between faculty and students. Instructors at these colleges are expected to mentor students and are often evaluated on their work as mentors. At regional universities, especially the larger ones, it is still possible for Latino students to identify a professor to serve as a mentor. It is really up to the student to find an appropriate faculty member, and make the first overture. Some students are reluctant to approach a professor unless they have high marks in his or her courses, or someone has recommended that they talk with the instructor. A Latino student should not hesitate to ask a professor to serve as a mentor. Faculty mentoring frequently results in students earning higher grades, developing a portfolio for use in applying to a graduate program, and a letter of recommendation.

When a faculty mentor gets to know a student and his or her career interests, this relationship invariably leads to a strong letter of recommendation for the Latino students. And in some cases, a faculty mentor actually contacts a colleague teaching in a graduate program and provides supportive commentary about the student. I have seen Latino students getting admitted to selective graduate programs because of the support provided by a faculty mentor.

Many faculty members often receive information from different sources about new graduate programs, scholarships and grants, and jobs as researchers or teaching assistance. It is important, therefore, for a Latino student to work with a faculty member, ask about graduate study, and what financial and employment opportunities may be available. An important intangible benefit of working with a faculty member is the moral support provided. A good faculty member will get to know the Latino student, encourage the student, build up his or her confidence, and serve as a guide to help find the best graduate program for the student. Consequently, a Latino student should not be shy about asking a professor to serve as a mentor.

The Latino student should also realize that a mentor need not be a faculty member or someone from the campus. A mentor from off the campus can be an invaluable asset for a student. There are various programs that link Latino students with professionals in the community, such as successful businessmen and businesswomen, elected political leaders, and well-regarded community leaders affiliated with nonprofit and community service groups. I will provide three examples. The Greenlining Institute in Berkeley, California, has a program that links Latino students with community leaders. The mentor helps the student by learning what his or her career goals are, and at times, by helping the student to better define what he or she wants to do. Often, a Latino student follows or serves as an observer in what the mentor does professionally. Most of the placements are with successful business leaders, such as small business owners, bank officers, and corporate middle management people. Ideally, a mentor should be Hispanic. However, many corporate leaders who work closely with Latinos are non-Hispanics. However, they are carefully selected and screened by the Greenlining Institute to ensure that they want to work with a Latino student and can be an effective mentor.

A second kind of community mentor is one who helps the student find part-time employment, but with a specific orientation toward what a student's career goals may be. For example, a young Latina was mentored by a talented Latina head of a large community services center designed to assist Latino families. The director of the center met regularly with the Latina student and had her observe the different types of services provided by the center. At the end of each month, the director of the center would meet with the student and discuss what she had observed and learned. At the end of six months, the young Latina student had sharpened her view about a career and decided to do graduate work in social work and public health.

A third type of mentor is someone in public office, such as an elected official. Many Latino locally elected politicians recruit Latino students to participate in projects within their district. A Latino county supervisor in California each year selects a Latino student to serve as an intern in his office. He is but one of many Latino public officials who work with students and help them to understand the relationship of schooling to work as a political leader. Some mentors invite the students to board meetings where the routines of public office are played out. The mentor can also be an advisor and help the student formulate their educational program and crystallize their plans for graduate study.

Mentors are not only an invaluable source or advice and direction, but they can also be strong supporters and serve as references. A letter of recommendation from an influential mentor is important to a Latino student as he or she applies for graduate study.

4. *Internships and volunteer activities.* The best graduate programs do not rely exclusively on grades and test scores. Admissions officers at graduate programs look carefully at a student's activities outside the classroom, and they are very interested in a student's extracurricular activities and leadership potential. In numerous conversations I've had with deans of admission at the most selective graduate programs, considerable weight has been given to a student's extracurricular activities. A pair of examples will underscore this.

Joey, a talented Latina interested in getting a law degree, was encouraged by her faculty mentor at the University of Texas, San Antonio (UTSA), to consider working as an intern in a law firm. She did so during her junior year at UTSA. The following year one of the senior partners in the law firm recommended her to work as a research assistant for a judge, doing a special project. When Joey applied for law school, the judge with whom she worked called the dean of admission at Columbia University School of Law and praised the work Joey had done for him and strongly recommended her for admission to the law program. Joey applied to several Ivy League law schools and was very pleased when the law school at Columbia University offered her admission. The dean of admission at Columbia University said that Joey's grades and test scores were about the same as most of the best applicants. However, what made the law school select her was Joey's work as an intern in a law firm, and then with a judge. A senior partner in the law firm and the judge sent strong letters of recommendation on her behalf. This support made the difference in her application and resulted in her admission to the law school at Columbia University.

On a similar note, Max, a Puerto Rican, was a student at Lehman College, a part of the City University of New York. Born and raised in the Bronx, he had wanted to pursue a career in the film industry but doubted he could afford the tuition at New York University that had a recognized graduate film program. He came from a poor family and worked his way through Lehman and earned a GPA that was between a B+ and A− average. He had looked into various film programs and believed that the cost to attend one of the better programs was beyond what he and his single mom could afford.

Lehman College has always prided itself in the mentoring programs that link students with faculty. In his junior year, Max spoke with his faculty mentor about going to graduate school to study cinema. He was not optimistic about his chances to attend one of the best programs in film studies. His faculty mentor encouraged Max to do volunteer work on a film restoration project at New York University. For most of his junior and senior years at Lehman, Max worked about 15 hours a week on the film restoration project. In the summer between his junior and senior years, Max volunteered to work on a film project in New York sponsored by the Library of Congress. He worked 20 hours a week, and about 25 hours a week as a volunteer. It was a hardship. However, he met one of the film experts from the Library of Congress and shared his interest in getting a graduate degree in film studies.

The curator from the Library of Congress received a doctorate in film studies from the University of Southern California (USC). He encouraged Max to apply to USC. Max did so, and was surprised when USC accepted him into the master's in fine arts program in cinema. He was offered a scholarship, and a part-time job in the University Library's film collection. The volunteer work Max did, even though it prevented him from working at a full-time job to help pay for his schooling at Lehman, made his dream of earning a graduate degree in film possible.

Max's story is an intriguing one because it involved faculty mentoring, volunteer work, and networking. Max's mentor at Lehman helped him find a volunteer job. The volunteer work led to an important meeting. He met a Library of Congress specialist in film who just happened to be a USC graduate in cinema. Max got to know and impressed the Library of

Congress specialist and shared his interest in film, and his desire to enroll in a graduate program in cinema. Max's story may sound unique, but it is a true example of what can happen if a Latino student takes on a volunteer assignment.

Joey and Max also did something very important that other Latina and Latino students should consider carefully. They both developed a portfolio, something to share with people about their interests and accomplishments. Developing a portfolio is as important as selecting the right institution and academic program, earning high grades, learning to do well on standardized tests, and finding a mentor.

5. *Developing a portfolio.* Latino students are well served by developing a portfolio of important accomplishments during their college experience. What is a portfolio? Too many people think a portfolio is something that only artists and writers compile. However, a well-organized portfolio with items that document a Latino student's background can be very significant. A good portfolio is a record of an undergraduate student's accomplishments. The portfolio may include class assignments that were well regarded by an instructor, an advisor, a mentor, or a community resource person, along with samples of writing that earned high marks. A good portfolio also includes extracurricular activities that document a student's successful performance outside of the classroom and beyond the campus boundaries.

Consider the portfolio of Josefina, a Latina student in Florida. She wanted to get a graduate degree in nursing and eventually teach nursing. Josefina started a portfolio during her second year of college. She included a description of courses she had taken in which she had earned high marks. There were examples of reports and papers she had written that included praise from her instructors. Josefina also included a narrative about clubs she joined in college, including serving as an officer (treasurer and vice president) of a club for students in health sciences. Josefina had her supervisor at a hospital write a letter that detailed the volunteer work she did at the hospital. The letter praised Josefina's performance and commitment to the welfare of patients in the ward where she worked.

Josefina's portfolio was an impressive record of her academic achievements and extracurricular activities. When she applied for graduate study in nursing, she was accepted with a scholarship for the doctor of nursing practice program at the University of Texas Health Sciences Center, Houston. Her grades and test scores were very good; but what impressed the admissions officers at UT Health Sciences was her portfolio. A comprehensive, well-organized portfolio is an important asset for any Latino student planning to do graduate study.

Summary

- Latino students need to prepare for graduate study as early as possible.
- Make certain that your parents understand and support your desire to do graduate study.
- Begin a well-thought-out plan of things to do to go to graduate school.
- Identify a faculty member to serve as a mentor and to help develop a plan for graduate study.
- Be flexible in your plan and consider different options that might arise.
- Talk with graduates of professional and/or graduate schools that interest you.
- Gather as much information from target graduate schools as possible.

Finally, I want to underscore that earning a graduate degree is essential for any Latino student with potential. The added earning power provided by a graduate degree and the advantages it provides for leadership in our society must be understood and acted on by Latinos. Planning and perseverance are critical and family support essential. And most importantly, like a close friend told an audience of Latino parents and students, "You need *ganas* to get into graduate school."

References

Camara, Wayne (October, 2009). "The College Board." Presentation, National Forum.

Educational Testing Service, www.ets.org.

Graduate Record Examination, www.ets.org/gre.

Paredes, Raymund (1979). Transfer Alliance Program, University of California, Los Angeles.

Short Stories of How I Made It in College

"I believe I can fly
I believe I can touch the sky."

From the 1993 song, "I believe I can fly",
lyrics by and sung by Robert Kelly

Introduction

Leonard A. Valverde

In this section are stories told by persons who we believe you will identify with. The six stories are divided into two halves. Two persons tell their stories and emphasize their undergraduate education experience (to earn their bachelor's degree) and four persons who went beyond their undergraduate degree to get a master's, doctorate, or professional terminal degree, like a law degree. The selected six persons provide a cross section of Latino students to demonstrate the diversity among us: Latinos and Latinas, Mexican descent, mainland Puerto Ricans, Cubans, young and older, East, mid-West, Southwest, those coming from middle class, others from Barrios, starting at the community college and others at the university level, some going to college right after finishing high school and others after being out of high school for some years, and so forth. While there are differences in their background, you should note that all of them faced some kind of difficulty, but most importantly they were able to get through it. They are you and you are them. The only difference is time in years. They are older and you are probably younger. Take encouragement from their stories and believe! One story in particular is a family story; how going to college became a family tradition. This family tradition is being replicated more and more across the country with Latinos. But wait there is more.

Thousands of Inspirational Stories

Included in this section are only six personal stories of success. They are included to demonstrate that you can be just as successful in college as these six persons, if not more. In the first edition, 10 other personal stories were included. But there are literally thousands of stories like these-sixteen. If you cannot find yourself in some the personal stories in this section, then I encourage you to read about other prominent Latina and Latino public figures so as to gain inspiration. You can find their stories in books, magazines, television, and over the Internet. Let me briefly identify two such figures. One is Supreme Court Justice Sonia Sotomayor and the other is U.S. Senator Robert Menendez from New Jersey.

Justice Sotomayor grew up in New York City, lived in what was commonly referred to as projects, or low income apartments, in the south Bronx. Her father worked as a tool and die maker and died when she was only nine years old. As a result, she was raised in a single parent family. Her mother worked very hard as a nurse, struggled to buy a set of encyclopedias, and pushed her to learn English. She was inspired to become a judge by viewing a TV program called *Perry Mason*. Sotomayor studied hard and graduated from Cardinal Spellman High School, and then entered the Ivy League school of Princeton University. At first she was overwhelmed in college, and after she received a low mark on her first mid-term paper, she sought help with English and writing. Besides seeking help in her academic life, she became highly involved with Accion Puertorriauena and Third World Center. She claims that these groups provided her "with an anchor I needed to ground myself in the new and different world." After Princeton, she earned her law degree from one of the best law schools in the country, Yale University. To learn more about her, you can look up the book entitled, *Sonia Sotomayor: The True American Dream* by Antonia Felix.

Similarly, U.S. senator Robert Menendez came from a stable Latino family of seven, both parents, two sisters, and two brothers. He is the son of immigrants and grew up in a tenement building in Union City. He is the product of New Jersey public schools and went to college at St. Peter's college to get a BA and then on to Rutger's University to earn a JD degree. He entered into public service at an early age, as a college student. When he was 19 years old, he launched a petition drive to reform the local schools. Later he went on to become a local school board member, then became a city mayor and state legislator.

You might consider these two stories as amazing. Yet these two highly successful persons do not. Senator Menendez says his story is "the quintessential American story." Supreme Court Justice Sotomayor story is named as "The True American Dream." Thus the reality is you and thousands of others can achieve just as much. They are not the exception. Their stories demonstrate that by you and countless others going to college, their stories can become ordinary!

Before proceeding to the six stories, we need to point out that the profile of college going students has changed over time. The old profile was characterized with these common traits: white, more males than females, ages 18–21, enrolling right out of high school, mostly single, full-time students, living on campus, and supported by their parents. Usually this profile of student enrollment is referred to as the traditional student. But this profile is no longer the norm. Instead, the characteristics are as follows: percentage of whites has decreased and persons of color have increased; more females than males; agewise students are older; more likely to start college in two-year campuses and transferring to four year; part-time students; commuting to campus; working part time to support themselves; married or with children or as head of households; and taking more years to graduate from college, up from four years to six years. When college staffs started seeing the changing makeup of the entering student body, they began to refer to this new profile as the nontraditional student. But now, the nontraditional student is the norm. You probably fit the characteristics of the new profile more than the old profile. In short, Latinos and Latinas are the regular students.

Both the stories you are about to read or the aforementioned new profile should give you encouragement that you can be successful in college because you fit the new and current mold. Or said better and shorter by Cesar Chavez: *Si Se Puede!*

College Degree: From Believing It Not Possible to a Family Expectation

Terry Guzman

I met my husband, John, while attending a primarily Latino high school in the East Los Angeles area of Los Angeles. It was made famous by the motion picture, *Stand and Deliver*, Garfield High School. He was a junior and I was a sophomore. We were both enrolled in advanced classes for college bound students. Although, I was considered a college bound student, the idea of actually going to college was very foreign to me.

Looking back, I do not ever recall a teacher encouraging me, or my fellow classmates to attend college. After graduating and employed, I learned that Garfield High had one of the highest high school drop-out rates in the city and the one of the lowest college going rates! I excelled academically in high school. I was also very involved in student government, and an array of school organizations. Despite excellent grades and school involvement, I lacked the confidence to think I could attend college.

In my immediate family only two of my cousins had graduated from high school. My eldest sister had dropped out of high school to marry. Therefore, going to college appeared impossible. On the other hand, my future husband seemed very sure he would attend college.

Terry Guzman is a second generation American of Mexican Ancestry. Born in El Paso, Texas, her parents migrated to Los Angeles when she was young. She went to public school in the second-largest Spanish Speaking barrio in the world, East Los Angeles. When she entered school she spoke only Spanish. (Mexico City is the largest Spanish Speaking city in the world.) Despite going to a low-performing high school and other traditional odds against her, she was successful in earning a college degree! Read about her story and that of her family.

In retrospect, I surmise his determination to attend college arose from the fact that his older sister was attending college, and served as a positive role model for him. Therefore, his goal of earning a college degree was realistic to him. Unfortunately, his parents did not share in his goal. Although both high school graduates, they never encouraged him to attend college. They would have been satisfied with him securing a full-time job after high school.

Nonetheless, inspired by his sister, my future husband did enroll in a local community junior college, and worked part-time to pay for his education. His college education was disrupted by the escalation of the Vietnam War. He dropped out of school, and joined the Navy, where he served for four years. While in the service, he made a conscious decision to return to school upon discharge. He knew he could count on his G.I. Bill to assist him financially.

Upon his military discharge, he did return to a community college with an enhanced determination to graduate, and transfer to a four year university. His sister was working as an elementary school teacher at the time, and he decided to enter the education field as well. His goal was to become a high school history teacher. He wanted to impart his knowledge on others. He also wanted to encourage young Latino students to go on with their schooling, since this had been lacking in his own high school experience. Most importantly, as a high school teacher he would serve as a positive role model for the younger Latino generation.

The road I embarked on to earn a college education differed greatly from my husband's experience. I was born and raised in El Paso, Texas. My parents had only an elementary school education. When I entered first grade, I did not speak English, and my teacher did not speak Spanish. Despite the language barrier, I enjoyed school, and always did well academically. I liked my teachers, and wanted to be liked by them. I just did not know how one became a school teacher. I do not remember ever hearing the word "college" mentioned. I had the impression that only wealthy, and English speaking persons became teachers. No one in my family had attended college.

My family relocated to Los Angeles when I was thirteen. I enrolled in a local junior high school, and immediately went into culture shock. No one spoke Spanish on school grounds, and my new friends spoke of going to college after high school.

I attended high school and excelled in my studies. Interestingly, although I elected to be a college bound student, I chose a secretarial major. I knew that I would have to work after graduation to help my family. While a senior, I realized that perhaps I could go to college. I saw the opportunity to attend college, and decided to take advantage of it. I had been awarded a small scholarship to attend a community college. I wanted a better life for myself. If I was going to get out of poverty, I would need to attend college. Despite the protests of my parents, and the lack of encouragement from my teachers, I enrolled in a community college. I did have the emotional support from my future husband, since he was already attending.

After completing my general educations requirements, I transferred to the University of California at Los Angeles as a junior. I had been awarded financial assistance from the Educational Opportunity Program. At UCLA I continued to work part time as a research assistant, since my parents could not afford to help me financially. I left after one year to marry.

One year later, I enrolled at the California State University at Los Angeles. I worked part-time as a teacher's aide and attended school. The experience of working as a teacher's aide influenced my decision not to go into the teaching field. I didn't enjoy the education field. Realistically, I also could not afford to go to school for another year to earn a teaching credential. I felt the need to start working full-time as soon as possible. During my last quarter at Cal State LA, I was hired as a social worker with the County of Los Angeles. I was working full-time and going to school full-time. I graduated with a Bachelor's Degree in History from Cal State LA.

I enjoyed the social work field, because it gave me the chance to help others. But I also came to the conclusion that, I would have to expand my knowledge of social work in order to be more effective. After seven years of working full time, I enrolled in a two year Social Work Master's Degree Program at the University of California at Los Angeles. When I finished and earned my Master's Degree, my husband returned to school, and also completed a Master's Degree in Computer Science.

As previously discussed my eldest sister dropped out of high school to marry at the age of 15. At the age of thirty-five she applied for a position as a teacher's aide. Originally, she was going to apply to work in the school cafeteria. Since she had been assisting in her daughter's classroom, I encouraged her to apply for the teacher's aide position instead. She was hired and thoroughly enjoyed the experience.

After about three years, her coworker shared her idea of attending a community college, and asked my sister to join her. My sister discussed the possibility with me. She was afraid to go to college. Since she only had a ninth grade education, she lacked confidence in her learning abilities. I insisted she should at least try. I told her that she and her friend could be on the "buddy system." They could take the same classes, and help each other. I also informed her, I would be there to support her and help her with her studies. After much thought, she did decide to go. Our family was extremely proud to see her at the podium receiving her AA degree at the age of forty-five.

Her friend made the decision to become a teacher, and was transferring to a four year university. She asked my sister to join her. Again, my sister felt afraid. I had the impression my sister believed she had been lucky to graduate with her Associates' of Arts Degree. She did not have the confidence to attend a university. After much discussion, encouragement from me, her spouse, and her children she finally agreed to go. She graduated with a Bachelor's Degree in Education. She taught a kindergarten class in a Catholic school for seventeen years. As a consequence of her accomplishments, she began to talk to her children about the value of education, and encouraged them to attend college. She used herself as an example of what could be achieved, if the desire was there. As a result, her two youngest children went on to college, and both earned Master's Degree in the field of education. They are both successful school teachers.

Our new family tradition of attending college was readily transferred to our only son. As a child, we took him to visit various universities within the United States. The question for him was not whether he would attend college, but where he would go. At the early age of four years old he would inform people where he was going to college.

In our home, we often spoke of the importance of education, and the University of California at Los Angeles. Therefore at an early age he decided where he would attend college.

Fortunately, he was accepted at the University of California at Los Angeles, and we were able to pay for his education without a having financial burden. Nonetheless, he did work part-time which I believe enriched his college experience, as he was contributing to pay for his education. He graduated with a Bachelor's Degree in History,

Upon graduation, he started working with mentally challenged adults. He enjoyed working with this population. After one year, he decided to go back to school and obtain a teaching credential. He decided he wanted to be a Special Education Teacher. He had the idea that working with special needs children would be rewarding. Most importantly, he could make an impact with them when they were young. Teaching them knowledge and skills which would help them as independent adults. He earned his teaching credential, and then elected to enter a Special Education Master's Program. While he worked full-time, he did earn his Master's Degree in Special Education. He has worked as a Special Education teacher for the past eight years.

Continuing with our family tradition, our granddaughter will be expected to attend college. This is an expectation that her parents have expressed on numerous occasions. Funds are already being set aside to see this goal to fruition.

Attending college has now become a family tradition. Nieces and nephews are now constantly being encouraged to attend college. Some who are in elementary school have already decided where they will be going. In two generations, my family's views on education have changed dramatically. They view the college experience as a positive experience, and not a frightening or an unattainable one. My family now has the courage to not only attend college, but also seek advanced degrees.

Selection of College That Fits You—Helps Lead to Success

Leo Raul Valverde

Ancient Zen Proverb: When the student is ready, a teacher will appear.

I was born in East LA. But I didn't grow up in the barrio. I grew up in Austin, Texas. My family wasn't poor. We weren't rich either (the air conditioner was only used for "special" occasions). I attended public schools. I wasn't the first in my family to attend college—my parents claimed those honors.

Both of my parents are teachers. They didn't beat me over the head with education and stress the need to go to college. They simply led by example. Of course I realized fairly early what I wanted to be when I grew up.

It was the beginning of my eighth grade year. I was running for student council. All the candidates had to give their speeches on parent's night. Students, teachers, and parents would be there. *Aye dios mio!* I wrote my campaign speech—all one paragraph—and read it over and over. Then the night came. We candidates were brought on stage. There was a podium and microphone! We went in alphabetical order, so naturally I was last. As I watched my fellow classmates, I noticed something. They all got to the podium, read their speech, and never looked up at the audience. Finally my turn came. I started my speech

Leo Raul Valverde earned a law degree from Arizona State University, Tempe Campus. His bachelor's degree in political science and philosophy is from Trinity University in San Antonio, Texas. He has been a public defender with the Maricopa County Public Defender's Office and in private practice as criminal defense attorney. His interests in teaching has lead him to teach part time at the college level. He started a college saving fund for his daughter before her birthday of one year so she could go to the college of her choice.

173

and realized I knew it by heart. So I looked up. I made eye contact with the crowd. I could feel their attention on me. I gave my entire speech without looking at my paper. What a rush!

I won the election, played sports, got good grades—I was The Man . . . in eighth grade. And that's when I knew I wanted a career in politics or the law. I knew I had to go to college.

Things changed once I got to high school. I was no longer the big fish in the sea. I lost a student council election my freshman year and got cut from the basketball team my sophomore year. When class rankings came out I was somewhere in the 100's in a class of 600.

Then my whole world changed. My family moved from Austin to San Antonio after my sophomore year. The transition was hard. I was in a new school in a new city. It took me a while to make friends. But that gave me more time to study. And I studied hard. I was shocked when the class rankings came out in the beginning of senior year. I was ranked number 12 of 600 students!

My hard work, good grades, and class ranking opened up a great many opportunities. I was recruited to join the Academic Decathlon Team and made it! Our team even made it to State. I was elected President of the Spanish Honor Society. My confidence grew and suddenly I was thinking about Ivy League Schools. That's where great politicians and great lawyers came from— Harvard and Yale.

I was fortunate to attend a high school that promoted college attendance. There were college fairs where school recruiters came to our school. I did well in math and science. Some of my teachers encouraged me to become an engineer. But I loved social studies and government classes. I started to research schools for government and political science programs.

I wanted to try and head back to my place of birth. I had family in East LA. I didn't apply to a single school in Texas. Eventually I applied to Harvard, Yale, Stanford, UCLA, Claremont McKenna, and Pomona, the last two in southern California.

Harvard, Yale, and UCLA all sent me very polite rejection letters. Claremont McKenna and Pomona accepted me. AND I GOT INTO STANFORD! Stanford, one of the most prestigious universities in the world, wanted me. This was going to be a no-brainer right?

Nevertheless, I decided to visit Stanford and Claremont McKenna just to make sure. Claremont McKenna was in Los Angeles after all. What I found surprised me. Stanford was huge. A big campus with a large number of student enrollment. Very big classes. Claremont McKenna was small. Small campus. Small enrollment. Small classes. I liked small. I learned better in small classes.

After careful consideration I chose to attend Claremont McKenna College. That's right, I rejected Stanford. Stanford didn't fit me. I had to go to where I felt comfortable to be able to learn. Besides, attending Claremont would be my triumphant return to LA.

I graduated from John Marshall High School in 1990 and headed off to college. Claremont McKenna is a wonderful college. Beautiful campus, diverse student body, and fantastic faculty. I was able to visit with family on the weekends and learn during the week. But as the semester wore on, I never felt "at home." I missed my friends and my parents. Something just wasn't right. I was getting a great education but I began to have my doubts about living in LA.

I started to think of other schools I could attend. Schools that were closer to home in San Antonio. And there was a perfect school right under my nose. Trinity University in San Antonio is a small private, liberal arts schools with excellent academics. I talked with my parents about my feelings and thoughts. They understood and agreed with my decision. After one semester in LA, I transferred to Trinity.

I felt more comfortable at Trinity. A few of my high school classmates attended as well. I could visit my parents every Sunday to do laundry and have dinner. (A tradition that carries on to this day.) Because I was more comfortable I was able to study better. I felt more at ease with myself and my surroundings. I chose to major in Political Science with an eye toward attending law school.

As fate would have it, my parents moved from San Antonio to Phoenix just after my sophomore year. However, I chose to stay at Trinity and complete my education. I enjoyed the school enormously. I took any class related to the law. Some of the law courses were in the business department, communication department, and philosophy department. I also enjoyed many of the philosophy classes so much that I got a minor in Philosophy.

I was active in intramural sports and the campus radio. I acted in a play. I took ballroom dance. I helped to produce four popular multi-media lectures for a very distinguished philosophy professor. I did a lot of pleasure reading as well. I wanted to learn as much as I could—and not just about how to get into law school.

I also worked. I had part-time jobs all through college. I worked at a gym for one year and then a flower shop for two. These were off-campus jobs. They were great because I earned a little money and learned responsibility.

I loved to study in the library. There is something about the energy of a college library. Study groups met there. Knowledge lives there. I hung out there.

My grades were good but they were not great. I figured I would need great grades to get into law school. When it came time to take the LSAT I took a prep course and studied hard. I still had dreams of Harvard Law! Until my results came back. My score was average. Not great. Not terrible. Average. I figured I wouldn't get into any law school with good grades and an average LSAT score.

However, my parents, my professors, and my friends encouraged me to apply to law school. In 1997 I graduated from Trinity University with a BA in Political Science and a Minor in Philosophy. I had also been accepted to Arizona State University Law School. (Where I went on to meet some of my best friends in life—one of whom you will also meet in this collection of stories.)

I guess you could say that I made it in college because I wanted to make it—I chose to make it. When I was ready to learn my parents appeared. When I was ready to apply for college Academic Decathlon appeared. When I was ready for college Claremont McKenna appeared. When I was ready to come back to Texas, Trinity appeared. Everything happens for a reason.

Your education is like your life. You only get out what you put it. So don't be afraid to live. . . . Or learn.

Higher Education Opened Doors to Greater Opportunity

Tomas Morales

I was born in Puerto Rico as the third son of hard working parents who migrated to the Bronx in New York City before my first birthday. When I started public school, I was unable to speak English. Fortunately, my parents highly valued education and they closely monitored the education my brothers and I received from the New York City public education system.

Both my mother and father were extraordinary role models; their unwavering commitment to their own educational goals was inspirational. My father, an unskilled factory worker, enrolled in night school to complete courses for certification as a machinist. My mother, who never finished high school, at the age of thirty-six decided to return to school to earn a GED and subsequently enrolled in a community college. After earning her associate degree, she went on to complete a baccalaureate and a master's degree in social work. Ultimately, she retired as the Director of Social Work at a major community health care center. My parents' career paths demonstrated their commitment to and belief in the importance of higher education and to our family. It was not only excit-

---

Dr. Morales started college at State University of New York at Paltz and received his bachelor's degree (1975) in secondary education (major in history) and graduated cum laude. He continued his higher education by completing a master's program in educational administration and policy studies in 1978 at State University of New York at Albany. He returned to SUNY Albany and earned a doctorate in educational administration in 1998. As a result of his higher education work he has become the president of the College of Staten Island in the City University of New York.

ing, but also motivational to witness both my older brother and mother earn their master's degrees during the same week.

Throughout high school, I worked in restaurants, delivered newspapers, and mopped hallways to support myself. In my junior year, I was fortunate to be offered a position in a bank in New York's financial district; it was during this period that I realized that attending college was the pre-requisite to becoming a learned person. It soon became apparent to me that acquiring a liberal arts education was the necessary first step in the pursuit of a professional career.

A co-worker of mine from Brooklyn invited me to visit a state university north of New York City where his sister was attending. I was so impressed to meet a Latina from Brooklyn living in a residence hall on campus and pursuing a baccalaureate degree. She became yet another role model who encouraged me to apply for admission. At that time, my parents could not afford to pay my tuition, room, and board. So, I sought assistance in completing the various financial aid forms required to apply for both federal and state financial aid programs. Most colleges offer assistance for both applicants and their parents; however, it is important for admission applicants to complete the financial aid application early.

Upon completion of the admission application process, I received my offer of admission—I just couldn't contain my excitement. Immediately, I inquired on the status of my financial aid application. Following submission of required family income documentation, I received my financial aid award. Soon thereafter, I received an invitation to attend a summer orientation program. A new beginning was on the horizon.

After carefully reading *all* of the materials sent to new entrants, I realized that I should attend the orientation. Orientation was critically important to my transition as a freshman; it afforded me the opportunity to meet fellow students, professional staff, and faculty. Making new friends and getting to know the faculty and staff also eased the adjustment I had to make coming from the Bronx to a small upstate college town, a very different environment from where I was raised. I also learned of the student and academic support services that were available undergraduates. I continued to rely on my faculty advisor and professional staff whom I met at orientation throughout my undergraduate years, and, in fact, I still stay in touch with several of them today.

My involvement with several student organizations expanded my network of friends, faculty and staff advisors. Participating in these organizations honed my leadership skills, provided me with an opportunity to contribute to my community, and exposed me to invaluable learning opportunities outside the classroom. During my second year, I volunteered to serve as a peer counselor to new entrants, and I continued to serve in this capacity as an undergraduate. As I continued to progress as an undergraduate, I worked with the admissions office as a student recruiter visiting high schools, and I also accompanied the admissions professional staff to college information fairs. This was my initial opportunity to work for the College and gain experience as an admissions counselor intern. It was then that I realized I may want to pursue a career in higher education.

After my freshman year I began to work full-time in order to support my family. My need to work full-time while pursuing my undergraduate degree required that I carefully manage my time. I quickly realized that time management, or in other words, my ability to allocate my time wisely was absolutely essential to my academic success. Carefully, I mapped out my weekly schedule, outlining the number of hours I needed to attend class, including the commute time to the campus; the investment of time I had to reserve to complete reading assignments, to study, to take advantage of tutorial and student services, to participate in co-curricular activities, to meet my employment responsibilities, and of course, to spend time with my family.

Undoubtedly, I attribute my success as an undergraduate to the opportunity that I had to develop a mentoring relationship with the faculty in my major. It was my faculty advisor who I met as a freshman, as well as other faculty and staff at the College who inspired me to persist and graduate. Faculty and professional staff innately enjoy mentoring students and nurturing their development and transformation as undergraduates. I earned my baccalaureate degree with honors because I worked hard, took advantage of learning opportunities both in and outside the class, benefitted from a mentoring relationship with faculty and staff who were dedicated to my success and those of my fellow students. The College I attended created a sense of belonging for me and gave me the opportunity to volunteer and contribute to the campus community as a student leader.

Several months after I graduated, I applied for a professional position at my alma mater and was fortunate to be appointed as an academic advisor serving financially and academically disadvantaged students. I believe that I was selected by the search committee and appointing officer because of my experience as both a peer counselor and admission recruiter intern. My experiences as an undergraduate student leader, work study student, and my first professional experience was the beginning of my academic career in higher education.

As a young professional, I knew that completing a graduate degree was a requirement to furthering my career. I immediately applied to a graduate program at a sister campus which was over 70 miles one way. Working full-time, supporting my family, and commuting over 140 miles round trip was a sacrifice which I knew would pay off. To reiterate, I attribute my success in completing my Master's degree, again, to faculty with whom I worked closely. As a part-time student, it took me two years to complete my degree. During this period,

I accepted a position at an Ivy League institution joining an admissions and academic support and student services team. This was an exciting professional opportunity to work with faculty and staff to improve the academic success of undergraduate students. Later, I advanced to one of the State's flagship campuses in a similar position.

Throughout my career I have held positions in student affairs and academic affairs in three of the largest public systems of higher education in New York and California. Prior to assuming the presidency at the College of Staten Island/CUNY, I held the position of Provost and Vice President for Academic Affairs and Professor of Education at the California State University, Pomona.

It's Up to You

Christopher A. Flores

In 1994 I graduated from Arizona State University, earning a bachelor's degree in communications. Afterward, I continued on at ASU to get my JD degree from the Law school in 1997. After passing the bar in 1997, I spent two years at the Maricopa County Public Defender's Office, where I began defending clients charged with all levels of felonies. Since 2000 I have been in private practice, representing clients charged with crimes ranging from misdemeanors to major felonies in City, State, and Federal Courts throughout Arizona.

My inspiration to go to law school were my parents. My dad, Albert Flores, graduated from Arizona State Law School in 1974. My father was one of ten children. He came from very modest means. He and his family spent most of his early childhood in a tiny two bedroom house. The family later built the house that he spent the latter part of his childhood and high school years in. My parents met in high school and had my older brother at a young age. By the time my parents were 20 they had two children. My mother worked full time to put my dad through college and law school. My parents are still married and continue to work as hard as they did when I was young. My parents worked hard to give me small and big opportunities like: take me to baseball practice, to attend a college preparatory school, then college, and finally law school. I do

Chris Flores earned a JD degree from the Law School at Arizona State University at Tempe. He is in private practice as a criminal defense attorney in Phoenix, Arizona, where he was born, raised, and educated. He was an attorney with the Maricopa County Public Defender's Office for two years. He and his wife Tina are planning on having their two young daughters go to college.

believe that I was given important opportunities that other kids I grew up with did not have. Recognizing and taking advantage of those opportunities has put me where I am today.

My first trial in court was actually way before I graduated from law school. Sometime around 7th or 8th grade I was hanging out in the neighborhood with my group of buddies late at night. The police in the neighborhood of 48th and Southern were trying to keep us off the streets past curfew and would often give us a chase through the neighborhood. The group would disperse and usually nobody got caught but sometimes one or two unlucky kids would. One particular night I was the unlucky one to get caught hiding behind Eric S's parent's shed. I was cited and pled guilty in Juvenile Court. I took a diversion class that lasted all day and the citation was dismissed.

Cruising Central Avenue was popular for low-rider and classic car enthusiasts. I grew up working on vintage Chevy's with my dad in our driveway. Many weekend nights my brother and his friends would take me to cruise South Central Avenue until early morning on Friday or Saturday. Not too long after my first curfew citation, I was "cruising central" with my brother and my uncle. We were approached by an officer late at night, -he arrested me (being under age) for being out past curfew. A diversion class was not available for my second curfew citation. I was set on going to trial to avoid a conviction.

My "old man" had already established himself as a prominent trial attorney. I was sure to walk out of Juvenile Court with a not guilty given that my father, "Big Al," was representing me. Little did I know that as far as the "old man" was concerned, all he was doing was walking in with me. The rest was up to me! When the judge called my case, my attorney/dad, stepped aside and told me to handle the case. I was way more surprised than I was prepared, but I presented my defense and the judge found me not guilty. The swagger on the way out of court after my victory, compared to my humble walk into court, was noticeable. So my dad set me back down a couple of notches by letting me know two things. One, he and the judge were from the same small town and he used to shine the judge's shoes. Two, "now that you have won your first trial, there is only one way to go. . . . Down!"

Like most eighth graders, I thought that I knew what was best for me, and for sure my parents had no clue. My parents knew it would be best for me to go to a college preparatory in an unfamiliar area of Phoenix. The college prep had none of the comforts that the public school had. There were no old friends, no blue jeans, no wrestling, and no girls. I had to wear a collared shirt too! As an eighth grader I as a wrestler so had I gone to public high school I would have been as connected as much as a freshman could ever be. My brother was a senior and his friends knew me well. Thus I would be much more than comfortable. I would be hooked-up! Nobody from the neighborhood had ever heard about this college prep school, let alone went there. I remember the first day well. I am often reminded of it by a (now) good friend. That day he happened to be standing out in front of the school near the President of the school. At the time I didn't know Brian L. I didn't know anyone at the school. In fact, I didn't know the President was a priest. Both the President and Brian L. had to see me coming because I was the passenger in the only 1949 Chevy Pickup with primer paint in a line of shiny Mercedes and BMWs. When the lowered Chevy arrived at the student drop off point and I opened the door, empty beer cans fell to the ground! My first day at a new school and I was already known as the guy in the primer low-rider with beer cans falling out. Also my collared shirt didn't have an alligator and my khaki's were Dickies and not Ralph Loren. I felt like quitting before I even started. However, as time pasted I found this new school as an opportunity to meet people that I would have never been able to meet had I take the easy road and stayed back in the old neighborhood.

As a result of the college prep high school, I began college at ASU and spent most of my out of class time with my older brother. Despite the fact that my brother was smarter, more talented, and wittier than me, he was into the easy road and had little intent or desire to put in the work and time it takes to go to college. I knew this because I knew him better than I knew anyone. I would study and he would hang out with me for hours at a time at various coffee shops around Tempe. He would spend hours reading true crime paperbacks while I spent hours reading class materials. For me the setting of a coffee shop was the most conducive setting for studying. A coffee shop was not the most time efficient setting but I was not the type of person to get it done alone in the library. To be successful in college it takes plenty of study time and it can be easy to get "burnt out" so I believe you must have a "study style." Over the years of college and law school I saw various types of styles other students used. Some students allocated specific amounts of time to study each day. Some had to study in the same place or at the same time. Others used study partners or study groups. Still others found they had to study right after class or after a workout that cleared their minds. All successful students had a routine that was comfortable for them. Over time I learned that I had to be in a comfortable environment occasionally visiting with my brother. Most of my friends told me that studying in a coffee shop with distractions wouldn't be productive for them. I understood that. However, I found that I could not continually, day after day, go back to the quiet and boring library to do homework. I know I would have completed the work sooner in a library but over the long term I would not have made it. The key is to find the "study style" for works for you.

Sitting in class at ASU Law School, daily entertainment came in the form of reading the daily crime blog in the campus newspaper. One particular morning I learned that my own brother and a few others had been arrested for conspiracy to possess, sell, and distribute marijuana. Reading the story I immediately knew it was referring to my brother and best friend and that the story wasn't a mistake or another "Rick Flores." Reading about my brother's mistakes while I was sitting in a classroom wouldn't be the last time his attempts at the quick buck and shortcut to success would directly cross paths with my more traditional approach of building a future.

The next time came while I was a clerk at the Public Defender's Office and studying for the bar exam. The task of the law clerk was to handle all of the arraignments of the newly indicted defendants for all cases to be assigned to the Public Defender's Office. Sitting at the defense table, the law clerk gets to be front and center of every new felony in the county. About six years after my brother's first felony, he was arrested and indicted for similar charges. I had the distasteful opportunity to announce as the attorney for my own brother.

My brother got the news that I passed the bar exam in 1997 via a collect call from the Arizona State Penitentiary where he spent the next few years. I don't tell this story to judge or demean my brother, but rather to point out that some people have the ability and opportunity to get a higher education and mistakenly choose not to face the task. Some have fewer opportunities, but work hard and overcome obstacles and create opportunities for themselves.

Years of court appearances have past, and as a defense attorney I am in court every day and sometimes run into some of the old guys from the neighborhood. Many times they are in-custody as defendants awaiting trial. From the group of guys I used to hang out with in the neighborhood, none made it through high school, a few were killed in street crime, and some are in jail or prison. One day I saw an old friend, Joey S., in court. He was in custody. Joey S. was the leader of our group most likely because he was physically the biggest and most mature. The summer between eighth and ninth grade we were too young to work so we had plenty of time to cause trouble in the neighborhood. I was always involved in baseball, so late one afternoon I told Joey that I was disappointed that I had to leave the guys. I had to meet my dad so he could take me to baseball practice. Joey took me aside and told me to go, to get home, and to go to practice. He wished that he had someone to take him to practice. From that day on I realized that I was fortunate to have someone to take me to baseball practice. Years later when I saw Joey in court, I wondered if things would have been different for him if he had had positive role models.

Obstacles are inevitable and higher education is not a given. Many underprivileged people have taken a much more difficult path than I have to get through school. Likewise, many more fortunate people have failed to take advantage of opportunities and pursue a higher education. College and law school is available for all who want to apply themselves and those with the ability and desire to overcome obstacles. Whether the obstacles take the form of financial setbacks, time constraints, family issues, emergencies, or friends, in school you will have to overcome them, learn from them, and not let them keep you from pursuing your dreams. It is up to you!

Buena Suerte/Good Luck

Doctor, Doctor: Not Like Degrees on a Thermometer

Jose Angel Gutierrez

When I was a youngster my father wanted me to follow in his professional footsteps and become a medical doctor. He was from Mexico and practiced in South Texas during the 1930s to late 1950s. Each time the subject came up I thought to myself "No way Jose." In order to not disrespect or defy him I would say in Spanish of course, "I'd rather be a lawyer." I knew firsthand what terrible hours my dad put into his practice being the only Mexican health professional in the area: births in the middle of night, bleeding bodies on weekends by our front door; no money to pay for his services; and no hospital privileges at the local Anglo-owned facility so he did the best he could at home with the help of my mother, his medical and laboratory assistant. My dad's medical office and clinic took up the front half of our home. He was on call 24/7. I on the other hand need full uninterrupted 8 hours of sleep; no way I could become and remain a doctor.[1]

You can surmise from that frequent dialogue between us that I talked myself into the legal profession from an early age. There were no Chicano attorney role models in my hometown of Crystal City, Texas, while I was growing up. I did not even know what a lawyer was or did back then in the 1950s. The only attorneys I met were in *Piedras Negras, Coahuila, Mexico* when my dad would

---

Jose Angel Gutierrez is a professor at the University of Texas at Arlington. He has been a community leader having served as president of a school board and been a local judge; a political activist having founded the Raza Unida Party in Texas and a civil rights leader. He is most proud to say he helped all seven of his children to college, earn a degree, and some have advanced to earn master's and doctorates.

take our family across the river in Eagle Pass, Texas into *Piedras*. Sometimes he would meet with doctors and other professionals including bankers, pharmacists, and lawyers. I could tell who the professionals were, they wore suits and ties. The only Mexican in *Cristal* as we called out town that sported a suit and tie on occasion was my dad. And all the attorneys in Cristal were white men.

So-called informed adults suggested I become a lawyer because I was argumentative, loquacious, verbose, and opinionated not to mention assertive at an early age. During my high school years I was recruited to participate in the Interscholastic League Forensic competition. I had no clue what those words meant; my motivation to enter was to be near the white girls who recited poetry and were in school plays. I entered speech competitions, and won. In fact my junior year I became the 1961, 28-AA, State Champion in Declamation in Texas; first Chicano to win that title. The judges, local, district, state, all marveled that I spoke without an accent as they politely wrote in the evaluation or comment score cards. Other words used by judges to describe my performances were "articulate, poised, clear enunciation, exact pronunciation, and forceful." I guess they meant this was a new experience for them listening to a Chicano kid. The key to my linguistic success was Suse Salazar. My family enrolled me in a Chicano bilingual school for my Kindergarten pre-school training in the *barrio* of *Mexico Grande*. We had segregated schools in Cristal and the Mexican kids had to go to their school because we could not speak English. And, you were retained in grade level until you learned how to speak English properly; most Chicano kids dropped out of school by their teen years because of this language policy and segregation. The curriculum at the barrio school was similar to the League of United Latin American Citizens (LULAC) early childhood program dubbed the "Little School of 400" words in English. Ms. Salazar taught all the students the alphabet, multiplication tables, math, geography plus oratory, declamation, and poetry recital. Her "school" was situated in half of her grocery store. Our desks were fashioned out of wooden orange and apple crates and our seats were foot stools or shoe shine boxes. Every Friday was test day. Each student would stand front and center before her with both palms face up. If we could not recite the alphabet, vowels and consonants, do multiplication tables and math in Spanish and English, she would whack our hands with a pile of wooden rulers. You had to start over again and again until you got it right. I learned real quick to get it right the first time or suffer burning hands and tears down my cheeks.

In my pre-teen years I did not know what skills an attorney should possess. Being talkative as adults seem to think and say must have been one of these. Wrong! As an attorney I have learned to listen rather than talk; analyze rather than opine; speak when spoken to; refrain from arguing over belief, feelings, faith, and certainly not to engage in conversation someone dumber than

I; debate only when necessary; defer to gain strategic advantage; and to speak and write less. It is very hard to speak and write less; takes much discipline and practice. Try to say less and write concisely; it is very difficult.

By the time I got to college the counselors suggested I take government courses if I was going into "pre-law." In hindsight I could just as easily have taken a degree in English, Math, Science, even Economics and been better prepared for the rigors of law school and the practice of law. A Business degree prepares you for running your law office better than Government; and they do not teach you how to operate a law office in law school. The folks over in Education probably have it right. Teachers must first major in a content area then take course on how to teach. Law school should also teach the law then teach you how to practice law. Someone somehow determined that the course of study for those in "pre-law" was the Government degree.

As I approached graduation at Texas A & I University with my degree in Government, the prospects of being inducted forcibly into military service during the heyday of the Vietnam War was not appealing. We had the draft in place. After graduation I would not have a student deferment. Instead I continued my pursuit of law studies and sought admission into law school. Back in the day, the only four year college in South Texas was Texas A & I in Kingsville and all Chicanos and Chicanas gravitated to that school. The rich Anglos and Mexicans went to private schools in San Antonio such as St. Mary's University, Incarnate Word College, Our Lady of the Lake University or Trinity University. The only public law schools were at the University of Texas in Austin, Texas Tech in Lubbock (West Texas), and two in Houston. One of the Houston schools was the historic law school for blacks, Texas Southern University. The other which I attended was the University of Houston. In the late 1960s we also had segregation in higher education in Texas. In my entering class the summer of 1966 at Bates College of Law, University of Houston, there were hundreds of white boys from East Texas and only three Chicanos; no Chicanas, no blacks. I literally felt for the first time in my life as a *mosca en leche* and in *barrio ajeno*. Every time I spoke up in class both fellow students and professors would attack me for my views and interpretation of the law as applied to fact situations in cases we studied. I was perpetually wrong on the "law," they said. But I was not one to be shamed or browbeaten into submission with words and argument. They were not ready for me and I certainly was not ready for them. I kept up my fight in every class, every day for nine torturous months. The burden of working full time, carrying a full load of courses and putting up with the racist professors and fellow students made me quit. And I am not a quitter. I left for graduate school at St. Mary's University where my mentor Charlie Cotrell was now a professor. He got me a job with which to pay the pricey tuition and books. The study of law had been boring; mostly memorization of cases and what they call black letter law (statutes and codes). In law school when I would ask "Why?" regarding a rule or decision the response was "because of 600 years of Anglo Saxon common law." To which I then would further probe with, "So they made it up as they robbed, stole, plundered, raped, maimed and killed my people?" They call these rulings and decisions precedent, *stare decisis*, which must be followed in subsequent cases. This is a neat power trick: decide a case under common law; then all other cases that follow must be decided the same way. Wrong doing by Anglos became the law, the overused slogan of "the rule of law." Let me provide an example of a verbal battle I had as a first year law student at Bates. Adverse possession is the taking and holding someone else's property against their will for a period of years; then it becomes yours. Nice way to justify stealing Mexican lands, cattle, gold mines, oil fields, timber stands, grazing lands, water, and anything else you can hold adversely against the owner for a period of years. Ever hear the phrase "possession is 9/10ths of the law?" Now you know Anglo Saxon Common Law.

At St. Mary's I enrolled in a Master's program in Government and flourished among my peers and faculty mentors. When I asked a question in any course the response was like looking at facets of a diamond: "Read these articles, these books." I found many answers not just one: 600 years of Anglo Saxon Common Law. I continued to memorize as in law school but also learned to think critically, analyze, connect the dots, make logical inferences and assumptions, and recall bibliography. I learned to frame questions and posit hypotheses to research and test empirically; nothing like law school. I loved wandering in this fertile field of learning all the way to a Master's degree. Ever since 1963 when five Chicanos ran and won all the seats of the city council in Cristal I developed an interest in power relations and politics. I love political science. Now I love teaching what I have learned to others. By 1970, the University of Texas in Austin had developed a doctoral program in Mexican American Studies and I wanted to combine that field with Government and enrolled. I was the only Chicano in the entire University of Texas system enrolled in a PhD program in Government. The draft board however was still looking to get me into the military. And they did despite the fact that I had exemptions from the draft: married, had a son, and in graduate school. I had to quit my studies and report for duty.

Before I finish this quick read, let me make two important points. First, when I took my law school admissions test I did well and poorly in the Graduate Record Examination. In other words, the tests predicted I would be a good lawyer and not so good in graduate school. Not! I obtained my PhD first and loved every minute of the journey while I hated every second of law school. Second, I became a judge without a bar license before I became a lawyer. In Texas County Judges are elected and they perform both judicial functions and are the chief executive officer for county government. I was elected County Judge for Zavala County under the banner of the Raza Unida Party, a political party I founded with others in January, 1970.[2] When I returned from military training and served in the Army Reserve I re-enrolled in my PhD program. Every Tuesday at 3am I would begin the drive from Cristal to Austin for classes and return Thursday evening. By 1976 after twenty-five years of schooling I finished my studies and obtained my doctoral degree.

As the youngest Chicano County Judge in the state at age 29, I was holding court; having trials with juries, debating with licensed attorneys, prepared jury charges, and sentenced people for nearly two four-year terms. I was re-elected in 1978 but did not finish out the term. I sought the presidency of the Colegio Cesar Chavez in Mt. Angel, Oregon in 1981. I was not selected and began my career as an academic teaching at Oregon College of Education in Monmouth, Oregon.

I still wanted my law degree. I was admitted and offered a full scholarship to Willamette Law School in Salem, Oregon. Instead I returned to law school in Texas not Oregon and obtained my law degree within two years and three months from the same law school I attended in the late 1960s. I had changed a lot. I was ready for law school and they were ready for me by the 1980s. Not only was my name in history and political science books by then but also in law cases because of my activism and challenges to Anglo Saxon Common Law in courts, state and federal. Others and I acting in concert changed the law of the 1960s in Texas and across the nation under the banner of the Chicano Movement. I was admitted into the practice of law in 1989 and have combined both an academic career with the legal profession. I teach political science and practice law in multiple jurisdictions across the country from the federal Court of Claims in Washington, D.C. to various federal courts in Arizona, Oregon, and Texas as well as Texas courts, local to the Supreme Court. With a law degree I have earned more money than as an educator and made some fundamental changes in people's lives with my legal skills as their attorney.[3] I have been an Administrative Law Judge for the City of Dallas and serve on the Judicial Nominations Committee for municipal judges in that same city where I live. The members of this committee recommend to the Dallas City Council which municipal judges to appoint. With law derived money I have helped put all of my seven children through college and some of them even further into professional and graduate school. Olin, a son is also an attorney but has not taken the bar exam. Tozi, the eldest daughter is finishing her PhD in Leadership Studies. Adrian, the oldest son, has two Master's degrees. Three others have college degrees and one of these, Avina, is now talking about getting her Master's in Chicano Studies. My youngest daughter, Clavel will graduate next year with her Bachelor's degree. From reading this short article you know why I became a lawyer and a professor; you can make things happen instead of just watching or wondering what has happened.

Notes

1. See my book *The Making of a Chicano Militant: Lessons from Cristal*, Madison: University of Wisconsin Press, 1999; and, my 2005 book for a younger audience, *The Making of a Civil Rights Leader: Jose Angel Gutierrez*, Houston: Arte Publico Press for a more ample narrative on these experiences.

2. From 1970 to 1973 I was elected and served as member and President of the Board of Trustees for the Crystal City Independent School District; a mere eight years after my graduation from high school.

3. In 1997 I was the lead attorney for Chicano parents and students from the Tucson Unified School District. As part of the settlement in that federal case, CV97–18-TUC-RMB, the school district instituted Mexican American Studies the very program now under attack and banned in Arizona.

My College Experience

Onelia Garcia Lage

I always knew I'd go to college; it was an inherent part of my immigrant upbringing. In 1962 my parents left Cuba after the revolution. With a seven month old in arms, fleeing as political refugees, they left their careers, their business, their friends, their hometown, their church, their family and almost everything they ever held dear. Arriving in Miami without knowing English and no one to lend a helping hand, they quickly took comfort in their faith and their hope for a better future if not for themselves, then for me, their seven month old daughter. My mother was an elementary school teacher and my father had completed some college but did not graduate, choosing instead to stay in the family business. Thus, I grew up with the phrase from my father "what you have in your head no one can take away from you" and from my mother "women need to be educated so they can stand on their own two feet and not have to depend on anyone to support them."

Little did I know that the historic landmark, the Freedom Tower (Miami, Florida) that once was a haven for providing social services to Cuban immi-

Onelia G. Lage completed her pediatric training at Metropolitan Hospital Center's New York Medical College Program. She started her higher education at a two-year college earning an AA degree from Miami-Dade College, Florida. She is currently an associate professor of clinical pediatrician and the director of the Adolescent Community Health at the University of Miami, Leonard M Miller School of Medicine in Coral Gables, Florida. She was appointed by the governor of Florida to serve on the Florida Board of Medicine, serving as vice chair in 2009 and chair in 2010. She is the first Hispanic woman and pediatrician to serve in this distinguished position.

grants including my family, would become a part of the college that opened its doors to my future—Miami Dade Community College now Miami Dade College. In 1979 when I received my letter of acceptance along with a full tuition scholarship entitled Scholar's Grant for two years at the community college and two years at a newly opened university, economic times were not unlike those of today, very hard! The recession of the 1970s had left my father, the only breadwinner in our home, struggling to make ends meet and necessitating that he rethink our future. He had lost his small business in a dire economy and once again had to start from scratch just as he did after arriving from Cuba in 1962. One of the most salient phrases I frequently heard my father say was "a man is not measured by the number of times he falls down but by the number of times he picks himself up." This wisdom reflects the quality of resilience, an essential component of success and one commonly attributed to college students as well as many immigrants and all those who thrive in the land of opportunity. Resilience is a character trait that is important to pursue. Frequently it is so easy to become disappointed when your GPA drops or you don't get accepted in the college of your choice. Learning to pick yourself up after such setbacks and grow from your experiences will help you attain your goals more readily.

Armed with those important life lessons, grateful that I had earned my way to college and that I was able to give back to my parents who sacrificed so much for me and my education; I enrolled in Miami Dade College North campus in the pre-med track. My parents always told me that my only job was to get good grades. Even though I taught ballet classes to pay for my gas and minor expenses, my parents supported me morally and financially. I in turn brought in the A's. Many students are not as lucky as I was, and have to work several jobs to pay for college thus making it difficult to maintain their grades. Regardless, staying positive and focused is essential because in the end, sacrifice is what builds character. Men and women of character are needed in all walks of life. That, in essence, is the inconspicuous reward of a college/graduate level education. It transforms you from a caterpillar to a butterfly, more self-confident, mature, knowledgeable and of course more resilient to face whatever adversity may come.

College always brings change, growth, challenges and opportunities even when you stay at home and drive to school every day. It is a series of firsts for many. For me it would be my first time driving myself to school and the first time I would meet people from around the world as far as Africa, very unlike the homogeneous group of friends I was accustomed to in high school. On my way to school, I would pick up my cousin who was interested in the field of communications and journalism. Talk about resilience, my cousin was legally blind. I remember when she first arrived to this country. My mother in preparing me to understand the depth of her disability, would make me walk around the house with my eyes closed and had me do activities of daily living which we so often take for granted with my eyes closed. What an eye opener that was for me. In spite of her disability she was a top student who let nothing get in her way. She utilized special computers and recorders that helped with her note taking and reading. She was a living, breathing example that where there is a will there is a way! Our Community college was the school that supported her on the path to Director of Development of United Way Miami Dade, a leadership post she successfully holds today. She was and continues to be a source of inspiration to me.

The road to a college or other degree is not always clear or inspiring. As a matter of fact, it too often is wrought with doubt and frustration. For someone who had a history of being a top student and who always dreamt of becoming a pediatrician, I had my share of indecisions. Being in a serious relationship when I finished high school, made me have second thoughts about pursuing a medical career. I worried about how long it would take and if I would have enough time to spend with my future children. I worried if my future spouse would be supportive even though thus far he had been my biggest fan. Finally I worried about getting admitted to medical school and financing a high cost medical education. These were just a few of the concerns that crossed my mind on a regular basis. My father sat me down one day and reminded me to stay true to my dreams and not let fear hold me back so that I would not have regrets in the future. I went ahead and did what I often did when I was at a crossroads needing to make an important decision. I prayed for guidance. A favorite bible quote that has supported me throughout my life is "Trust in the Lord with all your heart and lean not on your own understanding; in all your ways acknowledge Him and He will direct your paths." Proverbs 3–5. Obtaining guidance from students that had been through the process already, talking to counselors, and utilizing mentors were other ways I helped shape my career goals. Thus in spite of my changing condition; I continued my pre-med track and graduated with highest honors and distinction. I made a decision with my husband and parents to pursue graduate medical education at an offshore school (Universidad Central del Este, D.R.) for both personal and financial reasons. If I had known what I know today, it is possible that I may have followed a different path to my dream of becoming a pediatrician. In the end, living in a developing country and broadening my horizon to the needs of our global community were truly a life changing experience that I am eternally grateful for.

More mundane things in a student's life are also life changing. These include getting to class every day, planning for class by reading ahead, taking notes, being honest when taking a test, studying all night, having serious discussions in class, being challenged, encouraged or discouraged by professors and many more. Discipline, hard work and dedication are pillars of excellence. Persist until you succeed, as stated by Og Mandino in his book, *The World's Greatest Salesman*, is an essential component of higher education. It is necessary to understand how you learn best and what results you get when you study using different methods. Know what works for you. For example, I found that individual studying was best for me and that most of the time group work left me feeling that I had not accomplished much. Getting a healthy dose of exercise is also important to maintain your energy and balance as well as for improving your mental focus. My passion aside from helping children and youth was dance. I was a member of a ballet company in college and thus had classes and rehearsals on an almost daily basis. Creative or athletic outlets as well as having fun are important tools for a student in order to prevent burn out. Achieving balance in your professional life is a constant struggle but a necessary one.

As I look back at my career path today, I am content and blessed. I achieved my life's purpose of becoming a pediatrician who specializes in the care of adolescent patients. As an academic faculty at the University of Miami medical school, I spend much of my time and energy mentoring young patients, pre-med students, medical students, and residents, many of whom are of low-income or underserved communities. I enjoy sharing my hard earned wisdom and hope they take advantage of my guidance. Almost 30 years after I graduated from Miami Dade College, I am still married to my high school sweetheart who continues to be a constant source of support in my career. Also, I was inducted into my Alma Mater's Alumni Hall of Fame at their 50th anniversary celebration something I never would have expected in 1979.

I am a mother of two amazing children, who have learned well what we have taught them—principally faith in God, love of family and passion for education and service. My daughter is currently a high school senior applying to top colleges in the nation and like her mom, dreams of becoming a pediatrician. My son is currently at Oxford University as a Rhodes scholar and a graduate of Harvard College. He hopes to make healthcare for the elderly everything we expect in compassion and quality for our own loved ones upon graduating from Harvard medical school in 2017.

A college/graduate education is an opportunity to rise above challenges but more importantly it is a call to serve and to give back; to help make the world better than when you received it. As my father said, it is something that no one can take from you; it is a gift that gives in perpetuity.

Part IV

College and University Directories

"Fired Up and Ready to Go."

President Barack Obama

College and University Directory—Overview

If you want to find gold, go to places where gold has been discovered! Or, if you want to buy an evening dress or a suit, you would not go to a hardware store! Once you are ready (after reading Steps 1, 2, and 3) to select colleges to apply to, this directory will point you to campuses that have been most successful with Latina or Latino students earning their college bachelorette degrees. This directory provides you with two directories (information about each college) and two lists in alphabetical order. The two directories are: (1) the top 20 community colleges across the country, which have graduated the most Latinos with either an Associate of Arts (AA) or Associate of Science (AS) degree. Almost all of those persons who earn an AA or AS degree transfer to a four-year college. (2) The second directory is of the top 50 universities across the country, which have graduated the most Latinos with either a BA or a BS degree. If you have read the other steps in the book, particularly Step 8, you will note that we have encouraged you to think about going beyond your undergraduate first degree and think about an advanced degree. So we provide you with two lists. One is the top 50 universities that graduate the most Latinos with a master's degree, and the other, the top 50 universities that graduate the most Latinos with a doctorate or a professional degree.

We share one more piece of information to encourage you to think about a master's and/or doctorate degree. As we wrote in the introduction to this book, there have been a number of studies showing that it is economically wise to get a college degree because you earn more. One of these studies is by the College Board. It found that those persons who have a master's degree earn on an average three times more than a high school graduate, and four times more if they have a terminal degree, such as a PhD or JD (College Board, 2008). Another way to look at advanced degrees is to consider the added time and cost as an investment, not an expenditure. What is the difference between the two? An investment typically provides you with a continued return. It pays you back and with more time you earn more. An expenditure is a one-time purchase, that is, you get a limited return. When you expend money for a new car, the value is limited to four or five years. After certain amount of years driving the car, you get little return when you sell it. Whereas, in an investment, when you buy a financial instrument like a bond, you earn an interest of a fixed percent as long as you own it. In addition, you get the principal, the amount you paid for it.

There are two other reasons why this directory is useful to you. First, the majority of Latinos who apply to go to college are firsts in their families to do so. Unlike other more traditional (white) groups, you do not have the same kind of access to information about applying to colleges because there are few others to talk to, such as parents or elder brothers or sisters who have gone to college before you. Second, it is less likely that college recruiters go to high schools located in communities that are predominately Latino. Because of these two conditions, you will have to be active in seeking information about applying and finding out what different colleges have to offer. This directory helps you to find meaningful information. All you need is a computer with Internet access.

Before sharing the information in the directory, let us remind you of some basic questions you need to ask yourself before you start to look at the two directory lists.

- Where do I want to start my college education? At a two- or four-year college?
- Do I want or have to stay near to family or can I move away?
- Do I prefer a large campus or a small enrollment campus?
- Does the college offer programs I'm interested in exploring as a major? For example, are they more science centered or liberal arts focused?
- How much financial aid is available or scholarships funds?
- What is the cost of attending per year?
- What percent of enrollment is Latino and what about Latino staff and faculty?
- If you are applying to a four-year institution, what are the admission criteria? For example, the lowest score on the SAT or the ACT, and lowest high school GPA to be qualified? (Remember two-year (community) colleges are open enrollment. All one needs is a high school diploma or a GED.)
- What are the deadlines for application? Where do I get the forms? Where and how do I submit them? By mail, electronically, and who sends what?

In answering these questions, for each person some questions are more important than others. For example, for some financial costs and aids may be paramount in importance. For another, staying close to family is more important. So you need to prioritize the questions. After you have prioritized the questions, collect information by talking to different persons, for example, to family members about moving away or staying close to home, to high school counselors or teachers about academic interests, or to business people in the area you are interested in, such as banking.

What kind of information will you find in the following directory? And how will it be helpful in answering some of the aforementioned questions? First, let's see what is provided, with a quick reason for its inclusion?

1. Rank order of institution by graduation success of Latinos, starting with the highest to lowest. (Reason = successfulness)

2. The actual number of bachelor degrees awarded to Latinos.

3. Name of college or university.

4. Address, general phone number. (Reason = location)

5. Web home address. (Reason = to get detailed and current information)

6. Tuition cost for attending. (Reason = financial aid help)

7. Student enrollment and Latino enrollment. (Reason = size matters and comfort level)

How will these seven items be helpful to you? Let's take them in the order given.

1, 2, and 3. Most important, who has a track record of being successful with Latinos? By success, we mean students obtaining their degrees. You want some assurance in advance that you will succeed, that is, if you apply yourself. After all, you will be investing much time (years) and money (thousands of dollars). The odds need to be as much in your favor as possible.

4. "Location, location, location." You have probably heard this expression mostly by real estate agents. You may want to go out of state or stay close to home. Where are campuses out of your state and near you? You may want to set a radius for yourself. That is, what is the farthest distance you may be willing to attend a college? Fifty miles one way, 100 miles, or 200 miles, and so forth.

5. To learn specific information to questions such as admission requirements, deadlines to meet, forms to fill out, and where to submit information for each institution you are interested in, you will need to look up the college's

website. Each college or university keeps its website up-to-date and provides you with more information than you need. By getting online, you can take a virtual tour, see photos of the campus, read about activities, news announcements, and so forth.

6. Regrettably, the cost of a higher education continues to increase almost annually. Now at least half of the college students graduate with a debt. Students and/or their families have to take loans. But don't let the debt factor keep you away from going to college. As we have discussed, after college you will earn more money over your lifetime than if you don't go. You will be able to pay off your student debt after a few short years. But you definitely should know what the cost of attending is and what institutional financial aids exist.

7. You have probably heard these two phrases: "The bigger the better" and "The more the merrier." Student enrollment indicates class sizes. That is, the greater the student body is in enrollment generally means that class sizes will be larger. If you want to be in small classes so you get to know your professors and vice versa, then big is not better. Most of us want to fit in. It means we want to be among our own kind, that is, people who know our traditions and culture. So we provide the percent of Latino students' enrollment. After all, college is not only about studying; it is about developing a social life, making friends for life, and a precursor to a professional network. In short, the more the merrier means your comfort level will likely be higher.

After collecting information from the directory, create a short list for yourself. You should have identified three or four colleges that fit your criteria and you would like to apply for admission. If any one of the colleges on your list is within a visit, you should go and take in a scheduled campus tour. Almost every college has tours set up for prospective students. Take a friend with you or a family member. This will afford you the opportunity to get a feel of the college, visit with students, ask questions to staff, see the facilities, pick up additional literature not given on the website, and so forth. Most importantly, ask about and talk with staff about any special or targeted programs for Latinos on campus. Also inquire about projects that might get you involved with the local Latino communities.

If you are applying to a four-year college, any one university will probably become your first choice. But don't apply to just one! Apply to two or three because of the competition. That is, a majority of universities get more student applications than the number they can admit in a freshman class. Many students meet the universities' admission criteria, but because of the large number of applications, universities have to turn students away.

Secondly, when applying you will note that universities have admission fees. If paying that admission fee is a hardship for you or your parents, ask for a fee waiver. Also, if this is the case, you should apply for financial aid simultaneously.

In closing, there are two last points to make. The first is the rank order of the top 50 colleges and top 20 community colleges. This rank order was taken from the *Hispanic Outlook in Higher Education* magazine. While this book is being published in 2012, the latest data are from 2010. However, the ranking of each institution changes only slightly over the years. If you want more current data, you can get a recent copy of the *Hispanic Outlook* and get the rankings. The magazine usually publishes its rankings in the fall of each year. Secondly, while the directory and lists are from across the country, you will note that the majority of the top 50 universities and top 20 colleges are located in California, Texas, New York, and Florida. The primary reason for this status is that these five states have 62 percent of the Latino population in the United States. If you include four more states (Illinois, Arizona, New Jersey, and Colorado), then these eight states combined have 75 percent of all Latinos in the United States.

Helpful Notes about Directory Information

Now that we are in the age of high technology and quick information access, it is strongly recommended that once you have identified a two-year college, a four-year university, a master's program, or a doctoral degree you are interested in, and want to gain more information about that, you should look up the institutional electronic website, more commonly referred to as its home page. In the two directories (top 20 community colleges and top 50 universities), we have listed the home website addresses for you. However, for the top 50 master's and top 50 doctors, you need to do the following. Type in the name of the institution on a search engine; currently Goggle and Bing are the two most commonly used search engines. Once you have the website address, simply type it in and you have immediate access to the most current and most comprehensive information possible about the institutions.

Secondly, information changes with time. One thing that also changes is the cost of attending a college. Each year the cost of courses offered to students typically go up. Admission requirements may change, or the way an institution wants you to apply, or the dates for applying change with each new calendar year. Therefore, the information in the directory about tuition and fees, enrollment numbers, percent of students by race and ethnicity, and degrees granted change with each year. The information provided in the following directory is to give you a general overview of institutions that match up well with Latinos. So the information is a good indicator of what to expect, but by the time you read it, it may be outdated. Therefore, once you identify an institution of interest, go to its website to find the most up-to-date information.

Third, a special note about tuition and fees listed in the directory. The amounts given are not commonly calculated in the same way by institutions. By this we mean, some institutions only provide costs on a semester basis, others on an annual basis, still others on a quarterly basis. Some only list tuition without fees, others include books and supplies, plus transportation and on-campus dorm cost. So what you see in the tuition and fees part are no longer accurate not only because of datedness but also because of the method used to calculate the cost. Remember there is stated cost and real cost to go to college. See Chapter 3 for more information.

Fourth, almost every home page of a university has a tab called "prospectus student." If you place the pointer to this tab, it will probably have a drop-down menu or list of items on the side you can click on. Typically, the information provided is application progress, dates to apply, cost and financial-aid information, contact information for you to ask questions, and so forth. Consequently, all of these reasons indicate that you should use the directory information only as a guide and starting point.

Sources

Hispanic Outlook in Higher Education 21, no. 2 (March 21, 2011). Also, see *Hispanic Outlook in Higher Education*, May 5, 2011 issue.

The College Board (2008). Write-up by Martin Wolk, www.lifeinc.today.msnbc.msn.com/2011/11/17/886.

Top 20 Two-Year or Community Colleges (Best Degree Completion, 2009 Data)

1
Associate Degrees Awarded to Latinos = 1,792
Name: El Paso Community College
Address: 9050 Vicount Blvd., El Paso, TX 79925. Phone: (915) 831-3722
Web address: www. epcc.edu
Tuition and fees, Full time (Fall '11)

   In-state $834/semester

   Nonresident $1,110/semester

Enrollment = 29,681

Latino	84%
Black	2.1%
White	7.3%

2
Associate Degrees Awarded to Latinos = 1,127
Name: Valencia Community College
Address: 8600 Valencia College Lane, Orlando, FL 32825.
Phone: (407) 299-5000
Web address: www.valenciacollege.edu
Tuition and fees, Full time (Fall '11)

In-state $1,188/semester
Nonresident $4,500/semester

Enrollment = 39,000

Latino	38%
Black	23.6%
White	56%

3

Associate Degrees Awarded to Latinos = 868
Name: Mt. San Antonio College
Address: 1100 N. Grand Ave., Walnut, CA 91789. Phone: (909) 274-7500
Web address: www.mtsac.edu
Tuition and fees, Full time (Fall '11)

In-state	$432/semester
Nonresident	$2,568

Enrollment = 58,615

Latino	44.5%
Black	6%
White	17.7%

4

Associate Degrees Awarded to Latinos = 846
Name: Riverside Community College
Address: 4800 Magnolia Ave., Riverside, CA 92506. Phone: (951) 222-8000
Web address: www.rcc.edu
Tuition and fees, Full time (Fall '11)

In-state	$432/semester
Nonresident	$2,544/semester

Enrollment = 19,000+

Latino	35%
Black	11%
White	35%

5

Associate Degrees Awarded to Latinos = 790
Name: Texas Southmost College
Address: 80 Ft. Brown, Brownsville, TX 78520
Web address: www.utb.edu
Tuition and fees, Full time (Fall '11)

In-state	$2,412/year
Nonresident	$6,768/year

Enrollment = 11,500

Latino	92%
Black	0.4%
White	3%

6

Associate Degrees Awarded to Latinos = 769
Name: East Los Angeles College
Address: 1301 Avenida Cesar Chavez, Monterey Park, CA 91754.
Phone: (323) 265-8650
Web address: www.elac.edu
Tuition and fees, Full time (Fall '11)

In-state	$312/semester
Nonresident	$2,160/semester

Enrollment = 57,340

Latino	64%
Black	3%
White	35%

7

Associate Degrees Awarded to Latinos = 695
Name: Southwestern College
Address: 900 Otay Lakes Rd. Chula Vista, CA 91910.
Phone: (619) 421-6700
Web address: www.swccd.edu
Tuition and fees, Full time (Fall '11)

In-state	$772/year
Nonresident	$6,048/year

Enrollment = 20,000+

Latino	Data not listed on their web page
Black	Data not listed.
White	Data not listed.

8

Associate Degrees Awarded to Latinos = 652
Name: Santa Ana College
Address: 1530 West 17th street, Santa Ana, CA 92706.
Phone: (714) 564-6000
Web address: www.sac.edu
Tuition and fees, Full time (Fall '11)

In-state	$4,920/year
Nonresident	No data

Enrollment = 40,000+

Latino	57%
Black	2%
White	17%

9

Associate Degrees Awarded to Latinos = 648
Name: Houston Community College
Address: 3100 Main St., Houston, TX 77002. Phone: (713) 718-2000
Web address: www.hccs.edu
Tuition and fees, Full time (Fall '11)

In-state	$804/semester
Nonresident	$1,860/semester

Enrollment = 60,000

Latino	34%
Black	31%
White	18%

10
Associate Degrees Awarded to Latinos = 632
Name: CUNY/Borough of Manhattan Community College
Address: 199 Chambers St. New York, NY 10007. Phone: (212) 220-8000
Web address: www.bmcc.cuny.edu
Tuition and fees, Full time (Fall '11)

In-state	$1,800/semester
Nonresident	$2,880/semester

Enrollment = 21,000

Latino	34.7%
Black	35.7%
White	15.1%

11
Associate Degrees Awarded to Latinos = 612
Name: Pima Community College
Address: 4905 E. Broadway Blvd., Tucson, AZ 85709.
Phone: (520) 206-4500
Web address: www.pima.edu
Tuition and fees, Full time (Fall '11)

In-state	$702/semester
Nonresident	$3,528/semester

Enrollment = 13,700

Latino	33.7%
Black	3.7%
White	40.4%

12
Associate Degrees Awarded to Latinos = 600
Name: Laredo Community College
Address Westend Washington St., Laredo, TX 78040.
Phone: (956) 722-0521
Web address: www.laredo.edu
Tuition and fees, Full time (Fall '11)

| In-state | $1,158/semester |
| Nonresident | $1,662/semester |

Enrollment = 10,000

Latino	78.6%
Black	0.14%
White	1.4%

13

Associate Degrees Awarded to Latinos = 573
Name: San Jacinto Community College
Address: 5800 Uvalde Rd., Houston, TX 77049. Phone: (281) 458-4050
Web address: www.sanjac.edu
Tuition and fees, Full time (Fall '11)

| In-state | $743/semester |
| Nonresident | $1,943/semester |

Enrollment = 7,000

Latino	46.6%
Black	17.8%
White	1.5%

14

Associate Degrees Awarded to Latinos = 567
Name: Lone Star College System
Address: 5000 research Forest Dr., Woodlands, TX 77381.
Phone: (832) 813-6500
Web address: www.lonestar.edu
Tuition ONLY, Full time (Fall '11)

| In-state | $1,544/semester |
| Nonresident | $1,724/semester |

Enrollment = 69,000

Latino	Data not posted on web page.
Black	Data not posted.
White	Data not found.

15

Associate Degrees Awarded to Latinos = 561
Name: Del Mar College
Address: 101 Balwin Blvd., Corpus Christi, TX 78404.
Phone: (361) 698-1200
Web address: www.delmar.edu
Tuition and fees, Full time (Fall '11)

In-state	$1,695/semester
Nonresident	$2,139/semester

Enrollment = 22,000

Latino	59.3%
Black	3%
White	31.4%

16

Associate Degrees Awarded to Latinos = 538
Name: Central New Mexico Community College
Address: 525 Buena Vista Dr., SE Albuquerque, NM 87106
Web address: www.cnm.edu
Tuition and fees, Full time (Fall '11)

In-state	$579/semester
Nonresident	$3,008/semester

Enrollment = 29,000

Latino	43%
Black	3.7%
White	37%

17

Associate Degrees Awarded to Latinos = 529
Name: Rio Hondo College
Address: 3600 Workman Mill Rd., Whittier, CA 90601.
Phone: (562) 692-0921
Web address: www.riohondo.edu
Tuition ONLY, Full time (Fall '11)

| In-state | $1,068/year |
| Nonresident | $5,316/year |

Enrollment = 25,000

Latino	67%
Black	2%
White	8%

18
Associate Degrees Awarded to Latinos = 523
Name: Chaffey College
Address: 5885 Haven Ave., Rancho Cucamonga, CA 91737-3002.
Phone: (909) 652-6000
Web address: www.chaffey.edu
Tuition and fees, Full time (Fall '11)

| In-state | $7,562/year |
| Nonresident | no data |

Enrollment = 19,000

Latino	47.5%
Black	10.8%
White	2.7%

19
Associate Degrees Awarded to Latinos = 523
Name: Fresno City College
Address: 1101 E. University Ave., Fresno, CA 93741
Web address: www.fresnocitycollege.edu
Tuition and fees, Full time (Fall '11)

| In-state | $4,317/semester |
| Nonresident | no data |

Enrollment = 25,000

Latino	42%
Black	8%
White	25%

20
Associate Degrees Awarded to Latinos = 511
Name: Cerritos College
Address: 11110 Alondra Blvd., Norwalk, CA 90650. Phone: (562) 860-2451
Web address: www.cerritos.edu
Tuition and fees, Full time (Fall '11)

In-state	$493/semester
Nonresident	no data

Enrollment = 24,355

Latino	55%
Black	7%
White	11.5%

Information source for all tables: Ranking, number of degrees awarded to Latinos and name of community college taken from *Hispanic Outlook in Higher Education Magazine* 21, no. 2 (March 21, 2011). All other information provided for each institution is taken from their respective websites.

Top 50 Universities (by Number of Degrees Awarded)

 # 1
Bachelor's Awarded to Latinos = 3,918
Name: Florida International University
Address: 11200 S.W. 8th Street, Miami, FL 33199. Phone: (305) 348-2000
Web address: www.fiu.edu
Tuition and fees, Full time (Fall '11)

In-state	$5,678
Out of state	$18,077

Undergraduate enrollment = 44,500

Latino	61%
Black	13%
White	15%

 # 2
Bachelor's Awarded to Latinos = 2,382
Name: University of Texas El Paso
Address: 500 W. University Ave., El Paso, TX 79968.
Phone: (915) 747-5000
Web address: www.utep.edu
Tuition and fees, Full time (Fall '11)

| In-state | $14,056 |
| Out of state | $21,496 |

Undergraduate enrollment = 18,160

Latino	76%
Black	2.8%
White	9.9%

Directory: Top 50 Universities

3

Bachelor's Awarded to Latinos = 2,360
Name: University of Texas Pan American
Address: 1201 W. University Dr., Edinburg, TX 78539.
Phone: (866) 441-utpa
Web address: www.utpa.edu
Tuition and fees, Full time (Fall '11)

| In-state | $15,367 |
| Out of state | $24,757 |

Undergraduate enrollment = 16,266

Latino	90%
Black	1%
White	4%

4

Bachelor's Awarded to Latinos = 1,779
Name: University of Texas San Antonio
Address: One UTSA Circle, San Antonio, TX 78244.
Phone: (210) 458-4011
Web address: www.utsa.edu
Tuition and fees, Full time (Fall '11)

| In-state | $4,761 |
| Out of state | $10,395 |

Total enrollment = 30,300

Latino	Data not posted on web page.
Black	Data not found.
White	Data not found.

Directory: Top 50 Universities

5
Bachelor's Awarded to Latinos = 1,680
Name: California State University Fullerton
Address: 800 N. State Street, Fullerton, CA 92831-3599.
Phone: (657) 278-2011
Web address: www.fullerton.edu
Tuition and fees, Full time (Fall '11)

In-state	$3,064/semester
Out of state	$8,644/semester

Undergraduate enrollment = 36,156

Latino	32%
Black	3%
White	30%

6
Bachelor's Awarded to Latinos = 1,651
Name: Arizona State University
Address: University Drive, Tempe, AZ 85287. Phone: (480) 965-9011
Web address: www.asu.edu
Tuition and fees, Full time (Fall '11)

In-state	$9,720
Out of state	$22,319

Undergraduate enrollment = 58,404

Latino	18.7%
Black	5.2%
White	61%

Directory: Top 50 Universities

7
Bachelor's Awarded to Latinos = 1,464
Name: San Diego State University
Address: 5500 Campanile Dr., San Diego, CA 92182.
Phone: (619) 594-5200

Web address: www.sdsu.edu
Tuition and fees, Full time (Fall '11)

In-state	$3,289
Out of state	no data

Undergraduate enrollment = 25,741

Latino	28.6%
Black	3.9%
White	40.3%

8

Bachelor's Awarded to Latinos = 1,438
Name: The University of Texas at Austin
Address: 1 University Station, Austin, TX 78712. Phone: (512) 471-3434
Web address: www.utexas.edu
Tuition and fees, Full time (Fall '11)

In-state	$9,418/semester
Out of state	$11,742/semester

Undergraduate enrollment = 40,000+

Latino	24%
Black	4%
White	51%

Directory: Top 50 Universities

9

Bachelor's Awarded to Latinos = 1,384
Name: University of Florida
Address: Gainesville, FL 32611. Phone: (352) 392-3261
Web address: www.ufl.edu
Tuition and fees, Full time (Fall '11)

In-state	$4,134/semester
Out of state	$16,704

Undergraduate enrollment = 50,000+

Latino	Data not posted on web page.
Black	Data not found.
White	Data not found.

10
Bachelor's Awarded to Latinos = 1,356
Name: California State University Long Beach
Address: 1250 Bellflower Blvd., Long Beach, CA 90840.
Phone: (562) 985-4111
Web address: www.csulb.edu
Tuition and fees, Full time (Fall '11)

| In-state | $6,240/two semesters |
| Out of state | $15,168/two semesters |

Undergraduate enrollment = 33,000

Latino	29%
Black	4.7%
White	27%

Directory: Top 50 Universities

11
Bachelor's Awarded to Latinos = 1,348
Name: California State University Northridge
Address: 18111 Nordhoff Street, Northridge, CA 91330.
Phone: (818) 677-1200
Web address: www.csun.edu
Tuition and fees, Full time (Fall '11)

| In-state | $3,244/semester |
| Out of state | $8,824/semester |

Undergraduate enrollment = 36,000

Latino	29%
Black	9%
White	30%

12
Bachelor's Awarded to Latinos = 1,296
Name: University of Central Florida
Address: 4000 Central Florida Blvd., Orlando, FL 32816.
Phone: (407) 823-2000
Web address: www.ucf.edu
Tuition and fees, Full time (Fall '11)

In-state	$5,296 for two semesters
Out of state	$11,160 for two semesters

Undergraduate enrollment = 47, 300+

Latino	12%
Black	8%
White	68%

Directory: Top 50 Universities

13
Bachelor's Awarded to Latinos = 1,109
Name: University of New Mexico, Main
Address: Albuquerque, NM 87131. Phone: (505) 277-0111
Web address: www.unm.edu
Tuition and fees, Full time (Fall '11)

In-state	$2,752 per semester
Out of state	$9,345 per semester

Undergraduate enrollment = 34,674

Latino	33%
Black	3%
White	41%

14
Bachelor's Awarded to Latinos = 1,098
Name: Texas State University
Address: 601 University Dr., Sn Marcos, TX 78666. Phone: (512) 245-2111
Web address: www.txstate.edu

Tuition and fees, Full time (Fall '11)

In-state	$19,814
Out of state	$29,640

Undergraduate enrollment = 22,331

Latino	26%
Black	6%
White	62%

Directory: Top 50 Universities

15
Bachelor's Awarded to Latinos = 1,076
Name: University of Houston
Address: 4800 Calhoun Rd. Houston, Texas 77004. Phone: (713) 743-2255
Web address: www.uh.edu
Tuition and fees, Full time (Fall '11)

In-state	$9,211/year
Out of state	$24,713/year

Undergraduate enrollment = 29,378

Latino	22.3%
Black	12.6%
White	34.1%

16
Bachelor's Awarded to Latinos = 1,059
Name: California State University Los Angeles
Address: 5151 State University Dr., Los Angeles, CA 90032-8580.
Phone: (323) 343-3000
Web address: www.calstatela.edu
Tuition and fees, Full time (Fall '11)

In-state	$19,609/year
Out of state	$28,120/year

Undergraduate enrollment = 13,250

Latino	51%
Black	6%
White	9%

Directory: Top 50 Universities

17
Bachelor's Awarded to Latinos = 1,031
Name: Texas A&M
Address: College Station, Texas 77843
Web address: www.tamu.edu
Tuition and fees, Full time (Fall '11)

In-state	$4,209/semester
Out of state	$8,904/semester

Undergraduate enrollment = 41,500

Latino	15.9%
Black	3.3%
White	72.4%

18
Bachelor's Awarded to Latinos = 992
Name: University of California Los Angeles
Address: Los Angeles, CA 90095. Phone: (310) 825-1091
Web address: www.ucla.edu
Tuition and fees, Full time (Fall '11)

In-state	$13,910/semester
Out of state	$36,788/semester

Undergraduate enrollment = 25,924

Latino	15.9%
Black	4.1%
White	32.6%

Directory: Top 50 Universities

19

Bachelor's Awarded to Latinos = 973
Name: California State University Fresno
Address: 5241 N. Maple Ave., Fresno, CA 93740. Phone: (559) 278-4240
Web address: www.csufresno.edu
Tuition and fees, Full time (Fall '11)

In-state	$3,131/semester
Out of state	$8,711/semester

Undergraduate enrollment = 21,500

Latino	36.1%
Black	5%
White	32.6%

20

Bachelor's Awarded to Latinos = 963
Name: University of Texas Brownsville
Address: 80 Ft. Brown, Brownsville, TX 78720. Phone: (956) 882-8277
Web address: www.utb.edu
Tuition and fees, Full time (Fall '11)

In-state	$2,997/semester
Out of state	$7,692/semester

Undergraduate enrollment = 15,230

Latino	92%
Black	0.4%
White	3%

Directory: Top 50 Universities

21

Bachelor's Awarded to Latinos = 938
Name: University of California Santa Barbara
Address: 552 University Rd., Santa Barbara, CA 93106.
Phone: (805) 893-8000

Web address: www.ucsb.edu
Tuition and fees, Full time (Fall '11)

In-state	$13,595/year
Out of state	$36,473/year

Undergraduate enrollment = 19,180

Latino	23%
Black	4%
White	48%

22

Bachelor's Awarded to Latinos = 925
Name: University of Arizona
Address: 1010 N. Highland, Tucson, AZ 85721.
Phone: (520) 621-7211
Web address: www.arizona.edu
Tuition and fees, Full time (Fall '11)

In-state	$4,650/semester
Out of state	$12,754/semester

Undergraduate enrollment = 29,719

Latino	30%
Black	2%
White	64%

Directory: Top 50 Universities

23

Bachelor's Awarded to Latinos = 911
Name: New Mexico State University
Address: Las Cruces, NM 88003. Phone: (575) 646-4111
Web address: www.nmsu.edu
Tuition and fees, Full time (Fall '11)

In-state	$2,400/semester
Out of state	$3,529/semester

Undergraduate enrollment = 18,552

Latino	44%
Black	3%
White	47%

24

Bachelor's Awarded to Latinos = 903
Name: California State University San Bernardino
Address: 5500 University Parkway, San Bernardino, CA 92407-2393.
Phone: (909) 537-2393
Web address: www.csusb.edu
Tuition and fees, Full time (Fall '11)

| In-state | $6,453/year |
| Out of state | $17,613/year |

Undergraduate enrollment = 17,852

Latino	40%
Black	11%
White	28%

Directory: Top 50 Universities

25

Bachelor's Awarded to Latinos = 893
Name: Florida State University
Address: 222 S. Copeland Street, Tallahassee, FL 32306.
Phone: (850) 644-2625
Web address: www.fsu.edu
Tuition and fees, Full time (Fall '11)

| In-state | $19,354/year |
| Out of state | $35,344/year |

Undergraduate enrollment = 31,036

Latino—All minorities equal 27.7%	
Black	
White	72.3%

26

Bachelor's Awarded to Latinos = 848
Name: San Francisco State University
Address: 1600 Holloway Ave., San Francisco, CA 94132.
Phone: (415) 338-1111
Web address: www.sfsu.edu
Tuition and fees, Full time (Fall '11)

In-state	$6,276/year
Out of state	$17,436/year

Undergraduate enrollment = 25,000

Latino	22.5%
Black	5.9%
White	33.7%

Directory: Top 50 Universities

27

Bachelor's Awarded to Latinos = 831
Name: Florida Atlantic University
Address: 777 Glades Rd., Boca Raton, FL 38431-6496.
Phone: (561) 292-3000
Web address: www.fau.edu
Tuition and fees, Full time (Fall '11)

In-state	$20,922/year
Out of state	$34,889/year

Undergraduate enrollment = 21,268

Latino	21%
Black	18%
White	52%

28

Bachelor's Awarded to Latinos = 830
Name: San Jose State University
Address: One Washington Sq., San Jose CA 95192. Phone: (408) 924-1000
Web address: www.SJSU.edu

Tuition and fees, Full time (Fall '11)

| In-state | $2,790/semester |
| Out of state | $5,580/semester |

Undergraduate enrollment = 26,796

Latino	22%
Black	4%
White	27%

Directory: Top 50 Universities

 # 29
Bachelor's Awarded to Latinos = 829
Name: University of South Florida-main
Address: 4202 E. Flowler Ave., Tampa, FL 33620. Phone: (813) 974-2011
Web address: www.usf.edu
Tuition ONLY, Full time (Fall '11)

| In-state | $2,865/semester |
| Out of state | $7,455/semester |

Undergraduate enrollment = 13,610

Latino	17.1%
Black	11.1%
White	60.8%

 # 30
Bachelor's Awarded to Latinos = 825
Name: California State Polytechnic University
Address: 3801 West Temple Ave., Pomona, CA 91768-2557.
Phone: (909) 869-7659
Web address: www.csupomona.edu
Tuition and fees, Full time (Fall '11)

| In-state | $18,600/year |
| Out of state | $22,920 |

Undergraduate enrollment = 20,000

Latino	Data not posted on web page.
Black	Data not found.
White	Data not found.

Directory: Top 50 Universities

 # 31
Bachelor's Awarded to Latinos = 796
Name: University of North Texas
Address: 1155Union Circle, Denton, TX 76201. Phone: (940) 565-2000
Web address: www.unt.edu
Tuition and fees, Full time (Fall '11)

| In-state | $3,653/semester |
| Out of state | $7,373/semester |

Total enrollment = 35,000

Latino	Data not found on web page.
Black	Data not found.
White	Data not found.

 # 32
Bachelor's Awarded to Latinos = 795
Name: University of California, Riverside
Address: 950 University Ave., Riverside, CA 92521. Phone: (951) 827-1012
Web address: www.ucr.edu
Tuition and fees, Full time (Fall '11)

| In-state | $4,535/ quarter |
| Out of state | $12,161/quarter |

Undergraduate enrollment = 18,242

Latino	28.9%
Black	7.9%
White	17%

Directory: Top 50 Universities

33
Bachelor's Awarded to Latinos = 793
Name: Texas A&M, Kingsville
Address: 700 University Blvd., Kingsville, TX 78363-8202.
Phone: (361) 593-3907
Web address: www.tamuk.edu
Tuition and fees, Full time (Fall '11)

In-state	$3,320/semester
Out of state	$8,015/semester

Undergraduate enrollment = 5,100

Latino	62%
Black	5%
White	27%

34
Bachelor's Awarded to Latinos = 782
Name: University of California, Berkeley
Address: Berkeley, CA 94720. Phone: (510) 642-6000
Web address: www.berkeley.edu
Tuition and fees, Full time (Fall '11)

In-state	$32,634/year
Out of state	$55,512/year

Undergraduate enrollment = 36,000

Latino	10.4%
Black	3%
White	33%

Directory: Top 50 Universities

35
Bachelor's Awarded to Latinos = 756
Name: Texas A&M International

Address: 5201 University Blvd., Laredo, Texas 78041 (956) 326-2235
Web address: www.tamiu.edu
Tuition and fees, Full time (Fall '11)

In-state	$3,279/semester
Out of state	$7,974/semester

Total enrollment = 7000

Latino	Data not posted on web page.
Black	Data not found.
White	Data not found.

36

Bachelor's Awarded to Latinos = 745
Name: University of Houston, Downtown
Address: One Main Street, Houston, TX 77002. Phone: (713) 221-8000
Web address: www.uhd.edu
Tuition and fees, Full time (Fall '11)

In-state	$4,604/year
Out of state	$12,044/year

Undergraduate enrollment = 7,891

Latino	40.1%
Black	32.2%
White	18.2%

Directory: Top 50 Universities

37

Bachelor's Awarded to Latinos = 742
Name: CUNY-Lehman College
Address: 2450 Bedford Park Blvd., Bronx, NY 10468.
Phone: (718) 360-8000
Web address: www.lehman.edu
Tuition ONLY, Full time (Fall '11)

In-state	$3,840/semester
Out of state	$8,160/semester

Undergraduate enrollment = 9,841

Latino	51.4%
Black	29.4%
White	10.5%

38
Bachelor's Awarded to Latinos = 704
Name: University of California, Davis
Address: 1 Shields Ave., Davis, CA 95616. Phone: (530) 752-1011
Web address: www.ucdavis.edu
Tuition and fees, Full time (Fall '11)

In-state	$13,079/year
Out of state	$35,958/year

Undergraduate enrollment = 24,737

Latino	11.3%
Black	3%
White	34.5%

Directory: Top 50 Universities

39
Bachelor's Awarded to Latinos = 687
Name: University of Texas Arlington
Address: 701 South Nedderman Dr., Arlington, TX 76019.
Phone: (817) 272-2011
Web address: www.uta.edu
Tuition and fees, Full time (Fall '11)

In-state	$8,500/year
Out of state	$16,560/year

Undergraduate enrollment = 25,106

Latino	16.9%
Black	14.1%
White	49.9%

 # 40

Bachelor's Awarded to Latinos = 677

Name: University of California, Irvine

Address: Irvine, CA 92697. Phone: (949) 824-5011

Web address: www.uci.edu

Tuition and fees, Full time (Fall '11)

In-state	$13,970/year
Out of state	$36,848/year

Undergraduate enrollment = 27,000

Latino	Data not posted on web page.
Black	Data not found.
White	Data not found.

Directory: Top 50 Universities

 # 41

Bachelor's Awarded to Latinos = 670

Name: University of Miami

Address: Coral Gables, FL 33124. Phone: (305) 284-2211

Web address: www.miami.edu

Tuition and fees, Full time (Fall '11)

In-state	$38,440/year
Out of state	Amount not provided on web page.

Undergraduate enrollment = 16,068

Latino	24%
Black	7%
White	53%

 # 42

Bachelor's Awarded to Latinos = 650

Name: California State University, Sacramento

Address: 6000 J Street, Sacramento, CA 95819. Phone: (916) 278-6011

Web address: www.csus.edu

Tuition and fees, Full time (Fall '11)

In-state	$3,286
Out of state	$8,866

Undergraduate enrollment = 25,900

Latino	16%
Black	7%
White	43%

Directory: Top 50 Universities

 # 43
Bachelor's Awarded to Latinos = 619
Name: California State University San Diego
Address: 5500 Campanile Dr., San Diego, CA 92182.
Phone: (619) 594-5200
Web address: www.sdsu.edu
Tuition and fees, Full time (Fall '11)

In-state	$23,820/year
Out of state	$34,456/year

Undergraduate enrollment = 27,741

Latino	26%
Black	3.5%
White	37.1%

 # 44
Bachelor's Awarded to Latinos = 594
Name: CUNY-John Jay College Criminal Justice
Address: 899 Tenth Ave., Manhattan, NY 10019.
Phone: (212) 237-8000
Web address: www.jjay.cuny.edu
Tuition and fees, Full time (Fall '11)

In-state	$2,565/semester
Out of state	$9,465/semester

Undergraduate enrollment = 15,206

Latino Only information provided is that 64% of underrepresented groups make up student enrollment.

Black

White

Directory: Top 50 Universities

 # 45

Bachelor's Awarded to Latinos = 561

Name: University of Incarnate Word

Address: 4301 Broadway, San Antonio, Texas 78209-6318.

Phone: (210) 829-6000

Web address: www.uiw.edu

Tuition only, Full time (Fall '11)

In-state	$10,950/semester
Out of state	no data

Undergraduate enrollment = 5,460

Latino	56.9%
Black	7%
White	21.9%

 # 46

Bachelor's Awarded to Latinos = 553

Name: University of Southern California

Address: Los Angeles, CA 90089. Phone: (213) 740-2311

Web address: www.usc.edu

Tuition and fees, Full time (Fall '11)

In-state	$42,818/year
Out of state	no data

Undergraduate enrollment = 17,500

Latino	13.6%
Black	4.4%
White	43%

Directory: Top 50 Universities

 # 47

Bachelor's Awarded to Latinos = 538
Name: Texas A&M Corpus Christi
Address: 6300 Ocean Dr., Corpus Christi, TX 78412.
Phone: (361) 825-5700
Web address: www.tamucc.edu
Tuition and fees, Full time (Fall '11)

In state	$3,559/semester
Out of state	$8,664/semester

Undergraduate enrollment = 10,000

Latino	39%
Black	5.1%
White	46%

 # 48

Bachelor's Awarded to Latinos = 532
Name: Montclair State University
Address: 1 Normal Ave., Upper Montclair, NJ 07043.
Phone: (973) 655-4000
Web address: www.montclair.edu
Tuition and fees, Full time (Fall '11)

In-state	$10,502
Out of state	$19,078

Undergraduate enrollment = 14,383

Latino	23%
Black	10%
White	56%

Directory: Top 50 Universities

 # 49

Bachelor's Awarded to Latinos = 522

Name: University of California Santa Cruz
Address: 552 University Rd., Santa Cruz, CA 93106. Phone: (805) 893-8000
Web address: www.ucsb.edu
Tuition and fees, Full time (Fall '11)

In-state	$4,064/semester
Out of state	$12,157/semester

Undergraduate enrollment = 18,807

Latino	23%
Black	3%
White	47%

50
Bachelor's Awarded to Latinos = 504
Name: Texas Tech University
Address: 2500 Broadway, Lubbock, TX 79409. Phone: (806) 742-2011
Web address: www.ttu.edu
Tuition and fees, Full time (Fall '11)

In-state	$22,437/year
Out of state	$31,827/year

Undergraduate enrollment = 30,000

Latino	13.4%
Black	4.3%
White	71.4%

Information Source for all tables: Rankings, number of degrees awarded to Latinos, and university name taken from *Hispanic Outlook in Higher Education* 21, no. 15 (May 2, 2011). All other information provide for each university is taken from their respective websites.

Top 50 Universities in United States That Granted the Largest Number of Master's Degrees to Latinos

Rank	University	Master's Awarded	Total	Latinos or Latinas	Percent
1	Florida International, Florida	1,014	370	644	43%
2	Nova Southeastern, Florida	798	255	543	19%
3	University of Texas, Pan American, Texas	511	156	355	78%
4	University of Texas, El Paso, Texas	506	182	324	57%
5	National University, California	491	146	345	14%
6	University of Southern California	467	184	283	10%
7	California State University, Los Angeles	375	118	256	28%
8	Lamar University, Texas	352	84	268	12%
9	Arizona State University	351	117	234	9%
10	California State University, Long Beach	343	112	231	19%
11	University of Texas San Antonio	332	117	215	38%

(Continued)

(Continued)

Rank	University	Master's Awarded	Total	Latinos or Latinas	Percent
12	California State University, Northridge	306	92	214	18%
13	New York University, New York	306	91	215	5%
14	University of Florida, Florida	295	139	156	8%
15	Azusa Pacific University, California	274	78	196	22%
16	Touro College, New York	267	46	221	10%
17	Columbia University, City of New York	266	112	154	4%
18	University of La Verne, California	264	56	209	27%
19	University of California, Los Angeles	264	98	166	10%
20	San Jose State University, California	252	65	187	9%
21	Texas A&M at Commerce	249	136	113	25%
22	University of Texas at Austin	249	106	143	9%
23	University of Miami, Florida	225	99	126	27%
24	University of New Mexico, Main	225	85	140	22%
25	San Diego State University, California	224	89	135	12%
26	University of South Florida, Main	224	75	149	10%
27	Barry University, Florida	221	52	169	26%
28	Northern Arizona University	216	54	162	13%

(Continued)

(Continued)

Rank	University	Master's Awarded	Total	Latinos or Latinas	Percent
29	New Mexico State University	215	70	145	27%
30	Texas State University, San Marcos	210	63	147	17%
31	Mercy College, New York	205	29	176	16%
32	California State University, Fullerton	203	58	145	15%
33	Texas A&M International University	194	57	137	61%
34	California State University, San Bernardino	190	57	133	24%
35	CUNY/Lehman College	188	45	143	22%
36	California State University at Dominguez Hills	188	51	137	22%
37	Texas A&M University Kingsville	186	57	129	38%
38	California State University, Fresno	186	51	135	21%
39	University of Central Florida	178	76	102	9%
40	New Mexico Highlands University	173	41	132	48%
41	Loyola Marymount University, California	162	49	113	23%
42	Harvard University, Massachusetts	159	75	84	4%
43	Our Lady of the Lake Univ. San Antonio	158	44	114	52%
44	Florida Atlantic University, Florida	158	56	102	13%
45	CUNY/Hunter College, New York	158	31	99	10%
46	University of North Texas, Texas	156	57	99	9%

(Continued)

(Continued)

Rank	University	Master's Awarded	Total	Latinos or Latinas	Percent
47	University of Texas, Brownsville	151	40	111	75%
48	University of Houston, Texas	151	62	89	9%
49	CUNY/ City College, New York	150	44	109	15%
50	George Washington University, DC	150	63	87	4%

Source

Hispanic Outlook in Higher Education, 21, no. 15 (May 2, 2011): 12.

Top 50 Universities in United States That Granted the Largest Number of Doctoral Degrees to Latinos

Rank	University	Doctoral Degree Awarded	Total	Latino or Latina	Percent
1	Nova Southeastern University, Florida	266	86	180	15%
2	University of Florida, Florida	175	68	107	8%
3	University of Texas at Austin	145	48	79	10%
4	University of Southern California	121	56	65	8%
5	University of Miami, Florida	110	34	76	13%
6	Florida International University, Florida	109	46	63	38%
7	University of New Mexico, Main	100	42	58	21%
8	University of California, Berkeley	84	38	46	7%
9	University of California, Los Angeles	82	36	46	6%

(Continued)

(Continued)

Rank	University	Doctoral Degree Awarded	Total	Latino or Latina	Percent
10	University of Texas Health Science, San Antonio	81	35	46	19%
11	Columbia University, New York	78	42	36	6%
12	Saint Thomas University, Florida	70	29	41	33%
13	Stanford University, California	70	34	36	7%
14	University of Illinois at Chicago	69	29	40	7%
15	Harvard University, Massachusetts	68	40	28	5%
16	University of Houston, Texas	67	23	44	9%
17	University of Michigan-Ann Arbor	67	29	38	4%
18	University of the Pacific, California	63	26	37	9%
19	New York University, New York	63	30	33	4%
20	University of Arizona, Arizona	61	21	40	7%
21	St. Mary's University, Texas	58	25	33	24%
22	George Washington University, DC	57	30	27	6%
23	American University, DC	56	20	36	11%
24	University of California, Davis	55	20	35	6%
25	Fordham University, New York	53	28	25	9%
26	University of Pennsylvania	53	24	29	4%

(Continued)

(Continued)

Rank	University	Doctoral Degree Awarded	Total	Latino or Latina	Percent
27	University of Wisconsin–Madison	51	25	26	4%
28	Arizona State University, Tempe	50	24	26	8%
29	Emory University, Georgia	45	25	20	7%
30	Texas A&M University, College Station	45	13	32	6%
31	Texas Tech University, Lubbock	42	20	22	10%
32	Loma Linda University, California	42	21	21	9%
33	University of Chicago, Illinois	42	17	25	6%
34	Barry University, Florida	41	16	25	12%
35	Loyola Marymount University, California	41	18	23	10%
36	University of California, San Diego	40	25	15	6%
37	University of California, Irvine	39	19	20	8%
38	Cornell University, New York	39	11	28	5%
39	Northwestern University, Illinois	38	18	20	4%
40	Georgetown University, DC	38	20	18	4%
41	Stetson University, Florida	37	20	17	11%
42	St. John's University, New York	36	14	22	6%
43	Duke University, North Carolina	36	19	17	4%
44	University of Iowa, Iowa	36	15	21	4%

(Continued)

(Continued)

Rank	University	Doctoral Degree Awarded	Total	Latino or Latina	Percent
45	Temple University, Pennsylvania	36	19	17	3%
46	University of Washington, Seattle	36	11	25	3%
47	University of Illinois, Urbana Champaign	35	21	14	3%
48	University of San Diego, California	34	16	18	9%
49	Hofstra University, New York	33	13	20	8%
50	Florida State University, Florida	33	17	16	5%

Source

Hispanic Outlook in Higher Education 21, no. 17 (May 2, 2011): 14.

PART V

Resource Guides

Additional Resources

To acquire more information to help you understand the world of higher education, we provide you with a selective list of national organizations, magazines, and newsletters that you can look up periodically while you are in college. The following list is a set of additional references other than those already cited throughout the book. On reading these information sources, you will be better able to understand what is taking place that can affect your college-going experience. You should consider this selected list as a start and not all-inclusive. Some of the sources you may want to read before applying to college, others after you have been admitted, and still others once you have completed your first degree. Once you look up and read any of these sources, they will lead you to other readings. Consider the list that follows as an essential list. The list of -14 is divided into three parts: national educational organizations (six), Latino organizations (six), and publications (two).

Part I: National Educational Organizations

American Association of Community Colleges (AACC)

Web address: www.aacc.nche.edu

AACC provides opportunities, resources, and information of colleges to improve student success, which include persistence, retention, program completion, and transfer. Furthermore, high priority is given to promoting diversity, inclusion, and equity among the nation's community colleges. AACC is the principal source of information to community colleges.

American Council on Education (ACE)

Web address: www.acenet.edu

ACE provides programmatic support to colleges and universities to increase the number of adult learners so that they may be ready for college and career. Among the services it offers to adults are transcript services, GED sample test questions, and GED testing services. It also provides military program services. It has a number of publications that are informative to various adult populations.

ACT

Web address: www.act.org

ACT is an independent, not-for-profit organization that provides a broad array of assessment and research services. Each year, ACT serves millions of people in high school, college, and professional associations. Many four-year colleges require a score on the ACT examination by students who are applying for admission.

The College Board

Web address: www.collegeboard.org

The College Board, headquartered in New York City, is best known to prospective college students through taking the SAT or Scholastic Aptitude Test. The SAT measures critical reading, math, and writing skills. Many four-year colleges and universities require a prospective student to have their SAT score submitted when making application for acceptance. Besides the SAT, they offer the PSAT for students to take prior to their senior year in high school. Besides testing, the College Board provides information for planning, for example, finding a college that fits you, learning about financial aid, and so forth. The College Board has a number of publications that may be of help to students.

Educational Testing Service (ETS)

Web address: www.ets.org

For high school students, ETS provides Advance Placement Programs to be in selected high schools where students can take college-level courses and earn credits for college admissions. For college graduates, ETS offers the GRE, which is required by a majority of universities when students are applying for a master's program or doctoral studies. ETS is headquartered in Princeton, New Jersey.

Lumina Foundation

Web address: www.luminafoundation.org

The Lumina Foundation is committed to enrolling and graduating more students from college. Its current goal is to increase the number by 60 percent by the year 2025. One of its subgoals is a project called Latino Student Success-Goal 2025. To learn more about Lumina activities, look up their many publications, such as the *Focus* magazine, podcasts, and newsletters. The Lumina Foundation for education is a private independent foundation headquartered in Indianapolis, Indiana.

Part II: Latino National Organizations

Hispanic Association of Colleges and Universities (HACU)

Web address: www.hacu.net

HACU was established in 1985 in San Antonio, Texas, and now represents more than 400 colleges and universities and is committed to making Hispanics successful in higher education in the United States and Puerto Rico. It provides scholarships and holds annual conference about current issues facing Hispanic college students.

Hispanic Scholarship Fund

Web address: www.hsf.net

Hispanic Scholarship Fund is located at 55 Second Street, Suite 1500, San Francisco, CA 94105. Voice telephone is +1-877-HSF-INFO. It primarily provides scholarships but also has useful publications such as *Roadmap to College Admissions* and *The Money Manuel*.

League of United Latin American Council (LULAC)

Web address: www.lulac.org

LULAC is the largest Latino civil rights and advocacy group in the United States. It was established in 1929 and is dedicated to work for the improvement of opportunities in every region of the United States, with emphasis on education. Among its educational agenda, there are scholarships, financial aids, career planning, test preparations, and internships.

Mexican American Legal Defense and Education Fund (MALDEF)

Web address: www.maldef.org

MALDEF is a national nonprofit civil rights organization formed in 1968 to protect the rights of Latinos in the United States. Founded in San Antonio, Texas, it is currently headquartered in Los Angeles, California, and maintains regional offices in Sacramento, San Antonio, Chicago, and Washington, DC.

National Council of La Raza (NCLR)

Web address: www.nclr.org

NCLR was established as a result the Civil Rights Movement of the 1960s. It grew out of its predecessor, the Southwest Council of La Raza. One of its early focuses was education, eliminating segregation and promoting equal educational opportunity. The present-day NCLR still has a major focus on education. Its headquarters are at 1126, 16th Street, SW#600, Washington, DC 20096-4845. Phone is +1-202-785-167.

Puerto Rican Legal Defense and Education Fund (PRLDEF)

Web address: www.latinojustice.org

PRLDEF protects opportunities for all Latinos to succeed in work and school, fulfill their dreams, and sustain their families and communities. PRLDEF aims to help students to secure access to a legal education by providing comprehensive array of educational support programs, for example, by providing a LSAT Prep Course. PRLDEF is located at 99 Hudson Street, 14th floor, New York, NY 10013-2815. Phone is +1-212-219-3360.

Part III: Publications

Hispanic Outlook in Higher Education Magazine

Web address: www.hispanicoutlook.com

Since 1989, the *Hispanic Outlook* magazine has been a top information news source and the sole Hispanic educational magazine of the higher education community and those involved in running Hispanic institutions of higher learning. Published twice a month, except from June to August, it has a readership of 50,000. It is located at 80 Route 4 East, Suite 203, Paramus, NJ 07652. Phone is +1-800-549-8280.

Chronicle of Higher Education (Weekly)

Web address: www.chronicle.com

The Chronicle is the number one source of news and information about colleges and universities. It provides extensive coverage in weekly print paper, including areas such as news, opinion and ideas, facts and figures, jobs, forums, and events. Daily publication is via the Internet. It publishes an Almanac issue, once a year, which reports on a state-by-state basis, therefore providing a national picture of the status quo at the start of a new academic year. *The Chronicle* is based in Washington, DC, and has readership of 315,000.

Access and Usefulness

As a reminder, like so much of the citations given throughout the book, access to the aforementioned resources is free. That is, you can go online and read the information posted by the various organizations on the websites. Resources in print, such as magazines and newspapers, can be read free by going to the campus library. Most colleges and university libraries subscribe to those listed earlier.

In conclusion, we stress again that some of the resources listed have more value due to timing, for example, when thinking of applying you should look up the College Board for test information, look HSF for scholarship help, or if a veteran look up ACE; when in your first semester or year of college, look up AACC if in a community college or HACU if in four-year college, and so forth. But equally important, as a college student or an adult in the 21st century, you should expand your knowledge base to include the nation's dynamics and more than just the subject matter you are learning in your college courses. You need to be informed about national issues and developments, due to the impact those have on you as a higher education learner. For example, learning about the country's economic situation and understanding what it means for your cost of going to college to earn an advance college degree. Or, reading about the changing population demographics and how the issue of diversity impacts you. Or, coming to know about global interconnection and how the issue of migration affects you. Or, how the technology era will have impact on you as a lifelong learner and your future career plans. Fundamentally, you will come to learn that higher education institutions are responding to the global shifts, trying to adapt, and stay competitive to enroll more students and help them to graduate. The more you know about these forces and changes, the better you will be able to succeed in your college and earn a degree.

About the Editor and Chapter Authors

Leonard A. Valverde started his higher education at East Los Angeles Community College, earning an associate of arts, then transferred to California State University at Los Angeles, and earned a BA in history with a minor in mathematics. After teaching junior high school math and directing a bilingual education program, he returned to California State University—Los Angeles and earned a master's degree in educational administration. After being a math education supervisor with the Los Angeles City Unified School District, he was awarded a Ford Foundation Fellowship at Claremont Graduate School, where he earned his doctor of philosophy.

Since 1973, he has been a professor and department chair at the University of Texas at Austin, a vice president for academic affairs and graduate dean at University of Texas at San Antonio, a College of Education dean at Arizona State University, and executive director of a five-state consortium, the Hispanic Border Leadership Institute, funded by the W.K. Kellogg Foundation.

He has published extensively, one of his books being *Leaders of Color in Higher Education*. He has traveled to Europe, Asian, Middle East, and South America to learn, consult, and has made formal presentations.

Chapter Authors

Dr. Silas H. Abrego became a member of the California State University at Fullerton in 1985 and on January 1, 2011, was appointed acting vice president for student affairs. As the university's chief student affairs officer, he has the responsibility for managing the following units within the division of student affairs: Athletic Academic Services, Career Center, College-Based Assistant Deans for Student Affairs, Dean of Students, Disabled Student Services, Educational Partnerships, Federal TRIO Programs, Financial Aid, Guardian Scholars Program, Housing and Residence Life, International Education and Exchange, Student Academic Services, Student Health and Counseling Center, the University Learning Center, and the Women's Center/Adult Re-entry/Veterans Student Services. He is also responsible for intercollegiate athletics and works collaboratively with Associated Students, Incorporated.

Prior to coming to the Titan family, Dr. Abrego served as coordinator of the California Education Policy Fellowship Program at the Institute for Educational Leadership, Tomas Rivera Center at Claremont Graduate School, and later as assistant to the dean/director of Special Projects, School of Education at the University of Southern California.

Dr. Abrego received his MA and EdD in higher education, governance, and management from the University of Southern California.

Dr. Baltazar Arispe y Acevedo Jr.'s academic preparation includes a baccalaureate degree in social science education (history and political science) from Southwest Texas State University (1969), a master's of science in curriculum and instruction from Western Michigan (1974) and a PhD in higher education management and research from the University of Texas at Austin (1979). He has also completed four postdoctoral assignments with HEW, the American Council of Education, League for Innovation, and American Association of Community Colleges.

He has more than 40 years of demonstrated successful experience at all levels of education and in the public and private sectors and currently is a tenured professor of educational administration and research with the College of Education at the University of Texas-Pan American.

His extensive career demonstrates his lifelong commitment to addressing quality of life issues in both urban and rural communities. He began his career as a kindergarten teacher in the Migrant Education Programs in Michigan and has taught at the high school level and in universities in Texas and Michigan. He has also served as a labor organizer, a college dean, a policy analyst with several policy institutes, a director for workforce and economic development with the

Dallas County Community College District, and was the founding president of the College Without Walls for the Houston Community College System.

He has published extensively and has served his communities as a member of more than 20 boards among those being Habitat for Humanity and the Michigan Governor's Education Taskforce. Dr. Acevedo has made more than 100 presentations to academic, public, and governmental organizations.

Jacob Fraire serves as vice president of student and institutional success at the nonprofit Texas Guaranteed Student Loan Corporation (TG). He leads TG's philanthropic investments, community affairs, and student success initiatives, collectively designed to increase college access and degree completion among students, with an emphasis on individuals who are from low-to-moderate income families. Mr. Fraire earned a bachelor's of science in computer science from St. Edward's University in Austin, Texas, and a master of public affairs from the Lyndon Baines Johnson School of Public Affairs at the University of Texas at Austin. From 1987 to 1998, he served as an education lobbyist in Washington, DC, representing, among others, the Hispanic Association of Colleges and Universities and research-intensive universities. Mr. Fraire was appointed to the Advisory Committee on Measures of Student Success by U.S. Education Secretary Arne Duncan. He has served on the board of directors for the Houston Hispanic Forum and as chair of the corporate board of advisors for the Council for Opportunity in Education.

Dr. Shernaz B. García is an associate professor of multicultural/bilingual special education in the department of special education at The University of Texas at Austin. She is a fellow in the Lawrence and Stel Marie Lowman College of Education Endowed Excellence Fund and area coordinator of the Multicultural/Bilingual Special Education graduate programs. Dr. García holds a doctorate (PhD) in special education administration from The University of Texas at Austin, and earned her master's degree (MS) in special education from George Peabody College for Teachers, Nashville, Tennessee. Her baccalaureate degree in French was completed at Poona University, India. In her role as the graduate advisor for the department of special education, Dr. García established a variety of advising supports and resources for graduate students, including a peer-mentoring system. She has 25 years of experience as a teacher educator, researcher, and administrator of multicultural or bilingual special education programs at the university level and is a nationally recognized expert in the field of bilingual or multicultural special education. Her research and teaching interests are focused on cultural influences on teaching and learning, factors contributing to educational risk for students from nondominant sociocultural and linguistic communities; prevention of and early intervention for academic underachievement; family–professional partnerships; and personnel preparation.

Patricia L. Guerra, PhD, is an assistant professor in the Education and Community Leadership program at Texas State University, San Marcos. She earned her BS with specialization in deaf education, MEd in curriculum and instruction, and PhD in educational administration with supervision, mid-management, and superintendent certifications from the University of Texas at Austin. Currently, Patricia teaches graduate courses in principal preparation, teacher leadership, and culturally responsive school improvement. Her research interests center on culturally responsive leadership and schooling, equity, and educator beliefs. Prior to Texas State University, Patricia was co-director of the Leadership for Equity and Access Project based at the University of Texas at Austin. She has also worked at the Southwest Educational Development Laboratory where she conducted educational research and served as a leader at both the school and district levels. Along with her work at the university, she works with educators in the field to develop culturally responsive classrooms and schools, and coauthors a regular column on "Cultural Proficiency" in the *Journal of Staff Development* (JSD) published by Learning Forward (formerly the National Staff Development Council).

Roberto Haro, a Mexican American scholar and advocate, is a retired professor and university executive and has worked in California, Maryland, and New York universities. He received the BA and two graduate degrees from the University of California, Berkeley, and a doctorate in higher education from the University of San Francisco. His scholarly publications include five monographs, and more than 80 articles and chapters. He is an expert on the Latino community in California and elsewhere and has developed a depth of knowledge about aviation from World War I to World War II.

Haro's novels, written under the pen name Roberto de Haro, include: *Twist of Fate: Love, Turbulence and the Great War* (Vantage Press, 2006). *Intermezzo of the Longing Hearts* (iUniverse Press, 2006), *The Mexican Chubasco* (Author-House Press, 2007), *Jolene's Last Gasp* (iUniverse Press, 2007), *Camino Doloroso* (AuthorHouse Press, 2008), and *Assassins' Raid: Killing Admiral Yamamoto* (iUniverse Press, 2009). *For Nadine's Love: A Warriors Quest* (CreateSpace Press, 2010), *Murder at the Villa Museum* (iUniverse Press, November 2010), and *The Wayward Zephyr* (AuthorHouse Press, 2011).

Haro lives in Marin County, California.

Henry T. Ingle is a senior associate with The Knowledge-Brokers Inc., a professional services educational planning and consulting firm in southern California. He completed his PhD at Stanford University in education and communications and holds undergraduate and master's degrees in communication and telecommunication media from University of Texas-El Paso and Syracuse University in New York.

He has been in the roles of international development, federal government executive, university professor, and administrator, worked in both public and private sectors in Washington, DC, California, Texas southwestern states, and internationally. He has been a professor at California State University-Chico and the University of Texas at El Paso, and vice chancellor for technology with San Diego Community Colleges.

He has served as a trustee of the College Board, is recipient of two international senior Fulbright Fellowships, and has a senior postdoctoral appointment with National Research Council/Ford Foundation.

Juan Valdez is a first-year anthropology graduate student at California State University, Fullerton. Juan was selected to the Graduate Assistant Program by Enhancing Post Baccalaureate Opportunities at CSUF for Hispanic Students (EPOCHS). His passion is to explore the Civil Rights movement of the 1960s in order to determine and validate the major impact this historical period has had on our society today. He has engaged in academic leadership and community advocacy on minority rights. Juan served as a leader on the Interclub Council of Humanities and Social Science, Lambda Alpha Anthropology Honor Student Society, MESA Cooperativa, and Anthropology Student Association. He tutors algebra and arithmetic on a volunteer basis and spends his summers helping with the preservation of endangered primates. He is a fervent advocate for education and equality, reflecting his own background as a native immigrant from Mexico.

Index

Latino student profile
development for graduate
admission, 151–59; while
enrolled in a two-year college,
143–45
Graduate Management Aptitude Test
(GMAT), 151
Graduate Record Exam (GRE), 34, 151
Graduate schools, considering, 33–34.
See also Advanced degrees;
Graduate admission preparation
Graduate study, defined, 142
Grants, 42, 46
GRE. See Graduate Record Exam
Groups, 31–32
Gutierrez, Jose Angel, 187–92
Guzman, Terry, 167–71

HACU. See Hispanic Association of
Colleges and Universities
Hardware, 104–5
Hermanos or hermanas (brothers or
sisters), 12, 17
High school: college planning steps
and, 35–39; information about
attending college and, 13, 17
Hispanic Association of Colleges and
Universities (HACU), 249;
website, 46
Hispanic College Fund, 25
Hispanic Outlook in Higher Education
magazine, 203, 250–51
Hispanic Scholarship Fund, 249;
website, 46
Houston Community College, 208
"How to Get a GED; A Step-by-Step
Process to Earn a GED"
(Education-Portal.com), 23

Income earnings, education and, 43
Incompletes, 61, 88, 93
Information collection, 12–14
Information Technology (IT)
department, 100

Ingle, Henry T. "Achieving Technology
Smartness and Proficiency:
A Suggested 8-Step Process,"
99–100. See also Technology
Intelligence, myths related to, 21–22,
32–33
Interest inventories, 120–21
Internet, information from, 12–13, 17.
See also Websites
Internships, 157–59
IT. See Information Technology (IT)
department

Junior Reserve Officer Training Corps
(ROTC), 24

Kaplan, 151
Kelly, Kevin, What Technology
Wants, 95
Kelly, Robert, 161

Lage, Onelia Garcia, 193–96
Language barriers, 89–90
Language policies, 82
Laredo Community College,
209–10
Latino faculty and staff, 14. See also
Stories of success
Latino focus programs, 14
Latino national organizations,
249–50; Hispanic Association
of Colleges and Universities
(HACU), 249; Hispanic Schol-
arship Fund, 249; League of
United Latin American Council
(LULAC), 249–50; Mexican
American Legal Defense and
Education Fund (MALDEF),
250; National Council of La Raza
(NCLR), 250; Puerto Rican
Legal Defense and Education
Fund (PRLDEF), 250
Latino profile development, for
graduate admission, 151–59

CPSIA information can be obtained
at www.ICGtesting.com
Printed in the USA
LVOW05*0253110817
544587LV00006B/71/P